Protestant Episcopal Church USA

Selections from the Psalms of David in Metre

Protestant Episcopal Church USA
Selections from the Psalms of David in Metre
ISBN/EAN: 9783743388017
Manufactured in Europe, USA, Canada, Australia, Japa
Cover: Foto ©Lupo / pixelio.de

Manufactured and distributed by brebook publishing software (www.brebook.com)

Protestant Episcopal Church USA

Selections from the Psalms of David in Metre

SELECTIONS

FROM THE

PSALMS OF DAVID

IN METRE;

WITH

HYMNS

SUITED TO THE

FEASTS AND FASTS OF THE CHURCH,

AND

OTHER OCCASIONS OF PUBLIC WORSHIP.

PRINTED BY G. E. EYRE AND W. SPOTTISWOODE.
Warehouses:
NEW YORK, 626, BROADWAY.
LONDON, 43, FLEET STREET, E. C.; EDINBURGH, 16, ELDER STREET.

"BY the Bishops, the Clergy, and the Laity of the Protestant Episcopal Church in the United States of America, in Convention, this twenty-ninth day of October, in the year of our Lord one thousand eight hundred and thirty-two; this book of Psalms in Metre, selected from the Psalms of David, with Hymns, is set forth, and allowed to be sung in all congregations of the said Church, before and after Morning and Evening Prayer, and also before and after Sermons, at the discretion of the Minister."

"And it shall be the duty of every Minister of any Church, either by standing directions, or from time to time, to appoint the portions of Psalms which are to be sung."

"And further, it shall be the duty of every Minister, with such assistance as he can obtain from persons skilled in music, to give order concerning the tunes to be sung at any time in his Church; and especially, it shall be his duty to suppress all light and unseemly music, and all indecency and irreverence in the performance, by which vain and ungodly persons profane the service of the Sanctuary."

SELECTIONS
FROM THE PSALMS OF DAVID IN METRE.

SELECTION 1. C. M.
From the i. Psalm of David.

HOW blest is he, who ne'er consents
  By ill advice to walk,
Nor stands in sinners' ways, nor sits
  Where men profanely talk;
2 But makes the perfect law of God
  His business and delight;
Devoutly reads therein by day,
  And meditates by night.
3 Like some fair tree, which, fed by streams,
  With timely fruit does bend,
He still shall flourish, and success
  All his designs attend.
4 Ungodly men, and their attempts,
  No lasting root shall find;
Untimely blasted, and dispersed
  Like chaff before the wind.
5 Their guilt shall strike the wicked dumb
  Before their Judge's face:
No formal hypocrite shall then
  Among the saints have place.
6 For God approves the just man's ways;
  To happiness they tend:
But sinners, and the paths they tread,
  Shall both in ruin end.

SELECTION 2. C. M
From the ii. Psalm of David.

THUS God declares his sovereign will:
  "The King that I ordain,
Whose throne is fix'd on Zion's hill,
  Shall there securely reign."

2 Attend, O earth, whilst I declare
    God's uncontroll'd decree:
"Thou art my Son; this day, my heir
    Have I begotten thee.
3 "Ask, and receive thy full demands;
    Thine shall the heathen be;
The utmost limits of the lands
    Shall be possess'd by thee."
4 Learn then, ye princes; and give ear,
    Ye judges of the earth;
Worship the Lord with holy fear;
    Rejoice with awful mirth.
5 Appease the Son with due respect,
    Your timely homage pay:
Lest he revenge the bold neglect,
    Incensed by your delay.
6 If but in part his anger rise,
    Who can endure the flame!
Then blest are they, whose hope relies
    On his most holy Name.

SELECTION 3. C. M.
From the iii. Psalm of David.

THOU, gracious God, art my defence;
    On thee my hopes rely:
Thou art my glory, and shalt yet
    Lift up my head on high.
2 Since whensoe'er, in my distress,
    To God I made my prayer,
He heard me from his holy hill;
    Why should I now despair?
3 Guarded by him I lay me down
    My sweet repose to take;
For I through him securely sleep,
    Through him in safety wake.
4 Salvation to the Lord belongs;
    He only can defend:
His blessing he extends to all
    That on his power depend.

SELECTION 4. C. M.
From the iv. Psalm of David.

CONSIDER that the righteous man
 Is God's peculiar choice;
And when to him I make my prayer,
 He always hears my voice.
2 Then stand in awe of his commands,
 Flee every thing that's ill;
Commune in private with your hearts,
 And bend them to his will.
3 The sacrifice of righteousness
 Present to God on high;
And let your hope, securely fix'd,
 On him alone rely.
4 While worldly minds impatient grow
 More prosperous times to see,
Still let the glories of thy face
 Shine brightly, Lord, on me.
5 So shall my heart o'erflow with joy,
 More lasting and more true
Then theirs, who stores of corn and wine
 Successively renew.
6 Then down in peace I'll lay my head,
 And take my needful rest;
No other guard, O Lord, I crave,
 Of thy defence possess'd.

SELECTION 5. C. M.
From the v. Psalm of David.

REGARD my words, O gracious Lord,
 Accept my secret prayer;
To thee alone, my King, my God,
 Will I for help repair.
2 Thou in the morn my voice shalt hear,
 And, with the dawning day,
To thee devoutly I'll look up,
 To thee devoutly pray.
3 Lord, I within thy house will come,
 In thy abundant grace;

And I will worship in thy fear,
　Tow'rd thy most holy place.
4 Let those, O Lord, who trust in thee,
　With shouts their joy proclaim;
Let them rejoice whom thou preserv'st,
　And all that love thy Name.
5 To righteous men, the righteous Lord
　His blessing will extend;
And with his favour all his saints,
　As with a shield, defend.

SELECTION 6.　S. M.
From the vi. Psalm of David.

IN mercy, not in wrath,
　Rebuke me, gracious God!
Lest, if thy whole displeasure rise,
　I sink beneath thy rod.
2 Touch'd by thy quickening power,
　My load of guilt I feel;
The wounds thy Spirit hath unclosed,
　O let that Spirit heal.
3 In trouble and in gloom,
　Must I for ever mourn?
And wilt thou not, at length, O God,
　In pitying love return?
4 O come, ere life expire,
　Send down thy power to save;
For who shall sing thy Name in death,
　Or praise thee in the grave?
5 Why should I doubt thy grace,
　Or yield to dread despair?
Thou wilt fulfil thy promised word,
　And grant me all my prayer.

SELECTION 7.　C. M.
From the viii. Psalm of David.

O THOU, to whom all creatures bow
　Within this earthly frame,
Through all the world how great art thou!
　How glorious is thy Name!

2 In heaven thy wond'rous acts are sung,
   Nor fully reckon'd there;
 And yet thou mak'st the infant tongue
   Thy boundless praise declare.
3 When heaven, thy beauteous work on high,
   Employs my wondering sight;
 The moon, that nightly rules the sky,
   With stars of feebler light;
4 O, what is man, that, Lord, thou lov'st
   To keep him in thy mind?
 Or what his offspring, that thou prov'st
   To them so wondrous kind?
5 Him next in power thou didst create
   To thy celestial train;
 Ordain'd with dignity and state
   O'er all thy works to reign.
6 They jointly own his powerful sway;
   The beasts that prey or graze;
 The bird that wings its airy way;
   The fish that cuts the seas.
7 O Thou, to whom all creatures bow
   Within this earthly frame,
 Through all the world how great art thou!
   How glorious is thy Name!

SELECTION 8. C. M.
From the ix. Psalm of David.

TO celebrate thy praise, O Lord,
   I will my heart prepare;
 To all the listening world thy works,
   Thy wondrous works declare.
2 The thought of them shall to my soul
   Exalted pleasure bring;
 Whilst to thy name, O thou Most High,
   Triumphant praise I sing.
3 The Lord for ever lives, who has
   His righteous throne prepared,
 Impartial justice to dispense,
   To punish or reward.

4 All those who have his goodness proved,
    Will in his truth confide;
Whose mercy ne'er forsook the man
    That on his help relied.
5 Sing praises therefore to the Lord,
    From Sion, his abode;
Proclaim his deeds, till all the world
    Confess no other God.

SELECTION 9. C. M.
From the xi. Psalm of David.

THE Lord a holy temple hath,
    And righteous throne, above;
Whence he surveys the sons of men,
    And how their counsels move.
2 If God the righteous, whom he loves,
    For trial does correct,
What must the sons of violence,
    Whom he abhors, expect!
3 Snares, fire, and brimstone, on their heads
    Shall in one tempest shower;
This dreadful mixture his revenge
    Into their cup shall pour.
4 The righteous Lord will righteous deeds
    With signal favour grace,
And to the upright man disclose
    The brightness of his face.

SELECTION 10. C. M.
From the xiii. Psalm of David.

HOW long wilt thou forget me, Lord?
    Must I for ever mourn?
How long wilt thou withdraw from me,
    Oh! never to return?
2 O hear, and to my longing eyes
    Restore thy wonted light;
Dawn on my spirit, lest I sleep
    In death's most gloomy night.
3 Since I have always placed my trust
    Beneath thy mercy's wing,

SELECTIONS OF PSALMS.

Thy saving health will come; and then
   My heart with joy shall spring.
4 Then shall my song, with praise inspired,
   To thee, my God, ascend;
Who to thy servant in distress
   Such bounty didst extend.

SELECTION 11. L. M.
From the xiv. Psalm of David.

THE Lord look'd down from heaven's high tower,
   And all the sons of men did view,
To see if any own'd his power,
   If any truth or justice knew;
2 But all, he saw, were gone aside,
   All were degenerate grown, and base;
None took religion for their guide,
   Not one of all the sinful race.
3 How will they tremble then for fear,
   When his just wrath shall them o'ertake:
For to the righteous God is near,
   And never will their cause forsake.
4 O, that from Sion he'd employ
   His might, and burst th' oppressive band!
Then shouts of universal joy
   Should loudly echo through the land.

SELECTION 12. C. M.
From the xv. Psalm of David.

LORD, who's the happy man that may
   To thy blest courts repair,
Not, stranger-like, to visit them,
   But to inhabit there?
2 'Tis he who walketh uprightly,
   Whom righteousness directs;
Whose generous tongue disdains to speak
   The thing his heart rejects.
3 Who never did a slander forge,
   His neighbour's fame to wound;
Nor hearken to a false report
   By malice whisper'd round.

4 Who vice, in all its pomp and power,
   Can treat with just neglect;
And piety, though clothed in rags,
   Religiously respect.
5 Who to his plighted vows and trust
   Has ever firmly stood;
And, though he promise to his loss,
   He makes his promise good.
6 Whose soul in usury disdains
   His treasure to employ;
Whom no rewards can ever bribe
   The guiltless to destroy.
7 The man, who by this righteous course
   Has happiness insured,
When earth's foundation shakes, shall stand,
   By Providence secured.

SELECTION 13. C. M.
From the xvi. Psalm of David.

MY grateful soul shall bless the Lord,
   Whose precepts give me light;
And private counsel still afford
   In sorrow's dismal night.
2 I strive each action to approve
   To his all-seeing eye;
No danger shall my hopes remove,
   Because he still is nigh.
3 Therefore my heart all grief defies,
   My glory does rejoice;
My flesh shall rest, in hope to rise,
   Waked by his powerful voice.
4 Thou, Lord, when I resign my breath,
   My soul from hell shalt free
Nor let thy Holy One in death
   The least corruption see.
5 Thou shalt the paths of life display,
   Which to thy presence lead;
Where pleasures dwell without allay,
   And joys that never fade.

SELECTIONS OF PSALMS.

SELECTION 14.
From the xviii. Psalm of David.
PART I. L. M.

NO change of time shall ever shock
  My firm affection, Lord, to thee;
For thou hast always been my rock,
  A fortress and defence to me.

2 Thou my deliverer art, my God;
  My trust is in thy mighty power:
Thou art my shield from foes abroad,
  At home, my safeguard and my tower.

3 To thee I will address my prayer,
  To whom all praise we justly owe;
So shall I, by thy watchful care,
  Be guarded safe from every foe.

PART II. L. M.

1 THOU suit'st, O Lord, thy righteous ways
  To various paths of human kind;
They who for mercy merit praise,
  With thee shall wondrous mercy find.

2 Thou to the just shalt justice show;
  The pure thy purity shall see:
Such as perversely choose to go,
  Shall meet with due returns from thee.

3 That he the humble soul will save,
  And crush the haughty's boasted might,
In me the Lord an instance gave,
  Whose darkness he has turn'd to light.

4 Who then deserves to be adored,
  But God, on whom my hopes depend?
Or who, except the mighty Lord,
  Can with resistless power defend?

5 Let the eternal Lord be praised,
  The rock on whose defence I rest!
To highest heavens his Name be raised,
  Who me with his salvation bless'd!

6 My God, to celebrate thy fame,
  My grateful voice to heaven I'll raise;

And nations, strangers to thy Name,
  Shall learn to sing thy glorious praise.

SELECTION 15.
From the xix. Psalm of David.
PART I. C. M.

THE heavens declare thy glory, Lord,
  Which that alone can fill;
The firmament and stars express
  Their great Creator's skill.

2 The dawn of each returning day
    Fresh beams of knowledge brings;
  And from the dark returns of night
    Divine instruction springs.

3 Their powerful language to no realm
    Or region is confined;
  'Tis nature's voice, and understood
    Alike by all mankind.

4 Their doctrine does its sacred sense
    Through earth's extent display;
  Its bright contents the circling sun
    Does round the world convey.

5 From east to west, from west to east,
    His ceaseless course he goes;
  And, through his progress, cheerful light
    And vital warmth bestows.

PART II. C. M.

1 GOD's perfect law converts the soul,
    Reclaims from false desires;
  With sacred wisdom his sure word
    The ignorant inspires.

2 The statutes of the Lord are just,
    And bring sincere delight;
  His pure commands, in search of truth,
    Assist the feeblest sight.

3 His perfect worship here is fix'd,
    On sure foundations laid;
  His equal laws are in the scales
    Of truth and justice weigh'd;

4 Of more esteem than golden mines,
    Or gold refined with skill;
  More sweet than honey, or the drops
    That from the comb distil.

5 My trusty counsellors they are,
    And friendly warnings give:
  Divine rewards attend on those
    Who by thy precepts live.

6 But what frail man observes how oft
    He does from virtue fall?
  O cleanse me from my secret faults,
    Thou God that know'st them all!

7 Let no presumptuous sin, O Lord,
    Dominion have o'er me;
  That, by thy grace preserved, I may
    The great transgression flee.

8 So shall my prayer and praises be
    With thy acceptance blest;
  And I, secure on thy defence,
    My strength and Saviour, rest.

SELECTION 16. S. M.
From the xx. Psalm of David.

MAY Jacob's God defend
    And hear us in distress;
  Our succour from his temple send,
    Our cause from Sion bless!

2 May he accept our vow,
    Our sacrifice receive,
  Our heart's devout request allow,
    Our holy wishes give!

3 O Lord, thy saving grace
    We joyfully declare;
  Our banner in thy Name we raise—
    "The Lord fulfil our prayer!"

4 Now know we that the Lord
    His chosen will defend;
  From heaven will strength divine afford,
    And will their prayer attend.

5 Some earthly succour trust,
   But we in God's right hand:
Lo! while they fall, so vain their boast,
   We rise, and upright stand.
6 Still save us, Lord; and still
   Thy servants deign to bless:
Hear, King of heaven, in times of ill,
   The prayers that we address.

SELECTION 17.
From the xxii. Psalm of David.
PART I. C. M.

MY God, my God, why leav'st thou me
   When I with anguish faint?
O, why so far from me removed,
   And from my loud complaint?
2 Lo! I am treated like a worm,
   Like none of human birth;
Not only by the great reviled,
   But made the rabble's mirth.
3 With laughter, all the gazing crowd
   My agonies survey;
They shoot the lip, they shake the head,
   And thus deriding say:
4 " In God he trusted, boasting oft
   That he was Heaven's delight;
Let God come down to save him now,
   And own his favourite."
5 Withdraw not, then, so far from me,
   When trouble is so nigh;
O send me help! thy help, on which
   Alone I can rely.

PART II. C. M.
1 LIKE water is my life pour'd out,
   My joints are out of frame;
My heart dissolves within my breast,
   Like wax before the flame.
2 My strength is like a potsherd dried,
   My tongue is parch'd with drought;

And to the dismal shades of death
  My fainting soul is brought.
3 Like dogs, to compass me, my foes
    In wicked counsel meet;
  They pierced my inoffensive hands,
    They pierced my harmless feet.
4 My body's rack'd, till all my bones
    Distinctly may be told;
  Yet such a spectacle of woe
    As pastime they behold.
5 As spoil, my garments they divide,
    Lots for my vesture cast:
  Therefore, O leave me not, my God,
    But to my succour haste.

PART III. C. M.

1 LORD, to my brethren I'll declare
    The triumphs of thy Name;
  In presence of assembled saints
    Thy glory thus proclaim:
2 "Ye worshippers of Jacob's God,
    All you of Israel's line,
  O praise the Lord, and to your praise
    Sincere obedience join.
3 " He ne'er disdain'd on low distress
    To cast a gracious eye;
  Nor turn'd from misery his face,
    But hears its humble cry."
4 Thus in thy sacred courts, will I
    My cheerful thanks express;
  In presence of thy saints perform
    The vows of my distress.
5 The meek companions of my grief
    Shall find my table spread;
  And all that seek the Lord shall be
    With joys immortal fed.
6 Then shall the glad converted world
    To God their homage pay;
  And scatter'd nations of the earth
    One sovereign Lord obey.

7 'Tis his supreme prerogative
    O'er all mankind to reign;
 'Tis just that he should rule the world,
    Who does the world sustain.
8 The rich, who are with plenty fed,
    His bounty must confess;
 The sons of want, by him relieved,
    Their generous patron bless.
9 With humble worship to his throne
    They all for aid resort;
 That power, which first their being gave,
    Alone can them support.
10 Then shall a chosen spotless race,
    Devoted to his Name,
 To their adoring sons his truth
    And glorious acts proclaim.

SELECTION 18. C. M.
From the xxiii. Psalm of David.

THE Lord himself, the mighty Lord,
    Vouchsafes to be my guide;
 The shepherd, by whose constant care
    My wants are all supplied.
2 In tender grass he makes me feed,
    And gently there repose;
 Then leads me to cool shades, and where
    Refreshing water flows.
3 He does my wandering soul reclaim,
    And, to his endless praise,
 Instruct with humble zeal to walk
    In his most righteous ways.
4 I pass the gloomy vale of death,
    From fear and danger free;
 For there his aiding rod and staff
    Defend and comfort me.
5 Since God doth thus his wondrous love
    Through all my life extend,
 That life to him I will devote,
    And in his temple spend.

SELECTION 19. C. M.
From the xxiv. Psalm of David.

THE spacious earth is all the Lord's,
  The Lord's her fulness is;
The world, and they that dwell therein,
  By sovereign right are his.

2 He framed and fix'd it on the seas;
  And his almighty hand
Upon inconstant floods has made
  The stable fabric stand.

3 But for himself, this Lord of all
  One chosen seat design'd;
O who shall to that sacred hill
  Deserved admittance find?

4 The man whose hands and heart are pure,
  Whose thoughts from pride are free;
Who honest poverty prefers
  To gainful perjury.

5 This, this is he, on whom the Lord
  Shall shower his blessings down;
Whom God, his Saviour, shall vouchsafe
  With righteousness to crown.

6 Such is the race of saints, by whom
  The sacred courts are trod;
And such the proselytes that seek
  Thy face, O Jacob's God.

7 Erect your heads, eternal gates;
  Unfold, to entertain
The King of glory: see! he comes
  With his celestial train.

8 Who is the King of glory? who?
  The Lord, for strength renown'd;
In battle mighty; o'er his foes
  Eternal victor crown'd.

9 Erect your heads, ye gates; unfold,
  In state to entertain
The King of glory: see! he comes
  With all his shining train.

10 Who is the King of glory? who?
 The Lord of hosts renown'd;
 Of glory he alone is King,
 Who is with glory crown'd.

SELECTION 20. S. M.
From the xxv. Psalm of David.

TO God, in whom I trust,
 I lift my heart and voice:
 O let me not be put to shame,
 Nor let thy foes rejoice.
2 Those who on thee rely,
 Let no disgrace attend;
 Be that the shameful lot of such
 As wilfully offend.
3 To me thy truth impart,
 And lead me in thy way;
 For thou art he that brings me help,
 On thee I wait all day.
4 Thy mercies and thy love,
 O Lord, recall to mind;
 And graciously continue still,
 As thou wert ever, kind.
5 Let all my youthful crimes
 Be blotted out by thee;
 And, for thy wondrous goodness' sake
 In mercy think on me.
6 His mercy and his truth
 The righteous Lord displays,
 In bringing wandering sinners home,
 And teaching them his ways.
7 He those in justice guides
 Who his direction seek;
 And in his sacred paths shall lead
 The humble and the meek.
8 Through all the ways of God
 Both truth and mercy shine,

To such as, with religious hearts,
  To his blest will incline.
9 Since mercy is the grace
  That most exalts thy fame,
  Forgive my heinous sin, O Lord,
  And so advance thy Name.
10 Whoe'er with humble fear
  To God his duty pays,
  Shall find the Lord a faithful guide,
  In all his righteous ways.
11 For God to all his saints
  His secret will imparts,
  And does his gracious covenant write
  In their obedient hearts.
12 To Israel's chosen race
  Continue ever kind;
  And, in the midst of all their wants,
  Let them thy succour find.

SELECTION 21. C. M.
From the xxvi. Psalm of David.*

JUDGE me, O Lord, for I the paths
  Of righteousness have trod;
  I shall not fail, who all my trust
  Repose on thee, my God.
2 I'll wash my hands in innocence,
  And round thine altar go;
  Pour the glad hymn of triumph thence,
  And thence thy wonders show.
3 My thanks I'll publish there, and tell
  How thy renown excels;
  That seat affords me more delight,
  In which thine honour dwells.

---

* Extract from the Journal of the General Convention, 1832.
  4. *Resolved,* As the sense and declaration of this Convention, that so much of the rubrics in the Form of Consecration of a Church or Chapel as requires the singing of "Psalm 26, verses 6, 7, and 8," will hereafter be duly complied with by singing verses 2 and 8, in the selection from the 26th Psalm, included in the Psalms in Metre authorized by these resolutions to be set forth.

SELECTION 22. C. M.
From the xxvii. Psalm of David.

WHOM should I fear, since God to me
   Is saving health and light?
Since strongly he my life supports,
   What can my soul affright?

2 Henceforth within his house to dwell
   I earnestly desire;
His wondrous beauty there to view,
   And of his will inquire.

3 For there I may with comfort rest,
   In times of deep distress;
And safe, as on a rock, abide
   In that secure recess.

4 When us to seek thy glorious face
   Thou kindly dost advise;
" Thy glorious face I'll always seek,"
   My grateful heart replies.

5 Then hide not thou thy face, O Lord,
   Nor me in wrath reject;
My God and Saviour, leave not him
   Thou didst so oft protect.

6 Though all of nearest earthly ties,
   Me, in my woe, forsake,
Yet thou, whose love excels them all,
   Wilt care and pity take.

7 Instruct me in thy paths, O Lord,
   My ways directly guide;
Lest sinful men, who watch my steps,
   Should see me tread aside.

8 I trusted that my future life
   Should with thy love be crown'd;
Or else my fainting soul had sunk,
   With sorrow compass'd round.

9 God's time with patient faith expect,
   Who will inspire thy breast
With inward strength; do thou thy part,
   And leave to him the rest.

SELECTION 23. C. M.
From the xxviii. Psalm of David.

ADORED for ever be the Lord;
   His praise I will resound,
From whom the cries of my distress
   A gracious answer found.

2 He is my strength and shield; my heart
   Has trusted in his Name;
And now relieved, my heart, with joy,
   His praises shall proclaim.

3 The Lord, the everlasting God,
   Is my defence and rock,
The saving health, the saving strength,
   Of his anointed flock.

4 O save and bless thy people, Lord,
   Thy heritage preserve;
Feed, strengthen, and support their hearts,
   That they may never swerve.

SELECTION 24. L. M.
From the xxix. Psalm of David.

YE that in might and power excel,
   Your grateful sacrifice prepare;
God's glorious actions loudly tell,
   His wondrous power to all declare.

2 To his great Name fresh altars raise;
   Devoutly due respect afford;
Him in his holy temple praise,
   Where he's with solemn state adored.

3 'Tis he that, with amazing noise,
   The watery clouds in sunder breaks;
The ocean trembles at his voice,
   When he from heaven in thunder speaks.

4 How full of power his voice appears!
   With what majestic terror crown'd!
Which from their roots tall cedars tears,
   And strews their scatter'd branches round.

5 God rules the angry floods on high;
   His boundless sway shall never cease;
His saints with strength he shall supply,
   And bless his own with constant peace.

SELECTION 25. C. M.
From the xxx. Psalm of David.

IN my distress to God I cried,
   Who kindly did relieve,
And from the grave's expecting mouth
   My hopeless life retrieve.

2 O to his courts, ye saints of his,
   With songs of praise repair;
With me commemorate his truth,
   And providential care.

3 His wrath has but a moment's reign,
   His favour no decay;
The night of grief is recompensed
   With joy's returning day.

4 Therefore, O Lord, I'll gladly sing
   Thy praise in grateful verse;
And, as thy favours endless are,
   Thy endless praise rehearse.

SELECTION 26. S. M.
From the xxxi. Psalm of David.

DEFEND me, Lord, from shame,
   For still I trust in thee;
As just and righteous is thy Name,
   From danger set me free.

2 Bow down thy gracious ear,
   And speedy succour send;
Do thou my steadfast rock appear,
   To shelter and defend.

3 To thee, the God of truth,
   My life, and all that's mine,
(For thou preserv'st me from my youth,)
   I willingly resign.

4 My hope, my steadfast trust,
   I on thy help repose:
That thou, my God, art good and just,
   My soul with comfort knows.

5 Whate'er events betide,
   Thy wisdom times them all;
Then, Lord, thy servant safely hide
   From those that seek his fall.

6 The brightness of thy face
   To me, O Lord, disclose;
And, as thy mercies still increase,
   Preserve me from my foes.

7 How great thy mercies are
   To such as fear thy Name,
Which thou, for those that trust thy care,
   Dost to the world proclaim!

8 O all ye saints, the Lord
   With eager love pursue;
Who to the just will help afford,
   And give the proud their due.

9 Ye that on God rely,
   Courageously proceed;
For he will still your hearts supply
   With strength in time of need.

SELECTION 27. L. M.
From the xxxii. Psalm of David.

HE'S blest, whose sins have pardon gain'd,
   No more in judgment to appear;
Whose guilt remission has obtain'd,
   And whose repentance is sincere.

2 No sooner I my wound disclosed,
   The guilt that tortured me within,
But thy forgiveness interposed,
   And mercy's healing balm pour'd in.

3 Sorrows on sorrows multiplied,
   The harden'd sinner shall confound;
But them who in His truth confide,
   Blessings of mercy shall surround.

4 His saints, that have perform'd his laws,
  Their life in triumph shall employ;
Let them, as they alone have cause,
  In grateful raptures shout for joy.

SELECTION 28.
From the xxxiii. Psalm of David.
PART I. C. M.

LET all the just to God, with joy,
  Their cheerful voices raise;
For well the righteous it becomes
  To sing glad songs of praise.

2 Let harps, and psalteries, and lutes,
  In joyful concert meet;
And new-made songs of loud applause
  The harmony complete.

3 For faithful is the word of God;
  His works with truth abound;
He justice loves, and all the earth
  Is with his goodness crown'd.

4 By his almighty word, at first,
  The heavenly arch was rear'd;
And all the beauteous hosts of light
  At his command appear'd.

5 Let earth, and all that dwell therein,
  Before him trembling stand:
For when he spake the word, 'twas made,
  'Twas fix'd at his command.

PART II. C. M.

1 WHATE'ER the mighty Lord decrees,
  Shall stand for ever sure;
The settled purpose of his heart
  To ages shall endure.

2 How happy then are they, to whom
  The Lord for God is known!
Whom he, from all the world besides,
  Has chosen for his own.

3 Our soul on God with patience waits;
  Our help and shield is he:

SELECTIONS OF PSALMS.

Then, Lord, let still our hearts rejoice,
  Because we trust in thee.
4 The riches of thy mercy, Lord,
  Do thou to us extend;
Since we, for all we want or wish,
  On thee alone depend.

SELECTION 29.
From the xxxiv. Psalm of David.
PART I. C.M.

THROUGH all the changing scenes of life,
  In trouble and in joy,
The praises of my God shall still
  My heart and tongue employ.
2 Of his deliverance I will boast,
  Till all that are distress'd
From my example comfort take,
  And charm their griefs to rest.
3 O magnify the Lord with me,
  With me exalt his Name:
When in distress to him I call'd,
  He to my rescue came.
4 The Angel of the Lord encamps
  Around the good and just;
Deliverance he affords to all
  Who on his succour trust.
5 O make but trial of his love,
  Experience will decide
How blest they are, and only they,
  Who in his truth confide.
6 Fear him, ye saints; and you will then
  Have nothing else to fear:
Make you his service your delight,
  Your wants shall be his care.

PART II. C. M.

1 APPROACH, ye children of the Lord,
  And my instruction hear;
I'll teach you the true discipline
  Of his religious fear.

2 Let him who length of life desires,
   And prosperous days would see,
 From slandering language keep his tongue
   His lips from falsehood free:
3 The crooked paths of vice decline,
   And virtue's ways pursue;
 Establish peace, where 'tis begun,
   And where 'tis lost, renew.
4 The Lord from heaven beholds the just
   With favourable eyes;
 And, when distress'd, his gracious ear
   Is open to their cries:
5 But turns his wrathful look on those
   Whom mercy can't reclaim,
 To cut them off, and from the earth
   Blot out their evil name.
6 Deliverance to his saints he gives,
   When his relief they crave;
 He's nigh to heal the broken heart,
   And contrite spirit save.
7 Great troubles may afflict the just,
   Yet God will save them still;
 The righteous he will keep from harm,
   And guard from every ill.
8 The wicked, from their wickedness,
   Their ruin shall derive;
 Whilst righteous men, whom they detest,
   Shall them and their's survive.
9 For God preserves the souls of those
   Who on his truth depend;
 To them, and their posterity,
   His blessing shall descend.

SELECTION 30. L. M.
From the xxxvi. Psalm of David.

O LORD, thy mercy, my sure hope,
   The highest orb of heaven transcends;
 Thy sacred truth's unmeasured scope
   Beyond the spreading sky extends.

2 Thy justice like the hills remains,
　　Unfathom'd depths thy judgments are;
　Thy providence the world sustains,
　　The whole creation is thy care.

3 Since of thy goodness all partake,
　　With what assurance should the just
　Thy sheltering wings their refuge make,
　　And saints to thy protection trust!

4 Such guests shall to thy courts be led,
　　To banquet on thy love's repast;
　And drink, as from a fountain's head,
　　Of joys that shall for ever last.

5 With thee the springs of life remain,
　　Thy presence is eternal day;
　O let thy saints thy favour gain,
　　To upright hearts thy truth display.

SELECTION 31.
From the xxxvii. Psalm of David.
PART I. II. 2.

THOUGH wicked men grow rich or great,
　　Yet let not their successful state
　　　Thy anger or thy envy raise;
　For they, cut down like tender grass,
　Or like young flowers away shall pass,
　　　Whose blooming beauty soon decays.

2 Depend on God, and him obey,
　So thou within the land shalt stay,
　　　Secure from danger and from want:
　Make his commands thy chief delight,
　And he, thy duty to requite,
　　　Shall all thy earnest wishes grant.

3 In all thy ways trust thou the Lord,
　And he will needful help afford,
　　　To perfect every just design:
　He'll make, like light, serene and clear,
　Thy clouded innocence appear,
　　　And as a mid-day sun to shine.

4 With quiet mind on God depend,
  And patiently for him attend,
    Nor envy the success of crime:
  For God will sinful men destroy;
  While they his presence shall enjoy,
    Who trust on him and wait his time.

PART II. II. 2.

1 THE good man's way is God's delight:
  He orders all the steps aright
    Of him that moves by his command;
  Though he sometimes may be distress'd,
  Yet shall he ne'er be quite oppress'd,
    For God upholds him with his hand.

2 With caution shun each wicked deed,
  In virtue's ways with zeal proceed,
    And so prolong your happy days:
  For God, who judgment loves, does still
  Preserve his saints secure from ill,
    While soon the wicked race decays.

3 The upright shall possess the land,
  His portion shall for ages stand;
    His mouth with wisdom is supplied,
  His tongue by rules of judgment moves,
  His heart the law of God approves;
    Therefore his footsteps never slide.

PART III. II. 2.

1 THE wicked I in power have seen,
  And like a bay-tree fresh and green,
    That spreads its pleasant branches round:
  But he was gone as swift as thought;
  And, though in every place I sought,
    No sign or track of him I found.

2 Observe the perfect man with care,
  And mark all such as upright are;
    Their roughest days in peace shall end;
  While on the latter end of those
  Who dare God's sacred will oppose,
    A common ruin shall attend.

3 God to the just will aid afford,
　Their only safeguard is the Lord;
　　Their strength in time of need is he;
　Because on him they still depend,
　The Lord will timely succour send,
　　And from the wicked set them free.

SELECTION 32.　C. M.
From the xxxviii. Psalm of David.

THY chastening wrath, O Lord, restrain,
　　Though I deserve it all;
　Nor let on me the heavy storm
　　Of thy displeasure fall.

2 My sins, which to a deluge swell,
　　My sinking head o'erflow,
　And, for my feeble strength to bear,
　　Too vast a burden grow.

3 But, Lord, before thy searching eyes
　　All my desires appear;
　The groanings of my burden'd soul
　　Have reach'd thine open ear.

4 Forsake me not, O Lord, my God,
　　Nor far from me depart;
　Make haste to my relief, O thou,
　　Who my salvation art.

SELECTION 33.　C. M.
From the xxxix. Psalm of David.

LORD, let me know my term of days,
　　How soon my life will end:
　The numerous train of ills disclose,
　　Which this frail state attend.

2 My life, thou know'st, is but a span,
　　A cipher sums my years!
　And every man, in best estate,
　　But vanity appears.

3 Man, like a shadow, vainly walks,
　　With fruitless cares oppress'd;
　He heaps up wealth, but cannot tell
　　By whom 'twill be possess'd.

4 Why then should I on worthless toys
   With anxious cares attend?
On thee alone my steadfast hope
   Shall ever, Lord, depend.
5 Lord, hear my cry, accept my tears,
   And listen to my prayer,
Who sojourn like a stranger here,
   As all my fathers were.
6 O spare me yet a little time;
   My wasted strength restore,
Before I vanish quite from hence,
   And shall be seen no more.

SELECTION 34. L. M.
From the xl. Psalm of David.

I WAITED meekly for the Lord,
   Till he vouchsafed a kind reply;
Who did his gracious ear afford,
   And heard from heaven my humble cry.
2 The wonders he for me has wrought
   Shall fill my mouth with songs of praise;
And others, to his worship brought,
   To hopes of like deliverance raise.
3 For blessings shall that man reward,
   Who on th' Almighty Lord relies;
Who treats the proud with disregard,
   And hates the hypocrite's disguise.
4 Who can the wondrous works recount,
   Which thou, O God, for us hast wrought!
The treasures of thy love surmount
   The power of numbers, speech, and thought.
5 I've learnt that thou hast not desired
   Offerings and sacrifice alone;
Nor blood of guiltless beasts required
   For man's transgression to atone.
6 I therefore come—come to fulfil
   The oracles thy books impart:
'Tis my delight to do thy will;
   Thy law is written in my heart.

7 In full assemblies I have told
  Thy truth and righteousness at large;
 Nor did, thou know'st, my lips withhold
  From uttering what thou gav'st in charge:
8 Nor kept within my breast confined
  Thy faithfulness and saving grace;
 But preach'd thy love, for all design'd,
  That all might that and truth embrace.
9 Then let those mercies I declared
  To others, Lord, extend to me;
 Thy loving-kindness my reward,
  Thy truth my safe protection be.

SELECTION 35. C. M.
From the xli. Psalm of David.

HAPPY the man whose tender care
  Relieves the poor distress'd!
 When troubles compass him around,
  The Lord shall give him rest.
2 The Lord his life, with blessings crown'd,
  In safety shall prolong;
 And disappoint the will of those
  That seek to do him wrong.
3 If he, in languishing estate,
  Oppress'd with sickness lie:
 The Lord will easy make his bed,
  And inward strength supply.
4 Secure of this, to thee, my God,
  I thus my prayer address'd:
 "Lord, for thy mercy, heal my soul,
  Though I have much transgress'd."
5 Thy tender care secures my life
  From danger and disgrace;
 And thou vouchsaf'st to set me still
  Before thy glorious face.
6 Let therefore Israel's Lord and God
  From age to age be bless'd;
 And all the people's glad applause
  With loud Amens express'd.

SELECTION 36. C. M.
From the xlii. Psalm of David.

AS pants the hart for cooling streams
  When heated in the chase;
So longs my soul, O God, for thee,
  And thy refreshing grace.

2 For thee, my God, the living God,
    My thirsty soul doth pine;
  O, when shall I behold thy face,
    Thou Majesty divine?

3 Why restless, why cast down, my soul?
    Trust God; who will employ
  His aid for thee, and change these sighs
    To thankful hymns of joy.

4 God of my strength, how long shall I,
    Like one forgotten, mourn;
  Forlorn, forsaken, and exposed
    To my oppressor's scorn?

5 My heart is pierced, as with a sword,
    While thus my foes upbraid:
  "Vain boaster, where is now thy God?
    And where his promised aid?"

6 Why restless, why cast down, my soul?
    Hope still; and thou shalt sing
  The praise of him who is thy God,
    Thy health's eternal spring.

SELECTION 37. II. 5.
From the xliii. Psalm of David.

AS pants the wearied hart for cooling springs,
  That sinks exhausted in the summer's chase,
So pants my soul for thee, great King of kings,
  So thirsts to reach thy sacred dwelling-place.

2 Why throb, my heart? Why sink, my saddening soul?
    Why droop to earth, with various woes oppress'd?
  My years shall yet in blissful circles roll,
    And peace be yet an inmate of this breast.

3 Lord, thy sure mercies, ever in my sight,
   My heart shall gladden through the tedious day;
 And midst the dark and gloomy shades of night,
   To thee, my God, I'll tune the grateful lay.
4 Why faint, my soul? why doubt Jehovah's aid?
   Thy God the God of mercy still shall prove;
 Within his courts thy thanks shall yet be paid:
   Unquestion'd be his faithfulness and love.

SELECTION 38. L. M.
From the xliii. Psalm of David.

LET me with light and truth be bless'd;
   Be these my guides to lead the way;
 Till on thy holy hill I rest,
   And in thy sacred temple pray.

2 Then will I there fresh altars raise
   To God, who is my only joy;
 And well-tuned harps, with songs of praise,
   Shall all my grateful hours employ.

3 Why then cast down, my soul? and why
   So much oppress'd with anxious care?
 On God, thy God, for aid rely,
   Who will thy ruin'd state repair.

SELECTION 39. C. M.
From the xlv. Psalm of David.

WHILE I the King's loud praise rehearse,
   Indited by my heart,
 My tongue is like the pen of him
   That writes with ready art.

2 How matchless is thy form, O King!
   Thy mouth with grace o'erflows;
 Because fresh blessings God on thee
   Eternally bestows.

3 Gird on thy sword, most mighty Prince;
   And, clad in rich array,
 With glorious ornaments of power,
   Majestic pomp display.

4 Ride on in state, and still protect
  The meek, the just, and true;
Whilst thy right hand, with swift revenge,
  Does all thy foes pursue.
5 How sharp thy weapons are to them
  That dare thy power despise!
Down, down they fall, while through their heart
  The piercing arrow flies.
6 But thy firm throne, O God, is fix'd,
  For ever to endure;
Thy sceptre's sway shall always last,
  By righteous laws secure.
7 Because thy heart, by justice led,
  Did upright ways approve,
And hated still the crooked paths,
  Where wandering sinners rove:
8 Therefore did God, thy God, on thee
  The oil of gladness shed;
And has, above thy fellows round,
  Advanced thy lofty head.

SELECTION 40. II. 2.
From the xlvi. Psalm of David.

GOD is our refuge in distress,
  A present help when dangers press,
    In him, undaunted we'll confide;
Though earth were from her centre tost,
And mountains in the ocean lost,
  Torn piecemeal by the roaring tide.
2 A gentler stream with gladness still
  The city of our Lord shall fill,
    The royal seat of God most high:
God dwells in Sion, whose fair towers
Shall mock th' assaults of earthly powers,
  While his almighty aid is nigh.
3 Submit to God's almighty sway,
  For him the heathen shall obey,
    And earth her sovereign Lord confess:

The God of hosts conducts our arms,
  Our tower of refuge in alarms,
  As to our fathers in distress.

SELECTION 41. L. M.
From the xlvii. Psalm of David.

O ALL ye people, clap your hands,
  And with triumphant voices sing;
No force the mighty power withstands
  Of God, the universal King.

2 He shall assaulting foes repel,
    And with success our battles fight;
  Shall fix the place where we must dwell,
    The pride of Jacob, his delight.

3 God is gone up, our Lord and King,
    With shouts of joy, and trumpet's sound;
  To him repeated praises sing,
    And let the cheerful song rebound.

4 Your utmost skill in praise be shown,
    For him who all the world commands;
  Who sits upon his righteous throne,
    And spreads his way o'er heathen lands.

SELECTION 42. C. M.
From the xlviii. Psalm of David.

THE Lord, the only God, is great,
    And greatly to be praised
  In Sion, on whose happy mount
    His sacred throne is raised.

2 In Sion we have seen perform'd
    A work that was foretold,
  In pledge that God, for times to come,
    His city will uphold.

3 Let Sion's mount with joy resound;
    Her daughters all be taught
  In songs his judgments to extol,
    Who this deliverance wrought.

4 Compass her walls in solemn pomp,
    Your eyes quite round her cast;

Count all her towers, and see if there
    You find one stone displaced.
5 Her forts and palaces survey,
    Observe their order well;
That to the ages yet to come
    His wonders you may tell.
6 This God is ours, and will be ours,
    Whilst we in him confide;
Who, as he has preserved us now,
    Till death will be our guide.

SELECTION 43.
From the 1. Psalm of David.
PART I. II. 2.

THE Lord hath spoke, the mighty God
    Hath sent his summons all abroad,
    From dawning light till day declines:
The listening earth his voice hath heard,
    And he from Sion hath appear'd,
    Where beauty in perfection shines.
2 Our God shall come, and keep no more
Misconstrued silence as before,
    But wasting flames before him send;
Around shall tempests fiercely rage,
Whilst he does heaven and earth engage
    His just tribunal to attend.
3 Assemble all my saints to me,
(Thus runs the great divine decree,)
    That in my lasting covenant live,
And offerings bring with constant care:
The heavens his justice shall declare,
    For God himself shall sentence give.

PART II. II. 2.

1 ATTEND, my people; Israel, hear;
    Thy strong accuser I'll appear;
    Thy God, thine only God, am I:
'Tis not of offerings I complain,
Which, daily in my temple slain,
    My sacred altar did supply.

2 The sacrifices I require
   Are hearts which love and zeal inspire,
     And vows with strictest care made good:
   In time of trouble call on me,
   And I will set thee safe and free,
     And thou shalt praise thy gracious God.

3 Consider this, ye thoughtless men!
   My vengeance shall not fall in vain,
     And none will dare your cause to own:
   Who praises me due honour gives;
   And to the man that justly lives
     My strong salvation shall be shown.

SELECTION 44. S. M.
From the li. Psalm of David.

HAVE mercy, Lord, on me,
   As thou wert ever kind;
Let me, oppress'd with loads of guilt,
   Thy wonted mercy find.

2 Wash off my foul offence,
   And cleanse me from my sin;
For I confess my crime, and see
   How great my guilt has been.

3 Against thee, Lord, alone,
   And only in thy sight,
Have I transgress'd; and, though condemn'd,
   Must own thy judgment right.

4 In guilt each part was form'd
   Of all this sinful frame;
In guilt I was conceived, and born
   The heir of sin and shame.

5 Yet, Lord, thy searching eye
   Does inward truth require;
And secretly with wisdom's laws
   My soul thou wilt inspire.

6 With hyssop purge me, Lord,
   And so I clean shall be:
I shall with snow in whiteness vie,
   When purified by thee.

7 Make me to hear with joy
    Thy kind forgiving voice;
  That so the bones which thou hast broke
    May with fresh strength rejoice.

8 Blot out my crying sins,
    Nor me in anger view:
  Create in me a heart that's clean,
    An upright mind renew.

9 Withdraw not thou thy help,
    Nor cast me from thy sight;
  Nor let thy Holy Spirit take
    His everlasting flight.

10 The joy thy favour gives
    Let me, O Lord, regain;
  And thy free Spirit's firm support
    My fainting soul sustain.

11 So I thy righteous ways
    To sinners will impart;
  Whilst my advice shall wicked men
    To thy just laws convert.

12 Could sacrifice atone,
    Whole flocks and herds should die;
  But on such offerings thou disdain'st
    To cast a gracious eye.

13 A broken spirit is
    By God most highly prized;
  By him a broken, contrite heart
    Shall never be despised.

14 Let Sion favour find,
    Of thy good will assured;
  And thy own city flourish long,
    By lofty walls secured.

15 The just shall then attend,
    And pleasing tribute pay;
  And sacrifice of choicest kind
    Upon their altar lay.

SELECTION 45. C. M.
From the lv. Psalm of David.

GIVE ear, thou Judge of all the earth,
And listen when I pray;
Nor from thy humble suppliant turn
Thy glorious face away.

2 My heart is pain'd: the shades of death
Their terrors round me spread;
While fearful tremblings seize my breast,
Horrors o'erwhelm my head.

3 And thus I breathe my heavy sigh
To Him who hears above:
"O that my soul on wings could fly,
And emulate the dove!

4 "Swift I'd escape, and flee afar,
Some secret place to find;
Hide from the world's distracting care,
And rest my weary mind:

5 "I'd wing my everlasting flight,
Bidding the world farewell,
From sin and strife, to realms of light,
Where peace and quiet dwell."

6 Thus will I call on God, who still
Shall in my aid appear;
At morn, at noon, at night I'll pray,
And he my voice shall hear.

SELECTION 46. C. M.
From the lvi. Psalm of David.

LORD, though at times surprised by fear,
On danger's first alarm,
Yet still for succour I depend
On thy almighty arm.

2 God's faithful promise I shall praise,
On which I now rely;
In God I trust, and, trusting him,
The arm of flesh defy.

3 I'll trust God's word, and so despise
  The force that man can raise;
To thee, O God, my vows are due,
  To thee I'll render praise.
4 Thou hast retrieved my soul from death,
  And thou wilt still secure
The life thou hast so oft preserved,
  And make my footsteps sure:
5 That thus, protected by thy power,
  I may this light enjoy;
And in the service of my God
  My lengthen'd days employ.

SELECTION 47. L. M.
From the lvii. Psalm of David.

O GOD, my heart is fix'd, 'tis bent,
  Its thankful tribute to present;
And, with my heart, my voice I'll raise,
To thee, my God, in songs of praise.
2 Awake, my glory; harp and lute,
  No longer let your strings be mute:
And I, my tuneful part to take,
Will with the early dawn awake.
3 Thy praises, Lord, I will resound
  To all the listening nations round:
Thy mercy highest heaven transcends,
Thy truth beyond the clouds extends.
4 Be thou, O God, exalted high;
  And as thy glory fills the sky,
So let it be on earth display'd,
Till thou art here, as there, obey'd.

SELECTION 48. L. M.
From the lxii. Psalm of David.

MY soul, for help on God rely,
  On him alone thy trust repose;
My rock and health will strength supply,
To bear the shock of all my foes.
2 God does his saving health dispense,
  And flowing blessings daily send;

He is my fortress and defence,
  On him my soul shall still depend.
3 In him, ye people, always trust;
  Before his throne pour out your hearts:
  For God, the merciful and just,
  His timely aid to us imparts.
4 The Lord has oft his will express'd,
  And I this truth have fully known;
  To be of boundless power possess'd,
  Belongs of right to God alone.
5 Though mercy is his darling grace,
  In which he chiefly takes delight;
  Yet will he all the human race
  According to their works requite.

SELECTION 49. II. 2.
From the lxiii. Psalm of David.

O GOD, my gracious God, to thee
  My morning prayers shall offer'd be,
  For thee my thirsty soul does pant;
My fainting flesh implores thy grace,
As in a dry and barren place,
  Where I refreshing waters want.
2 O, to my longing eyes once more,
  That view of glorious power restore,
    Which thy majestic house displays:
  Because to me thy wondrous love
  Than life itself does dearer prove,
    My lips shall always speak thy praise.
3 My life, while I that life enjoy,
  In blessing God I will employ,
    With lifted hands adore his name:
  As with its choicest food supplied,
  My soul shall be full satisfied,
    While I with joy his praise proclaim.
4 When down I lie, sweet sleep to find,
  Thou, Lord, art present to my mind,
    And when I wake in dead of night;

Because thou still dost succour bring,
Beneath the shadow of thy wing,
I rest with safety and delight.

SELECTION 50.
From the lxv. Psalm of David.
PART I. L. M.

FOR thee, O God, our constant praise
In Sion waits, thy chosen seat;
Our promised altars there we'll raise,
And all our zealous vows complete.

2 Thou, who to every humble prayer
Dost always bend thy listening ear,
To thee shall all mankind repair,
And at thy gracious throne appear.

3 Our sins, though numberless, in vain
To stop thy flowing mercy try;
Whilst thou o'erlook'st the guilty stain,
And washest out the crimson dye.

4 Bless'd is the man, who, near thee placed,
Within thy sacred dwelling lives!
'Tis there abundantly we taste
The vast delights thy temple gives.

PART II. L. M.

1 LORD, from thy unexhausted store,
Thy rain relieves the thirsty ground;
Makes lands, that barren were before,
With corn and useful fruits abound.

2 On rising ridges down it pours,
And every furrow'd valley fills:
Thou mak'st them soft with gentle showers,
In which a blest increase distils.

3 Thy goodness does the circling year
With fresh returns of plenty crown;
And where thy glorious paths appear,
The fruitful clouds drop fatness down.

4 They drop on barren deserts, changed
By them to pastures fresh and green:

The hills about, in order ranged,
  In beauteous robes of joy are seen.
5 Large flocks with fleecy wool adorn
  The cheerful downs; the valleys bring
A plenteous crop of full-ear'd corn,
  And seem, for joy, to shout and sing.

SELECTION 51.
From the lxvi. Psalm of David.
PART I. C. M.

LET all the lands, with shouts of joy,
  To God their voices raise;
Sing psalms in honour of his Name,
  And spread his glorious praise.
2 And let them say, How dreadful, Lord,
  In all thy works art thou!
To thy great power thy stubborn foes
  Shall all be forced to bow.
3 Through all the earth the nations round
  Shall thee their God confess;
And, with glad hymns, their awful dread
  Of thy great Name express.
4 O come, behold the works of God,
  And then with me you'll own,
That he to all the sons of men
  Has wondrous judgments shown.
5 O all ye nations, bless our God,
  And loudly speak his praise;
Who keeps our souls alive, and still
  Confirms our steadfast ways.

PART II. C. M.

1 MY offerings to God's house I'll bring,
  And there my vows will pay,
Which I with solemn zeal did make
  In trouble's dismal day.
2 O come, all ye that fear the Lord,
  Attend with heedful care;
Whilst I what God for me has done
  With grateful joy declare.

3 As I before his aid implored,
  So now I praise his Name;
But, if my heart to sin incline,
  My prayer will God disclaim.
4 But God to me, whene'er I cried,
  His gracious ear did bend;
And to the voice of my request
  With constant love attend.
5 Then bless'd for ever be my God,
  Who never, when I pray,
Withholds his mercy from my soul,
  Nor turns his face away.

SELECTION 52. S. M.
From the lxvii. Psalm of David.

TO bless thy chosen race,
  In mercy, Lord, incline;
And cause the brightness of thy face
  On all thy saints to shine:
2 That so thy wondrous way
  May through the world be known;
While distant lands their tribute pay,
  And thy salvation own.
3 Let differing nations join
  To celebrate thy fame;
Let all the world, O Lord, combine
  To praise thy glorious Name.
4 O let them shout and sing,
  With joy and pious mirth;
For thou, the righteous Judge and King,
  Shalt govern all the earth.
5 Let differing nations join
  To celebrate thy fame;
Let all the world, O Lord, combine
  To praise thy glorious Name.
6 Then God upon our land
  Shall constant blessings shower;
And all the world in awe shall stand
  Of his resistless power.

SELECTION 53. L. M.
From the lxviii. Psalm of David.

THE servants of Jehovah's will
  His favour's gentle beams enjoy;
Their upright hearts let gladness fill,
  And cheerful songs their tongues employ.

2 To him your voice in anthems raise,
    Jehovah's awful name he bears;
  In him rejoice, extol his praise,
    Who rides upon high-rolling spheres.

3 His chariots numberless, his powers
    Are heavenly hosts, that wait his will;
  His presence now fills Sion's towers,
    As once it honour'd Sinai's hill.

4 Ascending high, in triumph thou
    Captivity hast captive led,
  And on thy people didst bestow
    Thy gifts and graces freely shed.

5 E'en rebels shall partake thy grace,
    And humble proselytes repair
  To worship at thy dwelling-place,
    And all the world pay homage there.

6 For benefits each day bestow'd,
    Be daily his great Name ador'd,
  Who is our Saviour and our God,
    Of life and death the sovereign Lord.

SELECTION 54.
From the lxix. Psalm of David.
PART I. L. M.

SAVE me, O God, from waves that roll,
  And press to overwhelm my soul:
With painful steps in mire I tread,
And deluges o'erflow my head.

2 O Lord, to thee I will repair
    For help, with humble, timely prayer;
  Relieve me from thy mercy's store,
    Display thy truth's preserving power.

3 From threat'ning dangers me relieve,
  And from the mire my feet retrieve;
  From all my foes in safety keep,
  And snatch me from the raging deep.

4 Lord, hear the humble prayer I make,
  For thy transcending goodness' sake;
  Relieve thy supplicant once more
  From thy abounding mercy's store.

5 Reproach and grief have broke my heart;
  I look'd for some to take my part,
  To pity, or relieve my pain;
  But look'd, alas! for both in vain.

6 With hunger pined, for food I call,
  Instead of food they give me gall;
  And when with thirst my spirits sink,
  They give me vinegar to drink.

7 For new afflictions they procur'd
  For him who had thy stripes endur'd;
  And made the wounds thy scourge had torn,
  To bleed afresh with sharper scorn.

PART II. L. M.

1 MY soul, howe'er distress'd and poor,
  Thy strong salvation shall restore:
  Thy power with songs I'll then proclaim,
  And celebrate with thanks thy Name.

2 Our God shall this more highly prize
  Than herds or flocks in sacrifice;
  Which humble saints with joy shall see,
  And hope for like redress with me.

3 For God regards the poor's complaint,
  And frees the captive from restraint:
  Let heaven, earth, sea, their voices raise,
  And all the world resound his praise.

SELECTION 55. C. M.
From the lxxi. Psalm of David.

IN thee I put my steadfast trust,
  Defend me, Lord, from shame:

Incline thine ear, and save my soul,
  For righteous is thy Name.
2 Be thou my strong abiding-place,
   To which I may resort:
 Thy promise, Lord, is my defence,
   Thou art my rock and fort.
3 My steadfast and unchanging hope
   Shall on thy power depend;
 And I in grateful songs of praise
   My time to come will spend.
4 Thy righteous acts and saving health
   My mouth shall still declare;
 Unable yet to count them all,
   Though summ'd with utmost care.
5 While God vouchsafes me his support,
   I'll in his strength go on;
 All other righteousness disclaim,
   And mention his alone.
6 Thou, Lord, hast taught me from my youth,
   To praise thy glorious Name;
 And ever since, thy wondrous works
   Have been my constant theme.
7 Therefore, with psaltery and harp,
   Thy truth, O Lord, I'll praise;
 To thee, the God of Jacob's race,
   My voice in anthems raise.
8 Then joy shall fill my mouth, and songs
   Employ my cheerful voice;
 My grateful soul, by thee redeem'd,
   Shall in thy strength rejoice.

SELECTION 56. C. M.
From the lxxii. Psalm of David.

LO! hills and mountains shall bring forth
  The happy fruits of peace;
 Which all the land shall own to be
   The work of righteousness:
2 While David's Son our needy race
   Shall rule with gentle sway;

     And from their humble neck shall take
        Oppressive yokes away.
3 In every heart thy awful fear
      Shall then be rooted fast,
   As long as sun and moon endure,
      Or time itself shall last.
4 He shall descend like rain, that cheers
      The meadow's second birth;
   Or like warm showers, whose gentle drops
      Refresh the thirsty earth.
5 In his blest days the just and good
      Shall spring up all around:
   The happy land shall every where
      With endless peace abound.
6 His uncontroll'd dominion shall
      From sea to sea extend;
   Begin at proud Euphrates' stream,
      At nature's limits end.
7 To him the savage nations round
      Shall bow their servile heads;
   His vanquish'd foes shall lick the dust,
      Where he his conquest spreads.
8 The kings of Tarshish and the isles
      Shall costly presents bring;
   From spicy Sheba gifts shall come,
      And wealthy Saba's king.
9 To him shall every king on earth
      His humble homage pay;
   And differing nations gladly join
      To own his righteous sway.
10 For he shall set the needy free,
      When they for succour cry;
   Shall save the helpless and the poor,
      And all their wants supply.
11 For him shall constant prayer be made,
      Through all his prosperous days:
   His just dominion shall afford
      A lasting theme of praise.

12 The memory of his glorious Name
  Through endless years shall run;
  His spotless fame shall shine as bright
  And lasting as the sun.
13 In him the nations of the world
  Shall be completely bless'd,
  And his unbounded happiness
  By every tongue confess'd.
14 Then bless'd be God, the mighty Lord,
  The God whom Israel fears;
  Who only wondrous in his works
  Beyond compare, appears.
15 Let earth be with his glory fill'd,
  For ever bless his Name;
  Whilst to his praise the listening world
  Their glad assent proclaim.

SELECTION 57. L. M.
From the lxxiii. Psalm of David.

THY presence, Lord, hath me supplied,
  Thou my right hand support dost give;
  Thou first shalt with thy counsel guide,
  And then to glory me receive.
2 Whom then in heaven, but thee alone,
  Have I, whose favour I require?
  Throughout the spacious earth there's none,
  Compared with thee, that I desire.
3 My trembling flesh and aching heart
  May often fail to succour me;
  But God shall inward strength impart,
  And my eternal portion be.
4 For they that far from thee remove
  Shall into sudden ruin fall;
  If after other gods they rove,
  Thy vengeance shall destroy them all.
5 But as for me, 'tis good and just
  That I should still to God repair;
  In him I always put my trust,
  And will his wondrous works declare.

* X

SELECTION 58. C. M.

From the lxxiv. Psalm of David.

THINE is the cheerful day, O Lord;
　　Thine the return of night;
Thou hast prepared the glorious sun,
　　And every feebler light.

2 By thee the borders of the earth
　　In perfect order stand;
The summer's warmth, and winter's cold,
　　Attend on thy command.

SELECTION 59. IV. I.

From the lxxvi. Psalm of David.

THE Name of our God
　　In Israel is known;
His mansion beloved
　　Is Sion alone:
There broke he the arrows
　　The enemy hurl'd,
And honour'd his mountain
　　Above all the world.

2 The pride of thy foes
　　Is turn'd to thy praise;
Their fierceness o'erruled
　　Thy providence sways;
Their sin overflowing
　　Thy power will restrain;
Thy arm on the wicked
　　New glory will gain.

3 Ye nations, to God
　　Vow homage sincere;
Devote to him gifts,
　　Love, worship, and fear:
Before him, ye mighty,
　　Your spirits repress;
Ye high, and ye humble,
　　His wonders confess!

SELECTION 60. C. M.
From the lxxviii. Psalm of David.

HEAR, O my people; to my law
    Devout attention lend;
Let the instruction of my mouth
    Deep in your hearts descend.

2 My tongue shall oracles proclaim
    Which ancient times have known;
The truths which our forefathers' care
    To us has handed down.

3 We will not hide them from our sons,
    Our offspring shall be taught
The praises of the Lord, whose strength
    Has works of wonder wrought.

4 For Jacob he his law ordain'd,
    His league with Israel made;
With charge to be from age to age,
    From race to race, convey'd:

5 That generations yet to come
    Should to their unborn heirs
Religiously transmit the same,
    And they again to theirs.

6 To teach them that in God alone
    Their hope securely stands;
That they should ne'er his works forget,
    But keep his just commands.

SELECTION 61. L. M.
From the lxxx. Psalm of David.

O THOU whom heavenly hosts obey,
    How long shall thy fierce anger burn?
How long thy suffering people pray,
    And to their prayers have no return?

2 Thou brought'st a vine from Egypt's land;
    And, casting out the heathen race,
Didst plant it with thine own right hand,
    And firmly fix it in their place.

3 Before it thou preparedst the way,
　　And mad'st it take a lasting root;
　Which, bless'd with thy indulgent ray,
　　O'er all the land did widely shoot.

4 The hills were cover'd with its shade,
　　Its goodly boughs did cedars seem;
　Its branches to the sea were spread,
　　And reach'd to proud Euphrates' stream.

5 To thee, O God of hosts, we pray,
　　Thy wonted goodness, Lord, renew;
　From heaven, thy throne, this vine survey,
　　And her sad state with pity view.

6 Behold the vineyard made by thee,
　　Which thy right hand did guard so long;
　And keep that branch from danger free,
　　Which for thyself thou mad'st so strong.

7 Do thou convert us, Lord, do thou
　　The lustre of thy face display;
　And all the ills we suffer now,
　　Like scatter'd clouds, shall pass away.

SELECTION 62. C. M.
From the lxxxi. Psalm of David.

TO God, our never-failing strength,
　　With loud applauses sing:
　And jointly make a cheerful noise
　　To Jacob's awful King.

2 Compose a hymn of praise, and touch
　　Your instruments of joy;
　Let psalteries and tuneful harps
　　Your grateful skill employ.

3 Let trumpets at the festival
　　Their joyful voices raise,
　To celebrate th' appointed time,
　　The solemn day of praise.

4 For this a statute was of old,
　　Which Jacob's God decreed
　To be with pious care observed,
　　By Israel's chosen seed.

SELECTION 63. C.M.
From the lxxxiv. Psalm of David.

O GOD of hosts, the mighty Lord,
   How lovely is the place,
Where thou, enthroned in glory, show'st
   The brightness of thy face!

2 My longing soul faints with desire
   To view thy blest abode;
My panting heart and flesh cry out
   For thee, the living God.

3 The birds, more happy far than I,
   Around thy temple throng;
Securely there they build, and there
   Securely hatch their young.

4 O Lord of hosts, my King and God,
   How highly bless'd are they,
Who in thy temple always dwell,
   And there thy praise display!

5 Thrice happy they, whose choice has thee
   Their sure protection made,
Who long to tread the sacred ways
   That to thy dwelling lead!

6 Who pass through parch'd and thirsty vales,
   Yet no refreshment want;
Their pools are fill'd with rain, which thou
   At their request dost grant.

7 Thus they proceed from strength to strength,
   And still approach more near;
Till all on Sion's holy mount
   Before their God appear.

8 Within thy courts one single day
   'Tis better to attend,
Than, Lord, in any other place
   A thousand days to spend.

9 Much rather in God's house will I
   The meanest office take,
Than in the wealthy tents of sin
   My pompous dwelling make.

10 For God, who is our sun and shield,
   Will grace and glory give;
   And no good thing will he withhold
   From them that justly live.

11 Thou God, whom heavenly hosts obey,
   How highly bless'd is he,
   Whose hope and trust, securely placed,
   Are still reposed on thee!

SELECTION 64. C. M.
From the lxxxv. Psalm of David.

O GOD our Saviour, all our hearts
   To thy obedience turn;
That, quench'd with our repenting tears,
   Thy wrath no more may burn.

2 For why should'st thou be angry still,
   And wrath so long retain?
Revive us, Lord, and let thy saints
   Thy wonted comfort gain.

3 Thy gracious favour, Lord, display,
   Which we have long implored;
And, for thy wondrous mercy's sake,
   Thy wonted aid afford.

4 God's answer patiently I'll wait;
   For he with glad success,
If they no more to folly turn,
   His mourning saints will bless.

5 To all that fear God's holy Name
   His sure salvation's near;
His glory in our happy land
   For ever shall appear.

6 For mercy now with truth is join'd;
   And righteousness with peace.
Like kind companions, absent long,
   With friendly arms embrace.

7 Truth from the earth shall spring, whilst heaven
   Shall streams of justice pour;
And God, from whom all goodness flows,
   Shall endless plenty shower.

8 Before him righteousness shall march,
    And his just paths prepare;
While we his holy steps pursue
    With constant zeal and care.

SELECTION 65. C. M.
From the lxxxvi. Psalm of David.

TO my complaint, O Lord my God,
    Thy gracious ear incline;
Hear me, distress'd, and destitute
    Of all relief but thine.

2 Do thou, O God, preserve my soul,
    That does thy Name adore;
Thy servant keep, and him whose trust
    Relies on thee, restore.

3 To me, who daily thee invoke,
    Thy mercy, Lord, extend;
Refresh thy servant's soul, whose hopes
    On thee alone depend.

4 Thou, Lord, art good; nor only good,
    But prompt to pardon too;
Of plenteous mercy to all those
    Who for thy mercy sue.

5 To my repeated humble prayer,
    O Lord, attentive be;
When troubled, I on thee will call,
    For thou wilt answer me.

6 Among the gods there's none like thee,
    O Lord, alone divine!
To thee as much inferior they,
    As are their works to thine.

7 Therefore their great Creator, thee
    The nations shall adore;
Their long-misguided prayers and praise
    To thy bless'd Name restore.

8 All shall confess thee great, and great
    The wonders thou hast done;
Confess thee God, the God supreme,
    Confess thee God alone.

9 Teach me thy way, O Lord, and I
　　From truth shall ne'er depart;
　In reverence to thy sacred Name
　　Devoutly fix my heart.

10 Thee will I praise, O Lord my God,
　　Praise thee with heart sincere;
　And to thy everlasting Name
　　Eternal trophies rear.

11 Thy boundless mercy shown to me
　　Transcends my power to tell;
　For thou hast oft redeem'd my soul
　　From lowest deeps of hell.

12 And thou thy constant goodness didst
　　To my assistance bring;
　Of patience, mercy, and of truth,
　　Thou everlasting spring!

SELECTION 66. II. 3.
From the lxxxvii. Psalm of David.

GOD'S temple crowns the holy mount,
　　The Lord there condescends to dwell:
His Sion's gates, in his account,
　　Our Israel's fairest tents excel:
Yea, glorious things of thee we sing,
O city of th' Almighty King!

2 Of honour'd Sion we aver,
　　Illustrious throngs from her proceed;
Th' Almighty shall establish her,
　　And shall enrol her holy seed:
Yea, for his people he shall count
The children of his favour'd mount.

3 He'll Sion find with numbers fill'd
　　Who celebrate his matchless praise;
Who, here, in hallelujahs skill'd,
　　In heaven their harps and hymns shall raise:
O Sion, seat of Israel's King,
Be mine to drink thy living spring!

SELECTION 67. L. M.
From the lxxxviii. Psalm of David.

GOD of my life, O Lord most high,
To thee by day and night I cry;
Vouchsafe my mournful voice to hear,
To my distress incline thine ear.

2 Like those whose strength and hopes are fled,
They number me among the dead;
Like those who, shrouded in the grave,
For thee no more remembrance have.

3 Wilt thou by miracle revive
The dead, whom thou forsook'st alive?
Shall the mute grave thy love confess,
A mouldering tomb thy faithfulness?

4 To thee, O Lord, I cry forlorn,
My prayer prevents the early morn:
Why hast thou, Lord, my soul forsook,
Nor once vouchsafed a gracious look?

5 Companions dear, and friends beloved,
Far from my sight thou hast removed:
God of my life, O Lord most high,
Vouchsafe to hear my mournful cry!

SELECTION 68. L. M.
From the lxxxix. Psalm of David.

THY mercies, Lord, shall be my song,
My song on them shall ever dwell;
To ages yet unborn, my tongue
Thy never-failing truth shall tell.

2 I have affirm'd, and still maintain,
Thy mercy shall for ever last;
Thy truth, that does the heavens sustain,
Like them shall stand for ever fast.

3 Thus spak'st thou by thy prophet's voice:
"With David I a league have made;
To him, my servant and my choice,
By solemn oath this grant convey'd:

4 "While earth, and seas, and skies endure,
Thy seed shall in my sight remain;

To them thy throne I will ensure,
   They shall to endless ages reign."
5 For such stupendous truth and love,
   Both heaven and earth just praises owe,
 By choirs of angels sung above,
   And by assembled saints below.
6 What seraph of celestial birth
   To vie with Israel's God shall dare?
 Or who among the gods of earth
   With our Almighty Lord compare?
7 With reverence and religious dread,
   His saints should to his temple press;
 His fear through all their hearts should spread,
   Who his almighty Name confess.
8 Lord God of armies, who can boast
   Of strength or power like thine renown'd?
 Of such a numerous, faithful host,
   As that which does thy throne surround?
9 Thou dost the lawless sea control,
   And change the prospect of the deep;
 Thou mak'st the sleeping billows roll;
   Thou mak'st the rolling billows sleep.
10 In thee the sovereign right remains
    Of earth and heaven; thee, Lord, alone,
 The world, and all that it contains,
    Their Maker and Preserver own.
11 Thine arm is mighty, strong thy hand,
    Yet, Lord, thou dost with justice reign;
 Possess'd of absolute command,
    Thou truth and mercy dost maintain.
12 Happy, thrice happy they, who hear
    Thy sacred trumpet's joyful sound;
 Who may at festivals appear,
    With thy most glorious presence crown'd.
13 Thy saints shall always be o'erjoy'd,
    Who on thy sacred Name rely;
 And, in thy righteousness employ'd,
    Above their foes be raised on high.

14 For in thy strength they shall advance,
    Whose conquests from thy favour spring:
  The Lord of hosts is our defence,
    And Israel's God our Israel's King.

SELECTION 69.
From the xc. Psalm of David.
PART I. C. M.

O LORD, the saviour and defence
    Of us thy chosen race,
  From age to age thou still hast been
    Our sure abiding place.

2 Before thou brought'st the mountains forth,
    Or th' earth and world didst frame,
  Thou always wast the mighty God,
    And ever art the same.

3 Thou turnest man, O Lord, to dust,
    Of which he first was made;
  And when thou speak'st the word, 'Return,'
    'Tis instantly obey'd.

4 For in thy sight a thousand years
    Are like a day that's past;
  Or like a watch in dead of night,
    Whose hours unminded waste.

5 Thou sweep'st us off as with a flood,
    We vanish hence like dreams:—
  At first we grow like grass, that feels
    The sun's reviving beams;

6 But howsoever fresh and fair
    Its morning beauty shows,
  'Tis all cut down, and wither'd quite,
    Before the evening close.

7 We by thine anger are consumed,
    And by thy wrath dismay'd;
  Our publick crimes and secret sins
    Before thy sight are laid.

8 Beneath thine anger's sad effects
    Our drooping days we spend;
  Our unregarded years break off,
    Like tales that quickly end.

9 Our term of time is seventy years,
 An age that few survive;
But if, with more than common strength,
 To eighty we arrive—
10 Yet then our boasted strength decays,
 To sorrow turn'd and pain:
So soon the slender thread is cut,
 And we no more remain.

PART II. C. M.

1 BUT who thine anger's dread effects
 Does, as he ought, revere?
And yet thy wrath does fall or rise,
 As more or less we fear.

2 So teach us, Lord, th' uncertain sum
 Of our short days to mind,
That to true wisdom all our hearts
 May ever be inclined.

3 O to thy servants, Lord, return,
 And speedily relent:
As we of our misdeeds, do thou
 Of our just doom repent.

4 To satisfy and cheer our souls,
 Thy early mercy send;
That we may all our days to come
 In joy and comfort spend.

5 To all thy servants, Lord, let this
 Thy wondrous work be known;
And to our offspring yet unborn,
 Thy glorious power be shown.

6 Let thy bright rays upon us shine,
 Give thou our work success;
The glorious work we have in hand
 Do thou vouchsafe to bless.

SELECTION 70.
From the xci. Psalm of David.
PART I. II. 2.

HE that has God his guardian made,
 Shall under the Almighty's shade
 Secure and undisturb'd abide:

Thus to my soul of him I'll say,
He is my fortress and my stay,
   My God, in whom I will confide.
2 His tender love and watchful care
Shall free thee from the fowler's snare,
   And from the noisome pestilence;
He over thee his wings shall spread,
And cover thy unguarded head;
   His truth shall be thy strong defence.
3 No terrors that surprise by night
Shall thy undaunted courage fright,
   Nor deadly shafts that fly by day;
Nor plague of unknown rise, that kills
In darkness, nor infectious ills
   That in the burning noon-tide slay.
4 Because, with well-placed confidence,
Thou mak'st the Lord thy sure defence,
   Thy refuge, even God most high;
Therefore no ill on thee shall come,
Nor to thy heaven-protected home
   Shall overwhelming plagues draw nigh.

PART II. III. 8.

1 GOD shall charge his angel legions
   Watch and ward o'er thee to keep;
Though thou walk through hostile regions,
   Though in desert wilds thou sleep.
2 On the lion vainly roaring,
   On his young, thy foot shall tread;
And, the dragon's den exploring,
   Thou shalt bruise the serpent's head.
3 Since, with pure and firm affection,
   Thou on God hast set thy love,
With the wings of his protection
   He will shield thee from above.
4 Thou shalt call on him in trouble,
   He will hearken, he will save;
Here for grief reward thee double,
   Crown with life beyond the grave.

SELECTION 71. C. M.
From the xcii. Psalm of David

HOW good and pleasant must it be
   To thank the Lord most high;
And with repeated hymns of praise
   His name to magnify!

2 With every morning's early dawn
   His goodness to relate;
And of his constant truth, each night,
   The glad effects repeat!

3 To ten-string'd instruments we'll sing,
   With tuneful psalteries join'd;
And to the harp with solemn sounds,
   For sacred use design'd.

4 For through thy wondrous works, O Lord,
   Thou mak'st my heart rejoice;
The thoughts of them shall make me glad,
   And shout with cheerful voice.

5 How wondrous are thy works, O Lord!
   How deep are thy decrees!
Whose winding tracks, in secret laid,
   No careless sinner sees.

6 He little thinks, when wicked men,
   Like grass, look fresh and gay,
How soon their short-lived splendour must
   For ever pass away.

7 But thou, my God, art still most high;
   And all thy lofty foes,
Who thought they might securely sin,
   Shall be o'erwhelm'd with woes.

8 But righteous men, like rising palms,
   Shall grow and flourish still;
Thy flock shall spread, like cedars choice,
   On Lebanon's high hill.

9 These, planted in the house of God,
   Within his courts shall thrive;
Their vigour and their lustre both
   Shall in old age revive.

SELECTIONS OF PSALMS.

10 Thus will the Lord his justice show;
   And God, my strong defence,
Shall due rewards to all the world
   Impartially dispense.

SELECTION 72. L. M.
From the xciii. Psalm of David.

WITH glory clad, with strength array'd,
   The Lord, that o'er all nature reigns,
The world's foundation strongly laid,
   And the vast fabric still sustains.

2 How surely stablish'd is thy throne!
   Which shall no change or period see;
For thou, O Lord, and thou alone,
   Art God from all eternity.

3 The floods, O Lord, lift up their voice,
   And toss the troubled waves on high;
But God above can still their noise,
   And make the angry sea comply.

4 Thy promise, Lord, is ever sure,
   And they that in thy house would dwell,
That happy station to secure,
   Must still in holiness excel.

SELECTION 73.
From the xciv. Psalm of David.
PART I. C.M.

SAY ye, the Lord shall not regard,
   Shall not your sins discern?
Take heed, ye foolish and unwise;
   When will ye wisdom learn?

2 Can He be deaf, who form'd the ear,
   Or blind who framed the eye?
Shall earth's great Judge not punish those
   Who his known will defy?

3 He fathoms all the hearts of men,
   To him their thoughts lie bare;
His eye surveys them all, and sees
   How vain their counsels are.

PART II. C. M.

1 BLESS'D is the man, whom thou, O Lord,
    In kindness dost chastise,
And by thy sacred rules to walk
    Dost lovingly advise.

2 This man shall rest and safety find
    In seasons of distress;
Whilst God prepares a pit for those
    That stubbornly transgress.

3 For God will never from his saints
    His favour wholly take;
His own possession and his lot
    He will not quite forsake.

4 The world shall yet confess thee just
    In all that thou hast done;
And those that choose thy upright ways
    Shall in those paths go on.

5 Long since had I in silence slept,
    But that the Lord was near,
To stay me when I slipp'd; when sad,
    My troubled heart to cheer.

6 My soul's defence is firmly placed
    In God, the Lord most high:
He is my rock, to which I may
    For refuge always fly.

SELECTION 74. L. M.
From the xcv. Psalm of David.

O COME, loud anthems let us sing,
Loud thanks to our Almighty King;
For we our voices high shall raise,
When our salvation's rock we praise.

2 Into his presence let us haste,
To thank him for his favours past;
To him address, in joyful songs,
The praise that to his Name belongs:

3 For God the Lord, enthroned in state,
Is with unrivall'd glory great;

    A King superior far to all
    Whom gods the heathen falsely call.
4 The depths of earth are in his hand,
    Her secret wealth at his command;
    The strength of hills that reach the skies,
    Subjected to his empire lies.
5 The rolling ocean's vast abyss
    By the same sovereign right is his;
    'Twas made by his almighty hand,
    That form'd and fix'd the solid land.
6 O let us to his courts repair,
    And bow with adoration there;
    Down on our knees devoutly all
    Before the Lord, our Maker, fall.
7 For he's our God, our Shepherd he,
    His flock and pasture-sheep are we:
    O then, ye faithful flock, to-day
    His warning hear, his voice obey.

SELECTION 75. II. 8.
From the xcvi. Psalm of David.

SING to the Lord a new-made song;
    Let earth in one assembled throng
        Her common Patron's praise resound:
    Sing to the Lord, and bless his Name,
    From day to day his praise proclaim,
        Who us has with salvation crown'd:
    To heathen lands his fame rehearse,
    His wonders to the universe.
2 He's great, and greatly to be praised;
    In majesty and glory raised
        Above all other deities;
    For pageantry and idols all
    Are they whom gods the heathen call;
        He only rules who made the skies:
    With majesty and honour crown'd,
    Glory and strength his throne surround.
3 Be glory then to him restored
    By all who have false gods adored:
        Ascribe due honour to his Name,

Peace-offerings on his altar lay,
Before his throne your homage pay,
   Which he, and he alone, can claim:
To worship at his sacred court,
Let all the trembling world resort.
4 Proclaim aloud, Jehovah reigns,
Whose power the universe sustains,
   And banish'd justice will restore;
Let therefore heaven new joys confess,
And heavenly mirth let earth express,
   Its loud applause the ocean roar,
Its mute inhabitants rejoice,
And for this triumph find a voice.
5 For joy let fertile valleys sing,
The cheerful groves their tribute bring,
   And tuneful harmonies awake:
Behold! in truth and justice clad,
God comes to judge the world he made,
   And to himself his throne to take:
He's come, to judge the world he's come,
With justice to reward and doom.

SELECTION 76.   L. M.
From the xcvii. Psalm of David.

JEHOVAH reigns, let all the earth
   In his just government rejoice;
Let all the lands, with sacred mirth,
   In his applause unite their voice.
2 Darkness and clouds of awful shade
   His dazzling glory shroud in state;
Judgment and righteousness are made
   The habitation of his seat.
3 For thou, O God, art seated high,
   Above earth's potentates enthron'd;
Thou, Lord, unrivall'd in the sky,
   Supreme by all the gods art own'd.
4 Ye who to serve this Lord aspire,
   Abhor what's ill, and truth esteem;
He'll keep his servants' souls entire,
   And them from wicked hands redeem.

5 For seeds are sown of glorious light,
    A future harvest for the just;
And gladness for the heart that's right,
    To recompense its pious trust.

6 Rejoice, ye righteous, in the Lord;
    Memorials of his holiness
Deep in your faithful breasts record,
    And with your thankful tongues confess.

SELECTION 77. C. M.
From the xcviii. Psalm of David.

SING to the Lord a new-made song,
    Who wondrous things has done;
With his right hand and holy arm,
    The conquest he has won.

2 The Lord has through th' astonish'd world
    Display'd his saving might,
And made his righteous acts appear
    In all the heathen's sight.

3 Of Israel's house his love and truth
    Have ever mindful been;
Wide earth's remotest parts the power
    Of Israel's God have seen.

4 Let therefore earth's inhabitants
    Their cheerful voices raise,
And all with universal joy
    Resound their Maker's praise.

5 With harp and hymns soft melody,
    Into the concert bring
The trumpet and shrill cornet's sound,
    Before th' Almighty King.

6 Let the loud ocean roar her joy,
    With all that seas contain;
The earth and her inhabitants
    Join concert with the main.

7 Let floods and torrents clap their hands,
    With joy their homage pay;
Let echoing vales, from hill to hill,
    Redoubled shouts convey:

8 To welcome down the world's great Judge,
  Who does with justice come,
And with impartial equity,
  Both to reward and doom.

SELECTION 78. C. M.
From the xcix. Psalm of David.

JEHOVAH reigns; let therefore all
  The guilty nations quake:
On cherubs' wings he sits enthroned;
  Let earth's foundations shake.

2 On Sion's hill he keeps his court,
  His palace makes her towers;
And thence his sovereignty extends
  Supreme o'er earthly powers.

3 Let therefore all with praise address
  His great and dreadful Name;
And with his unresisted might,
  His holiness proclaim.

4 For truth and justice, in his reign,
  Of strength and power take place;
His judgments are with righteousness
  Dispensed to Jacob's race.

5 Therefore exalt the Lord our God,
  Before his footstool fall;
And with his unresisted might,
  His holiness extol.

6 With worship at his sacred courts
  Exalt our God and Lord;
For he, who only holy is,
  Alone should be adored.

SELECTION 79. L. M.
From the c. Psalm of David.

WITH one consent let all the earth
  To God their cheerful voices raise;
Glad homage pay with awful mirth,
  And sing before him songs of praise.

2 Convinced that he is God alone,
  From whom both we and all proceed;

    We, whom he chooses for his own,
        The flock that he vouchsafes to feed.
3 O enter then his temple gate,
    Thence to his courts devoutly press;
  And still your grateful hymns repeat,
    And still his Name with praises bless.
4 For he's the Lord, supremely good,
    His mercy is for ever sure;
  His truth, which always firmly stood,
    To endless ages shall endure.

SELECTION 80.
From the cii. Psalm of David.
PART I. C. M.

WHEN I pour out my soul in prayer,
    Do thou, O Lord, attend;
To thy eternal throne of grace
    Let my sad cry ascend.
2 O hide not thou thy glorious face
    In times of deep distress;
Incline thine ear, and, when I call,
    My sorrows soon redress.
3 My days, just hastening to their end,
    Are like an evening shade;
My beauty does, like wither'd grass,
    With waning lustre fade.
4 But thine eternal state, O Lord,
    No length of time shall waste;
The memory of thy wondrous works
    From age to age shall last.

PART II. C. M.

1 GOD shall arise, and Sion view
    With an unclouded face:
For now her time is come, his own
    Appointed day of grace.
2 The Name and glory of the Lord
    All heathen kings shall fear,
When he shall Sion build again,
    And in full state appear.

3 For God, from his abode on high,
　　His gracious beams display'd;
　The Lord from heaven, his lofty throne,
　　Hath all the earth survey'd.

4 That they, in Sion, where he dwells,
　　Might celebrate his fame,
　And through the holy city sing
　　Loud praises to his Name.

PART III. C. M.

1 THE strong foundations of the earth
　　Of old by thee were laid;
　Thy hands, O Lord, the arch of heaven
　　With wondrous skill have made.

2 Whilst thou for ever shalt endure,
　　They soon shall pass away;
　And, like a garment often worn,
　　Shall tarnish and decay.

3 Like that, when thou ordain'st their change,
　　To thy command they bend;
　But thou continuest still the same,
　　Nor have thy years an end.

4 Thou to the children of thy saints
　　Shalt lasting quiet give;
　Whose happy race, securely fix'd,
　　Shall in thy presence live.

SELECTION 81. L. M.
From the ciii. Psalm of David.

MY soul, inspired with sacred love,
　　God's holy Name for ever bless;
　Of all his favours mindful prove,
　　And still thy grateful thanks express.

2 'Tis he that all thy sins forgives,
　　And after sickness makes thee sound;
　From danger he thy life retrieves,
　　By him with grace and mercy crown'd.

3 He with good things thy mouth supplies,
　　Thy vigour eagle-like restores;

He to the sufferer promptly flies,
  Who, wrong'd, his righteous help implores.

4 The Lord abounds with tender love,
  And unexampled acts of grace;
His waken'd wrath doth slowly move,
  His willing mercy flies apace.

5 God will not always harshly chide,
  But with his anger quickly part;
And loves his punishments to guide
  More by his love than our desert.

6 As high as heaven its arch extends
  Above this little spot of clay,
So much his boundless love transcends
  The small respects that we can pay.

7 As far as 'tis from east to west,
  So far has he our sins removed;
Who, with a father's tender breast,
  Has such as fear him always loved.

8 For God, who all our frame surveys,
  Considers that we are but clay;
How fresh soe'er we seem, our days
  Like grass or flowers must fade away.

9 Whilst they are nipp'd with sudden blasts,
  Nor can we find their former place,
God's faithful mercy ever lasts
  To those that fear him, and their race.

10 This shall attend on such as still
  Proceed in his appointed way;
And who not only know his will,
  But to it just obedience pay.

11 The Lord, the universal King,
  In heaven has fix'd his lofty throne:
To him, ye angels, praises sing,
  In whose great strength his power is shown.

12 Ye that his just commands obey,
  And hear and do his sacred will,
Ye hosts of his, this tribute pay,
  Who still what he ordains fulfil.

13 Let every creature jointly bless
    The mighty Lord; and thou, my heart,
With grateful joy thy thanks express,
    And in this concert bear thy part.

SELECTION 82. S. M.
From the ciii. Psalm of David.

O BLESS the Lord, my soul,
    His grace to thee proclaim;
And all that is within me, join
    To bless his holy Name.

2 O bless the Lord, my soul,
    His mercies bear in mind;
Forget not all his benefits,
    Who is to thee so kind.

3 He pardons all thy sins,
    Prolongs thy feeble breath;
He healeth thine infirmities,
    And ransoms thee from death.

4 He feeds thee with his love,
    Upholds thee with his truth;
And, like the eagle's, he renews
    The vigour of thy youth.

5 Then bless the Lord, my soul,
    His grace, his love proclaim;
Let all that is within me, join
    To bless his holy Name.

SELECTION 83.
From the civ. Psalm of David.
PART I. L. M.

BLESS God, my soul; thou, Lord, alone
    Possessest empire without bounds,
With honour thou art crown'd, thy throne
    Eternal majesty surrounds.

2 With light thou dost thyself enrobe,
    And glory for a garment take;
Heaven's curtain stretch beyond the globe,
    Thy canopy of state to make.

3 God builds on liquid air, and forms
    His palace-chambers in the skies;
The clouds his chariots are, and storms
    The swift-wing'd steeds with which he flies.

4 As bright as flame, as swift as wind,
    His ministers heaven's palace fill;
They have their sundry tasks assign'd,
    All prompt to do their sovereign's will.

5 In praising God while he prolongs
    My breath, I will that breath employ;
And join devotion to my songs,
    Sincere, as in him is my joy.

PART II. L. M.

1 HOW various, Lord, thy works are found,
    For which thy wisdom we adore!
The earth is with thy treasure crown'd,
    Till nature's hand can grasp no more.

2 All creatures, both of sea and land,
    In sense of common want agree;
All wait on thy dispensing hand,
    And have their daily alms from thee.

3 They gather what thy stores disperse,
    Without their trouble to provide;
Thou op'st thy hand, the universe,
    The craving world, is all supplied.

4 Thou for a moment hid'st thy face,
    The numerous ranks of creatures mourn;
Thou tak'st their breath, all nature's race
    Decay, and to their dust return.

5 Again thou send'st thy Spirit forth,
    Inspiring vital energies;
Nature's restored; replenish'd earth,
    Joyous, her new creation sees.

6 Thus through successive ages stands
    Firm fix'd thy providential care;
Pleas'd with the work of thine own hands,
    Thou dost the wastes of time repair.

SELECTION 84. II. 3.
From the civ. Psalm of David.

HOW manifold thy works, O Lord,
   In wisdom, power, and goodness wrought!
The earth is with thy riches stored,
   And ocean with thy wonders fraught:
Unfathom'd caves beneath the deep
For thee their hidden treasures keep.

2 By thee alone the living live,—
   Hide but thy face, their comforts fly;
They gather what thy seasons give,—
   Take thou away their breath, they die;
But send again thy Spirit forth,
And life renews the gladden'd earth.

3 Joy in his works Jehovah takes,
   Yet to destruction they return;
He looks upon the earth, it quakes,—
   Touches the mountains, and they burn.
But God for ever is the same;
Glory to his eternal Name!

SELECTION 85. C. M.
From the cv. Psalm of David.

O RENDER thanks, and bless the Lord,
   Invoke his sacred Name;
Acquaint the nations with his deeds,
   His matchless deeds proclaim.

2 Sing to his praise in lofty hymns,
   His wondrous works rehearse;
Make them the theme of your discourse,
   And subject of your verse.

3 Rejoice in his almighty Name,
   Alone to be adored;
And let their hearts o'erflow with joy,
   That humbly seek the Lord.

4 Seek ye the Lord, his saving strength
   Devoutly still implore;
And, where he's ever present, seek
   His face for evermore.

5 The wonders that his hands have wrought
    Keep thankfully in mind;
The righteous statutes of his mouth,
    And laws to us assign'd.

SELECTION 86. L. M.
From the cvi. Psalm of David.

O RENDER thanks to God above,
    The fountain of eternal love;
Whose mercy firm through ages past
Has stood, and shall for ever last.

2 Who can his mighty deeds express,
Not only vast, but numberless?
What mortal eloquence can raise
His tribute of immortal praise?

3 Happy are they, and only they,
Who from thy judgments never stray;
Who know what's right; nor only so,
But always practise what they know.

4 Extend to me that favour, Lord,
Thou to thy chosen dost afford;
When thou return'st to set them free,
Let thy salvation visit me.

5 O may I worthy prove to see
Thy saints in full prosperity!
That I the joyful choir may join,
And count thy people's triumph mine.

6 Let Israel's God be ever bless'd,
His Name eternally confess'd;
Let all his saints, with full accord,
Sing loud Amens—Praise ye the Lord!

SELECTION 87.
From the cvii. Psalm of David.
PART I. III. 1.

MAGNIFY Jehovah's Name;
    For his mercies ever sure,
From eternity the same,
    To eternity endure.

2 Let his ransom'd flock rejoice,
    Gather'd out of every land,
  As the people of his choice,
    Pluck'd from the destroyer's hand.

3 In the wilderness astray,
    In the lonely waste they roam,
  Hungry, fainting by the way,
    Far from refuge, shelter, home:—

4 To the Lord their God they cry;
    He inclines a gracious ear,
  Sends deliverance from on high,
    Rescues them from all their fear:

5 Them to pleasant lands he brings,
    Where the vine and olive grow;
  Where, from verdant hills, the springs
    Through luxuriant valleys flow.

6 O that men would praise the Lord,
    For his goodness to their race;
  For the wonders of his word,
    And the riches of his grace!

PART II. C. M.

1 THY wondrous power, Almighty Lord,
    That rules the boisterous sea,
  The bold adventurers record,
    Who tempt that dangerous way.

2 At thy command the winds arise,
    And swell the towering waves;
  While they astonish'd mount the skies,
    And sink in gaping graves.

3 Dismay'd they climb the watery hills,
    Dismay'd they plunge again;
  Each like a tottering drunkard reels,
    And finds his courage vain.

4 Then to the Lord they raise their cries,
    He hears their loud request,
  He calms the fierce tempestuous skies,
    And lays the floods to rest.

5 Rejoicing, they forget their fears,
    They see the storm allay'd:
  The wish'd-for haven now appears;
    There, let their vows be paid!
6 O that the sons of men would praise
    The goodness of the Lord!
  And those who see his wondrous ways,
    His wondrous love record!

SELECTION 88. C. M.
From the cviii. Psalm of David.

O GOD, my heart is fully bent
    To magnify thy Name;
  My tongue with cheerful songs of praise
    Shall celebrate thy fame.
2 Awake, my lute; nor thou, my harp,
    Thy warbling notes delay;
  Whilst I with early hymns of joy
    Prevent the dawning day.
3 To all the listening tribes, O Lord,
    Thy wonders I will tell,
  And to those nations sing thy praise
    That round about us dwell;
4 Because thy mercy's boundless height
    The highest heaven transcends,
  And far beyond th' aspiring clouds
    Thy faithful truth extends.
5 Be thou, O God, exalted high
    Above the starry frame;
  And let the world, with one consent,
    Confess thy glorious Name.

SELECTION 89. II. 2.
From the cx. Psalm of David.

THE LORD unto my Lord thus spake:
    "Till I thy foes thy footstool make,
  Sit thou in state at my right hand:
  Supreme in Sion thou shalt be,
  And all thy proud opposers see
    Subjected to thy just command.

2 " Thee, in thy power's triumphant day,
  The willing people shall obey;
    And, when thy rising beams they view,
    Shall all, (redeem'd from error's night,)
    Appear more numerous and bright
      Than crystal drops of morning dew."
3 The Lord hath sworn, nor sworn in vain,
  That, like Melchizedech's, thy reign
    And priesthood shall no period see:
    Anointed Prince! thou, bending low,
    Shalt drink where darkest torrents flow,
      Then raise thy head in victory!

SELECTION 90. L. M.
From the cxi. Psalm of David.

PRAISE ye the Lord! our God to praise
  My soul her utmost power shall raise;
  With private friends, and in the throng
  Of saints, his praise shall be my song.
2 His works, for greatness though renown'd,
  His wondrous works with ease are found
  By those who seek for them aright,
  And in the pious search delight.
3 His works are all of matchless fame,
  And universal glory claim;
  His truth, confirm'd through ages past,
  Shall to eternal ages last.
4 By precepts he hath us enjoin'd
  To keep his wondrous works in mind;
  And to posterity record
  That good and gracious is our Lord.
5 His bounty, like a flowing tide,
  Has all his servants' wants supplied;
  And he will ever keep in mind
  His covenant with our fathers signed.
6 Just are the dealings of his hands,
  Immutable are his commands,
  By truth and equity sustain'd,
  And for eternal rules ordain'd.

7 He set his saints from bondage free,
And then establish'd his decree,
For ever to remain the same:
Holy and reverend is his Name.

8 Who wisdom's sacred prize would win,
Must with the fear of God begin:
Immortal praise and heavenly skill
Have they who know and do his will.

SELECTION 91. L. M.
From the cxii. Psalm of David.

THAT man is bless'd who stands in awe
Of God, and loves his sacred law;
His seed on earth shall be renown'd,
And with successive honours crown'd.

2 The soul that's fill'd with virtue's light
Shines brightest in affliction's night;
To pity the distress'd inclin'd,
As well as just to all mankind.

3 His liberal favours he extends,
To some he gives, to others lends;
Yet what his charity impairs,
He saves by prudence in affairs.

4 Beset with threatening dangers round,
Unmoved shall he maintain his ground:
The sweet remembrance of the just
Shall flourish when he sleeps in dust.

SELECTION 92. II. 2.
From the cxiii. Psalm of David.

YE saints and servants of the Lord,
The triumphs of his Name record;
His sacred Name for ever bless:
Where'er the circling sun displays
His rising beams or setting rays,
Due praise to his great Name address.

2 God through the world extends his sway;
The regions of eternal day
But shadows of his glory are:

With him whose majesty excels,
Who made the heaven in which he dwells,
  Let no created power compare.

3 Though 'tis beneath his state to view
In highest heaven what angels do,
  Yet he to earth vouchsafes his care;
He takes the needy from his cell,
Advancing him in courts to dwell,
  Companion to the greatest there.

SELECTION 93. C. M.
From the cxv. Psalm of David.

LORD, not to us, we claim no share,
  But to thy sacred Name
Give glory, for thy mercy's sake,
  And truth's eternal fame.

2 Why should the heathen cry, "Where's now
  The God whom ye adore?"
Convince them that in heaven thou art,
  And uncontroll'd thy power.

3 O Israel, make the Lord your trust,
  Who is your help and shield;
Priests, Levites, trust in him alone,
  Who only help can yield.

4 Let all who truly fear the Lord,
  On him they fear rely;
Who them in danger can defend,
  And all their wants supply.

5 Of us he oft has mindful been,
  And Israel's house will bless:
Priests, Levites, proselytes, e'en all
  Who his great Name confess.

6 On you, and on your heirs, he will
  Increase of blessings bring:
Thrice happy you, who favourites are
  Of this almighty King!

7 Heaven's highest orb of glory he
  His empire's seat designed;

  And gave this lower globe of earth
   A portion to mankind.
8 They who in death and silence sleep,
  To him no praise afford;
But we will bless for evermore
  Our ever-living Lord.

SELECTION 94. C. M.
From the cxvi. Psalm of David.

MY soul with grateful thoughts of love
  Entirely is possess'd,
Because the Lord vouchsafed to hear
  The voice of my request.

2 Since he has now his ear inclined,
  I never will despair;
But still in all the straits of life
  To him address my prayer.

3 With deadly sorrows compass'd round,
  With pains of hell oppress'd,
When troubles seized my aching heart,
  And anguish rack'd my breast,—

4 On God's almighty Name I call'd,
  And thus to him I pray'd;
"Lord, I beseech thee save my soul,
  With sorrows quite dismay'd."

5 How just and merciful is God,
  How gracious is the Lord:
Who saves the harmless, and to me
  Does timely help afford.

6 Then, free from pensive cares, my soul,
  Resume thy wonted rest;
For God has wondrously to thee
  His bounteous love express'd.

7 When death alarm'd me, he removed
  My dangers and my fears;
My feet from falling he secured,
  And dried my eyes from tears.

8 Therefore my life's remaining years,
  Which God to me shall lend,

Will I, in praises to his Name,
  And in his service, spend.
9 In God I trusted, and of him
  Did boast in greatest fear;
Though in my trouble I exclaim'd,
  All men are insincere.
10 O what return to God shall I
  For all his goodness make?
I'll praise his name, and with glad zeal
  The cup of blessing take.
11 I'll pay my vows among his saints,
  Whose blood (howe'er despised
By wicked men) in God's account
  Is always highly prized.
12 To thee I'll offerings bring of praise;
  And while I bless thy Name,
The just performance of my vows
  To all thy saints proclaim.
13 They in Jerusalem shall meet,
  And in thy house shall join
To bless thy Name with one consent,
  And mix their songs with mine.

SELECTION 95. C. M.
From the cxvii. Psalm of David.

WITH cheerful notes let all the earth
  To heaven their voices raise;
Let all, inspired with godly mirth,
  Sing solemn hymns of praise.
2 God's tender mercy knows no bound,
  His truth shall ne'er decay:
Then let the willing nations round
  Their grateful tribute pay.

SELECTION 96. C. M.
From the cxviii. Psalm of David.

O PRAISE the Lord, for he is good,
  His mercies ne'er decay:
That his kind favours ever last,
  Let thankful Israel say.

2 Their sense of his eternal love
   Let Aaron's house express;
 And that it never fails, let all
   That fear the Lord confess.
3 Far better 'tis to trust in God,
   And have the Lord our friend,
 Than on the greatest human power
   For safety to depend.
4 The Lord has been my help; the praise
   To him alone belongs;
 He is my Saviour and my strength,
   He only claims my songs.
5 Joy fills the dwelling of the just,
   Whom God has saved from harm;
 For wondrous things are brought to pass
   By his almighty arm.
6 He, by his own resistless power,
   Has endless honour won;
 The saving strength of his right hand
   Amazing works has done.
7 God will not suffer me to fall,
   But still prolongs my days;
 That, by declaring all his works,
   I may advance his praise.
8 When God had sorely me chastised,
   Till quite of hopes bereaved,
 His mercy from the gates of death
   My fainting life reprieved.
9 Then open wide the temple gates
   To which the just repair,
 That I may enter in, and praise
   My great Deliverer there.
10 Within those gates of God's abode
   To which the righteous press,
 Since thou hast heard, and set me safe,
   Thy holy Name I'll bless.
11 That which the builders once refused
   Is now the corner-stone:

This is the wondrous work of God,
  The work of God alone.

12 This day is God's; let all the land
  Exalt their cheerful voice:
"Lord, we beseech thee, save us now,
  And make us still rejoice."

13 Him that approaches in God's name
  Let all th' assembly bless;
"We that belong to God's own house
  Have wish'd you good success."

14 God is the Lord, through whom we all
  Both light and comfort find;
Fast to the altar's horns with cords
  The chosen victim bind.

15 Thou art my Lord, O God, and still
  I'll praise thy holy Name;
Because thou only art my God,
  I'll celebrate thy fame.

16 O then with me give thanks to God,
  Who still does gracious prove;
And let the tribute of our praise
  Be endless as his love.

SELECTION 97.
From the cxix. Psalm of David.
PART I. ALEPH. C. M.

HOW bless'd are they who always keep
  The pure and perfect way;
Who never from the sacred paths
  Of God's commandments stray!

2 How bless'd, who to his righteous laws
  Have still obedient been;
And have, with fervent humble zeal,
  His favour sought to win!

3 Such men their utmost caution use
  To shun each wicked deed;
But in the path which he directs
  With constant care proceed.

4 Thou strictly hast enjoin'd us, Lord,
    To learn thy sacred will;
  And all our diligence employ
    Thy statutes to fulfil.

5 O then that thy most holy will
    Might o'er my ways preside;
  And I the course of all my life
    By thy direction guide.

6 Then with assurance should I walk,
    From all confusion free;
  Convinced, with joy, that all my ways
    With thy commands agree.

7 My upright heart shall my glad mouth
    With cheerful praises fill,
  When, by thy righteous judgments taught,
    I shall have learn'd thy will.

8 So to thy sacred laws shall I
    Entire observance pay:
  O then forsake me not, my God,
    Nor cast me quite away!

PART II. BETH. C. M.

1 HOW shall the young preserve their ways
    From all pollution free?
  By making still their course of life
    With thy commands agree.

2 With hearty zeal for thee I seek,
    To thee for succour pray;
  O suffer not my careless steps
    From thy right paths to stray!

3 Safe in my heart, and closely hid,
    Thy word, my treasure, lies,
  To succour me with timely aid
    When sinful thoughts arise.

4 Secured by that, my grateful soul
    Shall ever bless thy Name;
  O teach me then by thy just laws
    My future life to frame!

5 My lips, unlock'd by pious zeal,
  To others have declared
How well the judgments of thy mouth
  Deserve our best regard.

6 Whilst in the way of thy commands,
  More solid joy I found,
Than had I been with vast increase
  Of envied riches crown'd.

7 Therefore thy just and upright laws
  Shall always fill my mind;
And those sound rules which thou prescrib'st
  Entire respect shall find.

8 To keep thy statutes undefaced
  Shall be my constant joy;
The strict remembrance of thy word
  Shall all my thoughts employ.

PART III. GIMEL. . C. M.

1 BE gracious to thy servant, Lord;
  Do thou my life defend,
That I according to thy word
  My time to come may spend.

2 Enlighten both my eyes and mind,
  That so I may discern
The wondrous things, which they behold,
  Who thy just precepts learn.

3 My fainting soul is almost pined,
  With earnest longing spent,
While always on the eager search
  Of thy just will intent.

4 Thy sharp rebuke shall crush the proud,
  Whom still thy curse pursues;
Since they to walk in thy right ways
  Presumptuously refuse.

5 But far from me do thou, O Lord,
  Contempt and shame remove;
For I thy sacred laws affect
  With undissembled love.

6 For thy commands have always been
   My comfort and delight;
 By them I learn with prudent care
   To guide my steps aright.

PART IV. DALETH. C. M.

1 MY soul, oppress'd with deadly care,
   Close to the dust doth cleave;
 Revive me, Lord, and let me now
   Thy promised aid receive.

2 To thee I still declared my ways,
   And thou inclin'dst thine ear;
 O teach me then my future life
   By thy just laws to steer!

3 If thou wilt make me know thy laws,
   And by their guidance walk,
 The wondrous works which thou hast done
   Shall be my constant talk.

4 But see, my soul within me sinks,
   Press'd down with weighty care:
 Do thou, according to thy word,
   My wasted strength repair.

5 Far, far from me, be all false ways
   And lying arts removed;
 But kindly grant I still may keep
   The path by thee approved.

6 Thy faithful ways, thou God of truth,
   My happy choice I've made;
 Thy judgments, as my rule of life,
   Before me always laid.

7 My care has been to make my life
   With thy commands agree;
 O then preserve thy servant, Lord,
   From shame and ruin free!

8 So in the way of thy commands
   Shall I with pleasure run;
 And, with a heart enlarged with joy,
   Successfully go on.

SELECTIONS OF PSALMS.

PART V. HE. C. M.

1 INSTRUCT me in thy statutes, Lord,
  Thy righteous paths display;
And I from them, through all my life,
  Will never go astray.

2 If thou true wisdom from above
  Wilt graciously impart,
To keep thy perfect laws I will
  Devote my zealous heart.

3 Direct me in the sacred ways
  To which thy precepts lead;
Because my chief delight has been
  Thy righteous paths to tread.

4 Do thou to thy most just commands
  Incline my willing heart;
Let no desire of worldly wealth
  From thee my thoughts divert.

5 From those vain objects turn mine eyes,
  Which this false world displays;
But give me lively power and strength
  To keep thy righteous ways.

6 Confirm the promise of thy word,
  And give thy servant aid,
Who to transgress thy sacred laws
  Is awfully afraid.

7 The censure and reproach I fear,
  In mercy, Lord, remove;
For all the judgments thou ordain'st
  Are full of grace and love.

8 Thou know'st how after thy commands
  My longing heart does pant;
O then make haste to raise me up,
  And promised succour grant.

PART VI. VAU. C. M.

1 THY constant blessing, Lord, bestow,
  To cheer my drooping heart;
To me, according to thy word,
  Thy saving health impart.

2 So shall I, whosoe'er upbraids,
    This ready answer make;
"In God I trust, who never will
    His faithful promise break."

3 Then let not quite the word of truth
    Be from my mouth removed;
Since still my ground of steadfast hope
    Thy judgments, Lord, have proved.

4 So I to keep thy righteous laws
    Will all my study bend;
And constantly my time to come
    In their observance spend.

5 My soul shall gladly walk at large,
    From all oppression free,
Since I resolved to make my life
    With thy commands agree.

6 My longing heart and ravish'd soul
    Shall both o'erflow with joy,
When in thy loved commandments I
    My happy hours employ.

7 Then will I to thy holy laws
    Lift up my willing hands;
My care and business then shall be
    To study thy commands.

PART VII. ZAIN. C. M.

1 ACCORDING to thy promised grace,
    Thy favour, Lord, extend;
Make good to me the word, on which
    Thy servant's hopes depend.

2 That only comfort in distress
    Did all my griefs control;
Thy word, when troubles hemm'd me round,
    Revived my fainting soul.

3 Thy judgments then, of ancient date,
    I quickly call'd to mind,
Till, ravish'd with such thoughts, my soul
    Did speedy comfort find.

4 Thy Name, that cheer'd my heart by day,
   Has fill'd my thoughts by night:
I then resolved by thy just laws
   To guide my steps aright.

5 That peace of mind, which has my soul
   In deep distress sustain'd,
By strict obedience to thy will
   I happily obtain'd.

PART. VIII. CHETH. C. M.

1 O LORD, my God, my portion thou
   And sure possession art;
Thy words I steadfastly resolve
   To treasure in my heart.

2 With all the strength of warm desire
   I did thy grace implore;
Disclose, according to thy word,
   Thy mercy's boundless store.

3 With deep reflection and strict care
   On all my ways I thought;
And so, reclaim'd to thy just paths,
   My wandering steps I brought.

4 Prolonging not the time, my soul
   Resolved without delay
To watch, that I might never more
   From thy commandments stray

5 To such as fear thy holy Name
   Myself I closely join;
To all who their obedient wills
   To thy commands resign.

6 O'er all the earth thy mercy, Lord,
   Abundantly is shed;
O grant that I may truly learn
   Thy sacred paths to tread.

PART IX. TETH. C. M.

1 WITH me, thy servant, thou hast dealt
   Most graciously, O Lord;
Repeated benefits bestow'd,
   According to thy word.

2 Teach me the sacred skill by which
   Right judgment is attain'd,
 Who in belief of thy commands
   Have steadfastly remain'd.

3 Before affliction stopp'd my course,
   My footsteps went astray;
 But I have since been disciplined
   Thy precepts to obey.

4 Thou art, O Lord, supremely good,
   And all thou dost is so;
 On me, thy statutes to discern,
   Thy saving skill bestow.

5 'Tis good for me that I have felt
   Affliction's chastening rod,
 That I may duly learn and keep
   The statutes of my God.

6 The law that from thy mouth proceeds,
   Of more esteem I hold
 Than richest mines, than thousand mines
   Of silver and of gold.

PART X. JOD. C. M.

1 TO me, who am the workmanship
   Of thy almighty hands,
 The heavenly understanding give
   To learn thy just commands.

2 My preservation to thy saints
   Strong comfort will afford,
 To see success attend my hopes,
   Who trusted in thy word.

3 That right thy judgments are, I now
   By sure experience see;
 And that in faithfulness, O Lord,
   Thou hast afflicted me.

4 O let thy tender mercy now
   Afford me needful aid;
 According to thy promise, Lord,
   To me, thy servant, made!

5 To me thy saving grace restore,
   That I again may live;
Whose soul can relish no delight
   But what thy precepts give.

6 In thy blest statutes let my heart
   Continue always sound;
That guilt and shame, the sinner's lot,
   May never me confound.

PART XI. CAPH. C. M.

1 MY soul with long expectance faints
   To see thy saving grace;
Yet still on thy unerring word
   My confidence I place.

2 My very eyes consume and fail
   With waiting for thy word;
O when wilt thou thy kind relief
   And promised aid afford?

3 Thy wonted kindness, Lord, restore,
   My drooping heart to cheer;
That by thy righteous statutes I
   My life's whole course may steer.

PART XII. LAMED. C. M.

1 FOR ever and for ever, Lord,
   Unchanged thou dost remain;
Thy word, establish'd in the heavens,
   Does all their orbs sustain.

2 Through circling ages, Lord, thy truth
   Immovable shall stand,
As doth the earth which thou uphold'st
   By thine almighty hand.

3 All things the course by thee ordain'd
   E'en to this day fulfil;
They are the faithful subjects all,
   And servants of thy will.

4 Unless thy sacred law had been
   My comfort and delight,
I must have fainted and expired
   In dark affliction's night.

5 Thy precepts therefore from my thoughts
   Shall never, Lord, depart;
 For thou by them hast to new life
   Restored my dying heart.
6 I've seen an end of what we call
   Perfection here below;
 But thy commandments, like thyself,
   No change or period know.

PART XIII. MEM. C. M.

1 THE love that to thy laws I bear
   No language can display;
 They with fresh wonders entertain
   My raptured thoughts all day.
2 My feet with care I have refrain'd
   From every sinful way,
 That to thy sacred word I might
   Entire obedience pay.
3 I have not from thy judgments stray'd,
   By vain desires misled;
 For, Lord, thou hast instructed me
   Thy righteous paths to tread.
4 How sweet are all thy words to me;
   O what divine repast!
 How much more grateful to my soul
   Than honey to my taste!
5 Taught by thy sacred precepts, I
   With heavenly skill am blest;
 Through which the treacherous ways of sin
   I utterly detest.

PART XIV. NUN. C. M.

1 THY word is to my feet a lamp,
   The way of truth to show;
 A watch-light, to point out the path
   In which I ought to go.
2 I've vow'd, and from my covenant, Lord,
   Will never start aside,
 That in thy righteous judgments I
   Will steadfastly abide.

3 Let still my sacrifice of praise
    With thee acceptance find;
  And in thy righteous judgments, Lord,
    Instruct my willing mind.
4 Thy testimonies I have made
    My heritage and choice;
  For they, when other comforts fail,
    My drooping heart rejoice.
5 My heart with early zeal began
    Thy statutes to obey;
  And, till my course of life is done,
    Shall keep thine upright way.

PART XV. SAMECH. C. M.

1 DECEITFUL thoughts and practices
    I utterly detest;
  But to thy law affection bear
    Too great to be express'd.
2 My hiding-place, my refuge-tower,
    And shield art thou, O Lord;
  I firmly anchor all my hopes
    On thy unerring word.
3 Away from me, ye wicked men,
    Approach not my abode;
  For firmly I resolve to keep
    The precepts of my God.
4 According to thy gracious word,
    From danger set me free;
  Nor make me of those hopes ashamed,
    That I repose on thee.

PART XVI. AIN. C. M.

1 MINE eyes, alas! begin to fail,
    In long expectance held;
  Till thy salvation they behold,
    And righteous word fulfill'd.
2 To me, thy servant in distress,
    Thy wonted grace display,
  And discipline my willing heart
    Thy statutes to obey.

3 On me, devoted to thy fear,
 Thy sacred skill bestow,
That of thy testimonies I
 The full extent may know.
4 Thy laws and precepts I account
 In all respects divine;
They teach me to discern the right
 And all false ways decline.

PART XVII. PE. C. M.

1 THE wonders which thy laws contain,
 No words can represent;
Therefore to learn and practise them
 My zealous heart is bent.
2 The very entrance to thy word
 Celestial light displays,
And knowledge of true happiness
 To simplest minds conveys.
3 With eager hopes I waiting stood,
 And fainting with desire,
That of thy wise commands I might
 The sacred skill acquire.
4 With favour, Lord, look down on me,
 Who thy relief implore;
As thou art wont to visit those
 Who thy blest Name adore.
5 Directed by thy heavenly word
 Let all my footsteps be;
Nor wickedness of any kind
 Dominion have o'er me.
6 On me, devoted to thy fear,
 Lord, make thy face to shine:
Thy statutes both to know and keep
 My heart with zeal incline.

PART XVIII. TSADDI. C. M.

1 THOU art the righteous Judge, in whom
 Wrong'd innocence may trust;
And, like thyself, thy judgments, Lord,
 In all respects are just.

2 Most just and true those statutes were
  Which thou didst first decree;
And all with faithfulness perform'd
  Succeeding times shall see.

3 Lord, each neglected word of thine,
  Howe'er by men despised,
Is pure, and for eternal truth
  By me, thy servant, prized.

4 Thy righteousness shall then endure
  When time itself is past;
Thy law is truth itself, that truth
  Which shall for ever last.

5 Though trouble, anguish, doubts, and dread,
  To compass me unite;
Beset with danger, still I make
  Thy precepts my delight.

6 Eternal and unerring rules
  Thy testimonies give:
Teach me the wisdom that will make
  My soul for ever live.

PART XIX. KOPH. C. M.

1 WITH my whole heart to God I call'd—
  Lord, hear my earnest cry!
And I thy statutes to perform
  Will all my care apply.

2 Again more fervently I pray'd—
  O save me, that I may
Thy testimonies fully know,
  And steadfastly obey!

3 My earlier prayer the dawning day
  Prevented, while I cried
To him, upon whose faithful word
  My hope alone relied.

4 Lord, hear my supplicating voice,
  And wonted favour show;
O quicken me, and so approve
  Thy judgments ever true!

5 Concerning thy divine commands
   My soul has known of old,
 That they were true, and shall their truth
   To endless ages hold.

PART XX. RESCH. C. M.

1 CONSIDER my affliction, Lord,
   And me from bondage draw;
 Think on thy servant in distress,
   Who ne'er forgets thy law.

2 Defend my cause, and me to save
   Thy timely aid afford;
 With beams of mercy quicken me,
   According to thy word.

3 From harden'd sinners thou remov'st
   Salvation far away;
 'Tis just thou should'st withdraw from them
   Who from thy statutes stray.

4 Since great thy tender mercies are
   To all who thee adore;
 According to thy judgments, Lord,
   My fainting hopes restore.

5 Consider, O my gracious God,
   How I thy precepts love;
 O therefore quicken me with beams
   Of mercy from above.

6 As from the birth of time thy truth
   Has held through ages past,
 So shall thy righteous judgments firm
   To endless ages last.

PART XXI. SCHIN. C. M.

1 THY sacred word my joyful breast
   With heavenly rapture warms;
 Nor conquest, nor the spoils of war,
   Have such transporting charms.

2 Perfidious practices and lies
   I utterly detest;
 But to thy laws affection bear,
   Too vast to be express'd.

3 Seven times a day, with grateful voice,
    Thy praises I resound,
  Because I find thy judgments all
    With truth and justice crown'd.

4 Secure, substantial peace have they
    Who truly love thy law;
  No smiling mischief them can tempt,
    Nor frowning danger awe.

5 For thy salvation I have hoped,
    And, though so long delay'd,
  With cheerful zeal and anxious care
    All thy commands obey'd.

6 Thy testimonies I have kept,
    And constantly obey'd;
  Because the love I bore to them
    Thy service easy made.

7 From strict observance of thy laws
    I never yet withdrew;
  Convinced that my most secret ways
    Are open to thy view.

PART XXII. TAU. C. M.

1 TO my request and earnest cry
    Attend, O gracious Lord;
  Inspire my heart with heavenly skill,
    According to thy word.

2 Let my repeated prayer at last
    Before thy throne appear;
  According to thy plighted word,
    For my relief draw near.

3 Then shall my grateful lips return
    The tribute of their praise,
  When thou thy counsels hast reveal'd,
    And taught me thy just ways.

4 My tongue the praises of thy word
    Shall thankfully resound;
  For thy commands are right, thy laws
    With truth and justice crown'd.

5 Let thy almighty arm appear,
  And bring me timely aid;
 For I the laws thou hast ordain'd
  My heart's free choice have made.
6 My soul has waited long to see
  Thy saving grace restored;
 Nor comfort knew, but what thy laws,
  Thy heavenly laws, afford.
7 Prolong my life, that I may sing
  My great Restorer's praise;
 Whose justice, from the depths of woe,
  My fainting soul shall raise.
8 Though like a sheep that's lost I've stray'd,
  And from thy ways declined,
 Do thou, O Lord, thy servant seek,
  Who keeps thy laws in mind.

SELECTION 98. C. M.
From the cxxi. Psalm of David.

TO Sion's hill I lift my eyes,
  From thence expecting aid;
 From Sion's hill, and Sion's God,
  Who heaven and earth has made.
2 He will not let thy foot be moved,
  Thy guardian will not sleep;
 Behold, the God who slumbers not,
  Will favour'd Israel keep.
3 Shelter'd beneath th' Almighty's wings,
  Thou shalt securely rest,
 Where neither sun nor moon shall thee
  By day or night molest.
4 From common accidents of life
  The Lord shall guard thee still;
 'Tis even he that shall preserve
  Thy soul from every ill.
5 At home, abroad, in peace, in war,
  Thy God shall thee defend;
 Conduct thee through life's pilgrimage,
  Safe to thy journey's end.

SELECTION 99. C. M.
From the cxxii. Psalm of David.

O 'TWAS a joyful sound to hear
   Our tribes devoutly say,
Up, Israel, to the temple haste,
   And keep your festal-day!

2 At Salem's courts we must appear,
   With our assembled powers,
In strong and beauteous order ranged
   Like her united towers.

3 'Tis thither, by divine command,
   The tribes of God repair,
Before his ark to celebrate
   His Name with praise and prayer.

4 O, ever pray for Salem's peace;
   For they shall prosp'rous be,
Thou holy city of our God,
   Who bear true love to thee.

5 May peace within thy sacred walls
   A constant guest be found;
With plenty and prosperity
   Thy palaces be crown'd.

6 For my dear brethren's sake, and friends
   No less than brethren dear,
I'll pray—May peace in Salem's towers
   A constant guest appear.

7 But most of all I'll seek thy good,
   And ever wish thee well,
For Sion and the temple's sake,
   Where God vouchsafes to dwell.

SELECTION 100. C. M.
From the cxxiv. Psalm of David.

HAD not the Lord, may Israel say,
   On Israel's side engaged,
The foe had quickly swallow'd us,
   So furiously he raged.

2 Had not the Lord himself vouchsafed
   To check his fierce control,

  The adversary's dreary flood
   Had overwhelm'd our soul.
3 But praised be our eternal Lord,
   Who left us not his prey;
  The snare is broke, his rage disarm'd,
   And we again are free.
4 Secure in God's almighty Name
   Our confidence remains;
  The God who made both heaven and earth,
   Of both sole monarch reigns.

SELECTION 101. C. M.
From the cxxv. Psalm of David.

WHO place on Sion's God their trust,
   Like Sion's rock shall stand;
  Like her immovably be fix'd
   By his almighty hand.
2 Look how the hills on every side
   Jerusalem enclose;
  So stands the Lord around his saints,
   To guard them from their foes.
3 Be good, O righteous God, to those
   Who righteous deeds affect;
  The heart that innocence retains,
   Let innocence protect.
4 All those who walk in crooked paths,
   The Lord shall soon destroy;
  Cut off th' unjust, but crown the saints
   With lasting peace and joy.

SELECTION 102. C. M.
From the cxxvii. Psalm of David.

WE build with fruitless cost, unless
   The Lord the pile sustain;
  Unless the Lord the city keep,
   The watchman wakes in vain.
2 In vain we rise before the day,
   And late to rest repair,
  Allow no respite to our toil,
   And eat the bread of care.

3 Supplies of life, with ease to them,
   He on his saints bestows;
He crowns their labours with success,
   Their nights with safe repose.

SELECTION 103. C. M.
From the cxxviii. Psalm of David.

THE man is bless'd that fears the Lord,
   Nor only worship pays,
But keeps his steps confined with care
   To his appointed ways.

2 He shall upon the sweet returns
   Of his own labour feed;
Without dependence live, and see
   His wishes all succeed.

3 Who fears the Lord shall prosper thus;
   Him Sion's God shall bless,
And grant him all his days to see
   Jerusalem's success.

SELECTION 104. S. M.
From the cxxx. Psalm of David.

FROM lowest depths of woe
   To God I send my cry;
Lord, hear my supplicating voice,
   And graciously reply.

2 Should'st thou severely judge,
   Who can their trial bear?
But thou forgiv'st, lest we despond,
   And quite renounce thy fear.

3 My soul with patience waits
   For thee, the living Lord;
My hopes are on thy promise built,
   Thy never-failing word.

4 My longing eyes look out
   For thy enlivening ray,
More duly than the morning watch
   To spy the dawning day.

5 Let Israel trust in God,
   No bounds his mercy knows;

  The plenteous source and spring from whence
   Eternal succour flows:
6 Whose friendly streams to us
  Supplies in want convey;
 A healing spring, a spring to cleanse
  And wash our guilt away.

SELECTION 105. III. 1.
From the cxxxi. Psalm of David.

LORD, for ever at thy side
 Let my place and portion be:
Strip me of the robe of pride,
 Clothe me with humility.

2 Meekly may my soul receive
  All thy Spirit hath reveal'd;
 Thou hast spoken—I believe,
  Though the oracle be seal'd.

3 Humble as a little child,
  Weaned from the mother's breast,
 By no subtleties beguiled,
  On thy faithful word I rest.

4 Israel! now and evermore
  In the Lord Jehovah trust;
 Him, in all his ways, adore,
  Wise, and wonderful, and just.

SELECTION 106. C. M.
From the cxxxii. Psalm of David.

O WITH due reverence let us all
 To God's abode repair;
And, prostrate at his footstool fall'n,
 Pour out our humble prayer.

2 Arise, O Lord, and now possess
  Thy constant place of rest;
 Be that, not only with thy ark,
  But with thy presence bless'd.

3 Clothe thou thy priests with righteousness,
  Make thou thy saints rejoice;
 And, for thy servant David's sake,
  Hear thy anointed's voice.

4 Fair Sion does, in God's esteem,
    All other seats excel;
  His place of everlasting rest,
    Where he desires to dwell.

5 Her store th' Almighty will increase,
    Her poor with plenty bless;
  Her saints shall shout for joy, her priests
    His saving health confess.

SELECTION 107. C. M.
From the cxxxiii. Psalm of David.

HOW vast must their advantage be,
    How great their pleasure prove,
  Who live like brethren, and consent
    In offices of love.

2 True love is like the precious oil,
    Which, pour'd on Aaron's head,
  Ran down his beard, and o'er his robes
    Its costly fragrance shed.

3 'Tis like refreshing dew, which does
    On Hermon's top distil;
  Or like the early drops that fall
    On Sion's favour'd hill.

4 For Sion is the chosen seat
    Where the Almighty King
  The promis'd blessing has ordain'd,
    And life's eternal spring.

SELECTION 108. C. M.
From the cxxxiv. Psalm of David.

BLESS God, ye servants, that attend
    Upon his solemn state;
  That in his temple's hallow'd courts
    With humble reverence wait.

2 Within his house lift up your hands
    And bless his holy Name:
  From Zion bless thy Israel, Lord,
    Who earth and heaven didst frame.

SELECTION 109. C. M.
From the cxxxv. Psalm of David.

O PRAISE the Lord with one consent,
   And magnify his Name;
Let all the servants of the Lord
   His worthy praise proclaim.

2 Praise him, all ye that in his house
   Attend with constant care;
With those that to his outmost courts
   With humble zeal repair.

3 For God his own peculiar choice
   The sons of Jacob makes;
And Israel's offspring for his own
   Most valued treasure takes.

4 That God is great, we often have
   By glad experience found;
And seen how he, with wondrous power,
   Above all gods is crown'd.

5 For he, with unresisted strength,
   Performs his sovereign will,
In heaven and earth, and watery stores
   That earth's deep caverns fill.

6 Their just returns of thanks to God
   Let grateful Israel pay;
Nor let anointed Aaron's race
   To bless the Lord delay.

7 Their sense of his unbounded love
   Let Levi's house express;
And let all those who fear the Lord,
   His name for ever bless.

8 Let all with thanks his wondrous works
   In Sion's courts proclaim;
Let them in Salem, where he dwells,
   Exalt his holy Name.

SELECTION 110. II. 4.
From the cxxxvi. Psalm of David.

TO God, the mighty Lord,
   Your joyful thanks repeat;

To him due praise afford,
  As good as he is great.
    For God does prove
      Our constant friend;
    His boundless love
      Shall never end.

2 To him, whose wondrous power,
    All other gods obey,
  Whom earthly kings adore,
    Your grateful homage pay.
      For God, &c.

3 By his almighty hand
    Amazing works are wrought;
  The heavens by his command
    Were to perfection brought.
      For God, &c.

4 He spread the ocean round
    About the spacious land;
  And bade the rising ground
    Above the waters stand.
      For God, &c.

5 By him the heavens display
    Their numerous hosts of light,
  The sun to rule by day,
    The moon and stars by night.
      For God, &c.

6 He, in our depth of woes,
    On us with favour thought;
  And from our cruel foes
    In peace and safety brought.
      For God, &c.

7 He does the food supply
    On which all creatures live:
  To God, who reigns on high,
    Eternal praises give.
      For God will prove
        Our constant friend;
      His boundless love
        Shall never end.

SELECTION 111. L. M.
From the cxxxvii. Psalm of David.

WHEN we, our weary limbs to rest,
   Sat down by proud Euphrates' stream,
We wept, with doleful thoughts oppress'd,
   And Sion was our mournful theme.

2 Our harps, that when with joy we sung,
   Were wont their tuneful parts to bear,
With silent strings neglected hung
   On willow trees that wither'd there.

3 O Salem, our once happy seat,
   When I of thee forgetful prove,
Let then my trembling hand forget
   The speaking strings with art to move.

4 If I to mention thee forbear,
   Perpetual silence be my doom;
Or if my chiefest joy compare
   With thee, Jerusalem, my home!

SELECTION 112. C. M.
From the cxxxviii. Psalm of David.

WITH my whole heart, my God and King,
   Thy praise I will proclaim;
Before the mighty I will sing,
   And bless thy holy Name.

2 I'll worship at thy sacred seat,
   And, with thy love inspired;
The praises of thy truth repeat,
   O'er all thy works admired.

3 Thou graciously inclin'dst thine ear,
   When I to thee did cry;
And, when my soul was press'd with fear,
   Didst inward strength supply.

4 For God, although enthroned on high,
   Does thence the poor respect;
The proud, far off, his scornful eye
   Beholds with just neglect.

5 Though I with troubles am oppress'd,
   He shall my foes disarm,

Relieve my soul when most distress'd,
    And keep me safe from harm.

6 The Lord, whose mercies ever last,
    Shall fix my happy state;
And, mindful of his favours past,
    Shall his own work complete.

SELECTION 113. L. M.
From the cxxxix. Psalm of David.

THOU, Lord, by strictest search hast known
    My rising up and lying down;
My secret thoughts are known to thee,
Known long before conceived by me.

2 Thine eye my bed and path surveys,
    My public haunts and private ways:
Thou know'st what 'tis my lips would vent,
My yet unutter'd words' intent.

3 Surrounded by thy power I stand,
    On every side I find thy hand:
O skill for human reach too high!
Too dazzling bright for mortal eye!

4 From thy all-seeing Spirit, Lord,
    What hiding-place does earth afford?
O where can I thy influence shun,
Or whither from thy presence run?

5 If up to heaven I take my flight,
    'Tis there thou dwell'st, enthroned in light;
If to the world unseen, my God,
There also hast thou thine abode.

6 If I the morning's wings could gain,
    And fly beyond the western main;
E'en there, in earth's remotest land,
I still should find thy guiding hand.

7 Or, should I try to shun thy sight
    Beneath the sable wings of night;
One glance from thee, one piercing ray,
Would kindle darkness into day.

8 The veil of night is no disguise,
   No screen from thy all-searching eyes;
   Through midnight shades thou find'st thy way,
   As in the blazing noon of day.
9 Thou know'st the texture of my heart,
   My reins and every vital part:
   I'll praise thee, from whose hands I came
   A work of such a wondrous frame.
10 Let me acknowledge too, O God,
   That since this maze of life I trod,
   Thy thoughts of love to me surmount
   The power of numbers to recount.
11 Far sooner could I reckon o'er
   The sands upon the ocean's shore;
   Each morn, revising what I've done,
   I find th' account but new begun.
12 Search, try, O God, my thoughts and heart,
   If mischief lurk in any part;
   Correct me where I go astray,
   And guide me in thy perfect way.

SELECTION 114. C. M.
From the cxli. Psalm of David.

LORD, in thy sight, O let my prayer
   Like morning incense rise;
My lifted hands accepted be
   As evening sacrifice.
2 From hasty language curb my tongue,
   And let a constant guard
Still keep the portal of my lips
   With wary silence barr'd.
3 From wicked men's designs and deeds
   My heart and hands restrain;
Nor let me share their evil works,
   Or their unrighteous gain.
4 Let upright men reprove my faults,
   And I shall think them kind;
Like healing oil upon my head
   I their reproof shall find.

SELECTION 115. C. M.
From the cxliii. Psalm of David.

LORD, hear my prayer, and to my cry
  Thy wonted audience lend;
In thy accustom'd faith and truth
  A gracious answer send.

2 Nor at thy strict tribunal bring
  Thy servant to be tried;
For in thy sight no living man
  Can e'er be justified.

3 To thee my hands in humble prayer
  I fervently stretch out;
My soul for thy refreshment thirsts,
  Like land oppress'd with drought.

4 Hear me with speed, my spirit fails;
  Thy face no longer hide,
Lest I become forlorn like them
  That in the grave reside.

5 Thy kindness early let me hear,
  Whose trust on thee depends:
Teach me the way where I should go,
  My soul to thee ascends.

6 Do thou, O Lord, from all my foes
  Preserve and set me free;
A safe retreat, a hiding-place,
  My soul implores from thee.

7 Thou art my God, thy righteous will
  Instruct me to obey;
Let thy good Spirit lead and keep
  My soul in thy right way.

8 O, for the sake of thy great Name,
  Revive my drooping heart;
For thy truth's sake, to me distress'd
  Thy saving health impart.

SELECTION 116. L. M.
From the cxliv. Psalm of David.

LORD, what's in man, that thou should'st love
  Of him such tender care to take?

What in his offspring could thee move
    Such great account of him to make?
2 The life of man does quickly fade,
    His thoughts but empty are and vain,
His days are like a flying shade,
    Of whose short stay no signs remain.
3 To thee, almighty King of kings,
    In new-made hymns my voice I'll raise;
And instruments of many strings
    Shall help me to adore and praise.

SELECTION 117.
From the cxlv. Psalm of David.
PART I. C. M.

THEE will I bless, my God and King,
    Thy endless praise proclaim;
This tribute daily I will bring,
    And ever bless thy Name.
2 Thou, Lord, beyond compare art great,
    And highly to be praised;
Thy majesty, with boundless height,
    Above our knowledge raised.
3 Renown'd for mighty acts, thy fame
    To future time extends;
From age to age thy glorious Name
    Successively descends.
4 Whilst I thy glory and renown,
    And wondrous works express,
The world with me thy might shall own,
    And thy great power confess.
5 The praise that to thy love belongs,
    They shall with joy proclaim;
Thy truth of all their grateful songs
    Shall be the constant theme.
6 The Lord is good; fresh acts of grace
    His pity still supplies;
His anger moves with slowest pace,
    His willing mercy flies.
7 Thy love through earth extends its fame,
    To all thy works express'd;

These show thy praise, whilst thy great Name
  Is by thy servants bless'd.
8 They, with a glorious prospect fired,
  Shall of thy kingdom speak;
And thy great power, by all admired,
  Their lofty subject make.
9 God's mighty works of ancient date
  Shall thus to all be known;
And thus his kingdom's glorious state
  In all its splendour shown.
10 His steadfast throne, from changes free,
  Shall stand for ever fast;
His boundless sway no end shall see,
  But time itself outlast.

PART II. C. M.

1 THE Lord does them support that fall,
  And makes the prostrate rise:
For his kind aid all creatures call,
  Who timely food supplies.
2 Whate'er their various wants require,
  With open hand he gives;
And so fulfils the just desire
  Of every thing that lives.
3 How holy is the Lord, how just,
  How righteous all his ways!
How nigh to him, who with firm trust
  For his assistance prays!
4 He grants the full desires of those
  Who him with fear adore;
And will their troubles soon compose,
  When they his aid implore.
5 The Lord preserves all those with care
  Whom grateful love employs;
But sinners, who his vengeance dare,
  In justice he destroys.
6 My time to come, in praises spent,
  Shall still advance his fame;
And all mankind, with one consent,
  For ever bless his Name.

SELECTION 118. III. 3.
From the cxlv. Psalm of David.

GOD, my King, thy might confessing,
   Ever will I bless thy Name;
Day by day thy throne addressing,
   Still will I thy praise proclaim.

2 Honour great our God befitteth;
   Who his majesty can reach?
Age to age his works transmitteth,
   Age to age his power shall teach.

3 They shall talk of all thy glory,
   On thy might and greatness dwell,
Speak of thy dread acts the story,
   And thy deeds of wonder tell.

4 Nor shall fail from memory's treasure,
   Works by love and mercy wrought;
Works of love surpassing measure,
   Works of mercy passing thought.

5 Full of kindness and compassion,
   Slow to anger, vast in love,
God is good to all creation;
   All his works his goodness prove.

6 All thy works, O Lord, shall bless thee,
   Thee shall all thy saints adore;
King supreme shall they confess thee,
   And proclaim thy sovereign power.

7 They thy might, all might excelling,
   Shall to all mankind make known;
And the brightness of thy dwelling,
   And the glories of thy throne.

8 Ever, God of endless praises,
   Shall thy royal might remain;
Evermore thy brightness blazes,
   Ever lasts thy righteous reign.

9 Them that fall the Lord protecteth,
   He sustains the bow'd and bent:
Every eye from thee expecteth,
   Fix'd on thee, its nourishment.

10 Thou to all, great God of nature,
    Giv'st in season due their food;
Spread'st thy hand, and every creature
    Satisfiest still with good.

11 God is just in all he doeth,
    Kind is he in all his ways;
He his ready presence showeth,
    When a faithful servant prays.

12 Who sincerely seek and fear him,
    He to them their wish will give;
When they call, the Lord will hear them,
    He will hear them, and relieve.

13 From Jehovah all who prize him
    Shall his saving health enjoy:
All the wicked who despise him,
    He will in their sin destroy.

14 Still, Jehovah, thee confessing,
    Shall my tongue thy praise proclaim;
And may all mankind with blessing
    Ever hail thy holy Name.

SELECTION 119. C. M.
From the cxlvi. Psalm of David.

O PRAISE the Lord, and thou, my soul,
    For ever bless his Name:
His wondrous love, while life shall last,
    My constant praise shall claim.

2 On princes, on the sons of men,
    Let none for aid rely;
They cannot help, they turn to dust,
    And all their counsels die.

3 Then happy he, who Jacob's God
    For his protector takes;
Who still, with well-placed hope, the Lord
    His constant refuge makes.

4 The Lord, who made both heaven and earth,
    And all that they contain,
Will never quit his steadfast truth,
    Nor make his promise vain.

5 The poor, oppress'd, from all their wrongs
  Are eased by his decree;
 He gives the hungry needful food,
  And sets the prisoners free.
6 By him the blind receive their sight,
  The weak and fall'n he rears;
 With kind regard and tender love
  He for the righteous cares.
7 The strangers he preserves from harm,
  The orphan kindly treats;
 Defends the widow, and the wiles
  Of wicked men defeats.
8 The God that does in Sion dwell,
  Is our eternal King:
 From age to age his reign endures;
  Let all his praises sing.

SELECTION 120. II. 2.
From the cxlvi. Psalm of David.

I'LL praise my Maker with my breath,
 And when my voice is lost in death,
  Praise shall employ my nobler powers:
 My days of praise shall ne'er be past,
 While life, and thought, and being last,
  Or immortality endures.
2 Why should I place in man my trust?
 E'en princes die and turn to dust,
  Vain is the help of flesh and blood;
 Their breath departs, their pomp and power,
 And thoughts, all vanish in an hour,
  Nor can they make their promise good.
3 Happy the man whose hopes rely
 On Israel's God: he made the sky,
  And earth, and seas, with all their train;
 He saves th' oppress'd, he feeds the poor;
 His truth for ever stands secure,
  And none shall find his promise vain.
4 The Lord gives eyesight to the blind,
 The Lord supports the sinking mind,
  He sends the righteous strength and peace,

He helps the stranger in distress,
The widow and the fatherless,
  And to the prisoner grants release.

5 God shall the wicked overturn,
On them his wrath shall ever burn,
  Sinners shall perish in their ways:
Sion! the God thy sons adore,
He, he is King for evermore;
  The Lord thy God for ever praise!

SELECTION 121.
From the cxlvii. Psalm of David.
PART I. C. M.

O PRAISE the Lord with hymns of joy,
  And celebrate his fame;
For pleasant, good, and comely 'tis
  To praise his holy Name.

2 His holy city God will build,
  Though levell'd with the ground;
Bring back his people, though dispersed
  Through all the nations round.

3 He kindly heals the broken hearts,
  And all their wounds does close;
He tells the number of the stars,
  Their several names he knows.

4 Great is the Lord, and great his power,
  His wisdom has no bound;
The meek he raises, and throws down
  The wicked to the ground.

5 To God the Lord, a hymn of praise
  With grateful voices sing;
To songs of triumph tune the harp,
  And strike each warbling string.

6 He covers heaven with clouds, and thence
  Refreshing rain bestows;
And on the mountains, through his care,
  The grass in plenty grows.

7 His care the beasts that loosely range
  With timely food supplies;

He feeds the ravens' tender brood,
    And stops their hungry cries.
8 The Lord to him that fears his Name
    His tender love extends;
To him that on his boundless grace
    With steadfast hope depends.

9 Let Sion and Jerusalem
    To God their praise address;
Whose strength secures their lasting gates,
    Who does their children bless.

PART II. L. M.

1 JEHOVAH speaks: swift from the skies
To earth the sovereign mandate flies;
The elements confess their Lord,
With prompt obedience to his word;

2 The thick-descending flakes of snow
O'er earth a fleecy mantle throw;
And glitt'ring frost o'er all the plains
Binds nature fast in icy chains.

3 He speaks: the ice and snow obey,
And nature's fetters melt away;
Softly the vernal breezes blow,
And murmuring waters freely flow.

4 But nobler works his grace record;
To Israel he reveals his word;
To them, his chosen flock, alone,
He makes his sacred precepts known.

5 Such bliss no heathen nation shares,
His oracles are only theirs:
Let Israel then their voices raise,
And bless their God in songs of praise.

SELECTION 122. II. 4.

From the cxlviii. Psalm of David.

YE boundless realms of joy,
    Exalt your Maker's fame;
His praise your song employ
    Above the starry frame:

Your voices raise,
Ye Cherubim
And Seraphim,
To sing his praise.

2 Thou moon, that rul'st the night,
And sun, that guid'st the day,
Ye glittering stars of light,
To him your homage pay:
His praise declare,
Ye heavens above,
And clouds that move
In liquid air.

3 Let them adore the Lord,
And praise his holy Name,
By whose almighty word
They all from nothing came;
And all shall last,
From changes free;
His firm decree
Stands ever fast.

4 Let earth her tribute pay:
Praise him, ye dreadful whales,
And fish that through the sea
Glide swift with glittering scales;
Fire, hail, and snow,
And misty air,
And winds that where
He bids them blow.

5 By hills, and mountains, all
In grateful concert join'd;
By cedars stately tall,
And tress for fruit design'd;
By every beast,
And creeping thing,
And fowl of wing,
His Name be blest.

6 Let all of highest birth,
With those of humbler name,

  And judges of the earth,
   His matchless praise proclaim:
    In this design,
   Let youths with maids,
   And hoary heads
    With children, join.

7 United zeal be shown
  His wondrous fame to raise,
Whose glorious Name alone
  Deserves our endless praise;
   Earth's utmost ends
   His power obey;
   His glorious sway
    The sky transcends.

8 His chosen saints to grace,
  He sets them up on high;
And favours Israel's race,
  Who still to him are nigh:
   O therefore raise
   Your grateful voice,
   And still rejoice
    The Lord to praise!

SELECTION 123. IV. 1.

From the cxlix. Psalm of David.

O PRAISE ye the Lord,
  Prepare your glad voice,
His praise in the great
  Assembly to sing:
In their great Creator
  Let Israel rejoice;
And children of Sion
  Be glad in their King.

2 Let them his great Name
  Extol in their songs,
With hearts well attuned
  His praises express;
Who always takes pleasure
  To hear their glad tongues,

And waits with salvation
    The humble to bless.

3 With glory adorn'd,
    His people shall sing
To God, who their heads
    With safety doth shield;
Such honour and triumph
    His favour shall bring:
O therefore, for ever
    All praise to him yield!

SELECTION 124. L. M.
From the cl. Psalm of David.

O PRAISE the Lord in that blest place,
  From whence his goodness largely flows;
Praise him in heaven, where he his face,
  Unveil'd in perfect glory shows.

2 Praise him for all the mighty acts
    Which he in our behalf has done;
His kindness this return exacts,
    With which our praise should equal run.

3 Let the shrill trumpet's warlike voice
    Make rocks and hills his praise rebound;
Praise him with harp's melodious noise,
    And gentle psaltery's silver sound.

4 Let them who joyful hymns compose,
    To cymbals set their songs of praise;
To well-tuned cymbals, and to those
    That loudly sound on solemn days.

5 Let all that vital breath enjoy,
    The breath he does to them afford,
In just returns of praise employ;
    Let every creature praise the Lord!

END OF THE SELECTIONS OF PSALMS IN METRE.

A TABLE OF FIRST LINES,

SHOWING WHERE TO FIND EACH PSALM, AND PART OF A PSALM, BY THE BEGINNING.

		Selec.	Part.	Page.
According to thy promised grace	cxix.	97	7	89
Adored for ever be the Lord	xxviii.	23		21
Approach, ye children of the Lord	xxxiv.	29	2	25
As pants the heart for cooling streams	xlii.	36		32
As pants the wearied hart for cooling	xlii.	37		32
Attend, my people; Israel, hear	l.	43	2	36
Be gracious to thy servant, Lord	cxix.	97	3	86
Bless'd is the man, whom thou, O Lord	xciv.	73	2	64
Bless God, my soul; thou, Lord, alone	civ.	83	1	72
Bless God, ye servants, that attend	cxxxiv.	108		104
But who thine anger's dread effects	xc.	69	2	60
Consider my affliction, Lord	cxix.	97	20	97
Consider that the righteous man	iv.	4		5
Deceitful thoughts and practices	cxix.	97	15	94
Defend me, Lord, from shame	xxxi.	26		22
For ever and for ever, Lord	cxix.	97	12	92
For thee, O God, our constant praise	lxv.	50	1	42
From lowest depths of woe	cxxx.	104		102
Give ear, thou Judge of all the earth	lv.	45		39
God is our refuge in distress	xlvi.	40		34
God, my King, thy might confessing	cxlv.	118		113
God of my life, O Lord most high	lxxxviii.	67		57
God shall arise, and Sion view	cii.	80	2	69
God shall charge his angel legions	xci.	70	2	61
God's perfect law converts the soul	xix.	15	2	12
God's temple crowns the holy mount	lxxxvii.	66		56
Had not the Lord, may Israel say	cxxiv.	100		100
Happy the man whose tender care	xli.	35		31
Have mercy, Lord, on me	li.	44		37
Hear, O my people; to my law	lxxviii.	60		51
He's blest whose sins have pardon gain'd	xxxii.	27		23
He that has God his guardian made	xci.	70	1	60
How bless'd are they who always keep	cxix.	97	1	84
How blest is he who ne'er consents	i.	1		3
How good and pleasant must it be	xcii.	71		62
How long wilt thou forget me, Lord	xiii.	10		8
How manifold thy works, O Lord	civ.	84		74
How shall the young preserve their ways	cxix.	97	2	85
How various, Lord, thy works are found	civ.	83	2	73
How vast must their advantage be	cxxxiii.	107		104
I'll praise my Maker with my breath	cxlvi.	120		115
In mercy, not in wrath	vi.	6		6
In my distress to God I cried	xxx.	25		22
Instruct me in thy statutes, Lord	cxix.	97	5	88
In thee I put my steadfast trust	lxxi.	55		46
I waited meekly for the Lord	xl.	34		30
Jehovah reigns, let all the earth	xcvii.	76		66
Jehovah reigns, let therefore all	xcix.	78		68
Jehovah speaks: swift from the skies	cxlvii.	121	2	117
Judge me, O Lord, for I the paths	xxvi.	21		19
Let all the just to God, with joy	xxxiii.	28	1	24
Let all the lands, with shouts of joy	lxvi.	51	1	43

TABLE OF FIRST LINES.

	Selec.	Part.	Page.
Let me with light and truth be bless'd	xliii.	38	33
Like water is my life pour'd out	xxii.	17 2	14
Lo! hills and mountains shall bring forth	lxxii.	56	47
Lord, for ever at thy side	cxxxi.	105	103
Lord, from thy unexhausted store	lxv.	50 2	42
Lord, hear my prayer, and to my cry	cxliii.	115	110
Lord, in thy sight, O let my prayer	cxli.	114	109
Lord, let me know my term of days	xxxix.	33	29
Lord, not to us, we claim no share	cxv.	93	80
Lord, though at times surprised by fear	lvi.	46	39
Lord, to my brethren I'll declare	xxii.	17 3	15
Lord, what's in man that thou should'st	cxliv.	116	110
Lord, who's the happy man that may	xv.	12	9
Magnify Jehovah's name	cvii.	87 1	75
May Jacob's God defend	xx.	16	13
Mine eyes, alas! begin to fail	cxix.	97 16	94
My God, my God, why leav'st thou me	xxii.	17 1	14
My grateful soul shall bless the Lord	xvi.	13	10
My offerings to God's house I'll bring	lxvi.	51 2	43
My soul, for help on God rely	lxii.	48	40
My soul, howe'er distress'd and poor	lxix.	54 2	46
My soul, inspired with sacred love	ciii.	81	70
My soul, oppress'd with deadly care	cxix.	97 4	87
My soul, with grateful thoughts of love	cxvi.	94	81
My soul with long expectance faints	cxix.	97 11	92
No change of time shall ever shock	xviii.	14 1	11
O all ye people, clap your hands	xlvii.	41	35
O bless the Lord, my soul	ciii.	82	72
O come, loud anthems let us sing	xcv.	74	64
O God, my gracious God, to thee	lxiii.	49	41
O God, my heart is fix'd, 'tis bent	lvii.	47	40
O God, my heart is fully bent	cviii.	88	77
O God of hosts, the mighty Lord	lxxxiv.	63	53
O God our Saviour, all our hearts	lxxxv.	64	54
O Lord, my God, my portion thou	cxix.	97 8	90
O Lord, the Saviour and defence	xc.	69 1	59
O Lord, thy mercy, my sure hope	xxxvi.	30	26
O praise the Lord, and thou, my soul	cxlvi.	119	114
O praise the Lord, for he is good	cxviii.	96	82
O praise the Lord in that blest place	cl.	124	120
O praise the Lord with hymns of joy	cxlvii.	121 1	116
O praise the Lord with one consent	cxxxv.	109	105
O praise ye the Lord	cxlix.	123	119
O render thanks and bless the Lord	cv.	85	74
O render thanks to God above	cvi.	86	75
O Thou, whom heavenly hosts obey	lxxx.	61	51
O Thou, to whom all creatures bow	viii.	7	6
O 'twas a joyful sound to hear	cxxii.	99	100
O with due reverence let us all	cxxxii.	106	103
Praise ye the Lord; our God to praise	cxi.	90	78
Regard my words, O gracious Lord	v.	5	5
Save me, O God, from waves that roll	lxix.	54 1	45
Say ye, the Lord shall not regard	xciv.	73 1	63
Sing to the Lord a new-made song	xcvi.	75	65
Sing to the Lord a new-made song	xcviii.	77	67
That man is bless'd who stands in awe	cxii.	91	79
Thee will I bless, my God and King	cxiv.	117 1	111

TABLE OF FIRST LINES. 123

	Selec.	Part.	Page.
The good man's way is God's delight	xxxvii.	31	2	28
The heavens declare thy glory, Lord	xix.	15	1	12
The Lord a holy temple hath	xi.	9		8
The Lord does them support that fall	cxlv.	117	2	112
The Lord hath spoke, the mighty God	l.	43	1	36
The Lord himself, the mighty Lord	xxiii.	18		16
The Lord look'd down from heaven's high	xiv.	11		9
The Lord, the only God, is great	xlviii.	42		35
The LORD unto my Lord thus spake	cx.	89		77
The love that to thy laws I bear	cxix.	97	13	93
The man is blest that fears the Lord	cxxviii.	103		102
The Name of our God	lxxvi.	59		50
The servants of Jehovah's will	lxviii.	53		45
The spacious earth is all the Lord's	xxiv.	19		17
The strong foundations of the earth	cii.	80	3	70
The wicked I in power have seen	xxxvii.	31	3	28
The wonders which thy laws contain	cxix.	97	17	95
Thine is the cheerful day, O Lord	lxxiv.	58		50
Thou art the righteous Judge, in whom	cxix.	97	18	95
Though wicked men grow rich or great	xxxvii.	31	1	27
Thou, gracious God, art my defence	iii.	3		4
Thou, Lord, by strictest search hast known	cxxxix.	113		108
Thou suit'st, O Lord, thy righteous ways	xviii.	14	2	11
Through all the changing scenes of life	xxxiv.	29	1	25
Thus God declares his sovereign will	ii.	2		3
Thy chastening wrath, O Lord, restrain	xxxviii.	32		29
Thy constant blessing, Lord, bestow	cxix.	97	6	88
Thy mercies, Lord, shall be my song	xxxix.	68		57
Thy presence, Lord, hath me supplied	lxxiii.	57		49
Thy sacred word my joyful breast	cxix.	97	21	97
Thy wondrous power, Almighty Lord	cvii.	87	2	76
Thy word is to my feet a lamp	cxix.	97	14	93
To bless thy chosen race	lxvii.	52		44
To celebrate thy praise, O Lord	ix.	8		7
To God, in whom I trust	xxv.	20		18
To God, our never-failing strength	lxxxi.	62		52
To God, the mighty Lord	cxxxvi.	110		105
To me, who am the workmanship	cxix.	97	10	91
To my complaint, O Lord my God	lxxxvi.	65		55
To my request and earnest cry	cxix.	97	22	98
To Sion's hill I lift my eyes	cxxi.	98		99
We build with fruitless cost, unless	cxxvii.	102		101
Whate'er the mighty Lord decrees	xxxiii.	28	2	24
When I pour out my soul in prayer	cii.	80	1	69
When we, our weary limbs to rest	cxxxvii.	111		107
While I the King's loud praise rehearse	xlv.	39		33
Whom should I fear, since God to me	xxvii.	22		20
Who place on Sion's God their trust	cxxv.	101		101
With cheerful notes let all the earth	cxvii.	95		82
With glory clad, with strength array'd	xciii.	72		63
With me, thy servant, thou hast dealt	cxix.	97	9	90
With my whole heart, my God and King	cxxxviii.	112		107
With my whole heart to God I call'd	cxix.	97	19	96
With one consent let all the earth	c.	79		68
Ye boundless realms of joy	cxlviii.	122		117
Ye saints and servants of the Lord	cxiii.	92		79
Ye that in might and power excel	xxix.	24		21

TABLE,

TO FIND THE PSALMS IN THE FOREGOING SELECTIONS SUITED TO PARTICULAR SUBJECTS AND OCCASIONS.

Adoration of God, Selection 7, 50, 74, 75, 117. (See *Praise*.)
——— of the second Person in the Trinity, 41.
Advent, Selections proper for, 43, part i.; 68, 75, 76, 77.
Afflicted, prayer of, 10, 36, 37, 73, part ii.; 80, 97, part xi.; 115.
———, comfort of, 97, part vii.
———, complaint of, 36, 37, 80, part i.; 115.
———, Selection proper for, 97.
Afflictions, benefits of, 73, part ii.; 97, part ix., verse 3.
———, deliverance from them celebrated, 29, 87.
Aged saint, prayer of, 55, verse 6.
Almsgiving, 35, verses 1, 2, 3; 91.
Angels, guard the righteous, 29, verse 4; 70, part ii.
———, called on to praise the Lord, 81, verses 11, 12.
Ascension, 19, verses 6, 7, 8, 9, 10; 41, 53, verses 4, 5.
Ash-Wednesday, 44, 104. (See *Penitential*.)
Assistance from God, 112, 116.
Atheism, practical, punishment denounced against, 11.
Attributes of God, 30, 90, 117, 119, 120, 121.

Blessing of God, on temporal business and comforts, 102, 103.
Blessings promised to the righteous, 1, 27, 103.
Blood of Christ, cleansing from sin, prefigured by the ceremonies of the law, 44.
Brotherly love, 107.

Care of God over his saints, 29.
Charitable man, blessings promised to, 35, verses 1, 2, 3.
Charity to the poor. (See *Almsgiving*.)
Children, instructed in God's law, 60, verses 3, 6; 97, part ii.
Christ, the true David, 68. (See *David*.)
———, covenant made with him typified by David, 68.
———, divinity of, 39, verses 6—8; 41, 89.
———, his incarnation, 34, verse 6, &c.
———, David in the person of, describes his sorrows, and the malice, and persecution of his enemies, and prays for deliverance, 17, 34, 45.
———, his death and sufferings set forth in the person of David, 17, 34, 45, 54.
———, his resurrection predicted, 2, 13, 54, part ii.; 96, verse 11, &c.
———, his ascension celebrated, 19, 41, 53.
———, his exaltation in his human nature to his mediatorial kingdom, 2, 7, 56, 68, 89, 96, 106.
———, his glorification in his human nature, 7.
———, his *love to his Church* celebrated, 39.
———, his *glory* and *power*, 39.
———, his *kingdom* among the *Gentiles*, 56, 66, 89, 106.
———, a *Priest* and *King*, 89.
———, our strength and righteousness, 55.
———, his first and second coming, 43, 75, 76, 77.

TABLE OF SUBJECTS.

Christmas-day, 39, 64, last three verses; 68, 89, 106.
Church, built on Jesus Christ, 96, verse 11, &c.
———, gathered and settled, 106.
———, its *beauty, worship*, and *order*, 42, 99.
———, the *birth-place of saints*, 31.
———, *safety* and *joy* in it, 22, 42, 63.
———, destruction of its enemies, 59.
———, Gentiles gathered into it, 39, 41.
———, God defends it and fights for it, 16, 40, 101.
———, Christ's love to it, 39.
———, God's *presence* in it, and *delight* in it, 29, 106.
———, the garden of the Lord, 71, verses 8, 9.
———, the spouse of Christ, 39.
———, its increase, 52.
———, in affliction, 61.
———, comforted, 101.
———, the honour and safety of a nation, 42.
———, its festivals joyfully attended, 99.
Comfort and support in God, 4, 13, 27, 29, 40, 73, part ii., first three verses.
———, and support in sadness, prayed for, 80.
——————————— of God's Spirit, prayed for, 37, 38, 44.
Communion of saints, 107.
Compassion of God, 81, 82, 117, from verse 6.
Complaint of absence from publick worship, 36, 37.
——————— of sickness, 6.
——————— of temptation and spiritual afflictions, 36, 37.
——————— of heavy afflictions in mind and body, 80, 115.
Confession of sin, repentance and pardon, 27, 32, 44, 104, 115.
Confirmation, psalms proper for, 15, part ii.; 20, verse 5, &c.; 29, part ii., verse 1, &c.; 44, verse 8, &c.; 97, part ii. verse 1, &c.; part v., verse 1, &c.; part xiv., verse 1, &c.
Conscience, its guilt relieved, 27, 104.
Consecration of a church, 106. (See *Office of Consecration*.)
Contrition, an act of, 20, 44.
Converse with God, 49.
Conversion of Jews and Gentiles, 66, 75, 86.
Corruption of manners, general, 11.
Counsel and support from God, 13, 97.
Courage in death, 13.
Covenant made with Christ in the person of David, 68.
Creation and Providence, 28, 84, 109, 110, 121, 122.
Creatures, no trust in them, and God all-sufficient, 28, part ii.; 48, 119.
——————— praising God, 122.
David, in his sufferings, deliverances, kingdom, &c., a type of Christ, 2, 14, 17, 34, 39, 45, 54, 56, 68, 89, 96, 106. (See *Christ*.)
Death, courage in, 13, 18, verse 4.
———, deliverance from, 26, 96.
———, of Christ, 17, 54.
———, of saints and sinners, 31.
———, the effect of sin, 69.
Defence and salvation in God, 3, 14, 98.
Delaying sinners warned, 74, verse 7.
Delight in God, 14, 36, 37, 49, 57, 63.
Deliverance begun and perfected, 64.
——————— from despair, 14.
——————— from deep distress, 29, 34.
——————— from death, 26, 96.

TABLE OF SUBJECTS.

Deliverance from oppression and falsehood, 46.
———— from persecution, 5, 73.
———— from slander, 5, 26.
———— from shipwreck, 87, part ii.
———— by prayer, 29, 34.
Desertion and distress of soul, 10, 32, 115.
Desire of knowledge, 97, part v.
——— of holiness, 97, part v.
——— of comfort and succour, 97, part v., verse 6, &c.
——— of quickening grace, 97, part iv.
Desolations, the Church safe in them, 40.
Devotion, 108.
———— in sickness, 6, 33.
Direction prayed for, 20.
Distress relieved, 29, 34, 104.
Divinity of Christ, 89, 89.
Dominion of man, 7, verses 5, 6.
Doubts and fears suppressed, 3, 26, 36, 37.

Easter-Eve, psalms proper for, 13, verse 3, &c.; 34, verses 1, 2.
Easter, psalms proper for, 2, verse 2 to the end; 25, 47, 96.
Education, religious, 29, part ii.; 60, verse 3, &c.; 97, part ii.
End of righteous and wicked, 1, 31.
Enemies of Christ and the Church, (typified by the enemies of David and Israel,) 14, 59. (See *Christ, Church, David.*)
Envy and unbelief cured, 31.
Epiphany, season of, psalms proper for, 17, part iii., verse 6, &c.; 39, 42, 52, 56, 66, 75, 77. (See *Gentiles, Kingdom of Christ.*)
Equity and wisdom of Providence, 8.
Evening Psalm, 63, last stanza.
Evidences of grace, 12, 21.
Exaltation of Christ, 2, 7, 56, 89.
Examination, 113, last verse.

Faith in divine power and mercy, 47, 48, 104.
Faithfulness of God, 68, 85, 90, 117, 118, 119.
Family love and worship, 115.
Fear in the worship of God, 68, verse 7, &c.; 78.
——— and reverence of God, 28, part i., last verse, 103. (See *God, his power and majesty.*)
Fears and doubts suppressed, 3, 26, 29, 36, 37.
Formal worship, 43, part ii.
Forgiveness of sin prayed for, 32, 44. (See *Penitential, Pardon.*)
Frailty of man, 33, 69, 116.
Fretfulness discouraged, 31.
Friendship, its blessings, 107.
Funeral, psalms proper for, 33, 69, 116, verse 2.

Gentiles given to Christ, 2, 17, part iii., last five verses; 56.
———— gathered into the Church, 39, 41, 52, 66, 75.
———— owning the true God, 50, part i., verse 2; 52, 75, 77.
Glorification of Christ in his human nature, 7.
Glory of Christ, 39.
——— and grace promised, 63, 76, last three verses.
God, his greatness and glory, 7.
———, his perfections and providence extolled, 30, 50, part ii.; 85, 118, 121.
———, his goodness, &c., 81, 82, 117, part i., verse 6, &c.; 121.
———, his omniscience, 113.
———, his omnipresence, 113.

TABLE OF SUBJECTS.

God, his omnipotence, 53, 68, verse 6, &c.; 72, 75.
—, his justice, 80, verse 2 ; 71, last verse.
—, his sovereignty and goodness, 7, 92, 116.
—, his compassion, 82, 117, part i., verse 6, &c., and part ii.; 118, verse 5, &c.
—, his care of the saints, 3, 29.
—, our defence and salvation, 3, 28, part ii.; 93.
—, eternal, &c., 72.
—, eternal, and man mortal, 69, 80, part i.
—, faithfulness, 68, 90, 117, 118.
—, goodness and mercy, 81, 82, 117, 118.
—, goodness and truth, 117, 118, 119.
—, governing power and goodness, 51.
—, greatness and goodness, 63, 116, 117, 118, 121.
—, the Judge, 8, verse 3 ; 43, 76, 77, last verse.
—, his majesty, 49, 76.
—, his condescension, 92.
—, mercy and truth, 30, 82, 110, 117, 118.
—, made man, 7, verse 5, &c.
—, his perfections extolled, 30, 90, 117, 118, 119, 120, 121.
—, our portion, 4, 57.
—, his power and majesty, 53, 68, verse 6, &c.; 72, 75.
—, our preserver, 98, 112.
—, present in his Church, 40, 63.
—, our Shepherd, 18.
—, our support and comfort, 73, part ii.
—, supreme Governor, 74.
—, his vengeance and compassion, 53, 75.
—, unchangeable, 68, 90.
—, worthy of all praise, 117, 118, 119, 120, 124.
Good Friday, psalms proper for, 17, 34, 45, 54. (See *Christ*, his *sufferings* and *death*.)
Good Works, 4, 12, 86, verse 3, &c.; 91, 97.
Goodness of God celebrated, 81, 82, 121. (See *God*.)
Gospel, its blessings, glory, and success, 15, 39, 68, 77, 89, 90.
Grace, prayed for, 20, 36, 37, 38.
——, its evidences, 21.
——, without merit, 27.
—— of Christ, 39, 56.
—— and providence, 28, 30, 109, 110.
——, preserving and restoring, 27, 31, part ii.; 101, 112.
—— and glory, 63, two last verses ; 97, last three verses.
——, pardoning, quickening, and sanctifying, 97, part iii., part v., part viii., part x.
Greatness of God, and his goodness, 53, 116, 117, 118, 120, 121.
Guilt of conscience removed, 27, 44, 104.
Harvest, 50, part ii.; 121, verse 6, &c.
Health, sickness, and recovery, 6, 25, 32, 33, 69, 80, part i.; 94.
Hearing of prayer, 4, 50, part i.; 51, part ii.; 80, part i.
Heart, known to God, 113.
Heaven, 13, 19, verse 3, &c.; 76, verse 5.
Holiness, 4, 12, 19, verse 4, &c.; 86, verse 3, &c.; 91, 97.
Holy Spirit, supplication for, 36, 37, 44, verse 9, &c. (See *Grace*.)
Hope and trust in God, 3, 13, 14, 22, 26, 40, 46, 48, 55, 65, 93, verse 3, &c.; 101.
Humiliation, day of, psalms proper for. (See *Penitential Psalms*.)
Humility, profession of, 105.
Hypocrites and hypocrisy, 43, part ii.

TABLE OF SUBJECTS.

Incarnation of Christ, 34, verse 6, &c.
Institution of a minister, 99, 106, 107.
Instruction, spiritual, 20, verse 3; 29, part ii.; 97.
Instructive psalms, displaying the different characters and ends of good and bad men, 1, 5, 8, 9, 11, 12, 19, 20, 27, 29, 30, 31, 43, 57, 63, 70, 71, 73, 91, 97, 98, 101, 102, 103, 107.
Intercession, psalms of, 16, 52, 99, last four verses; 106.
Judgment, day of, 1, last three verses; 43, part i.; 75, last stanza; 76, 77, last verse. (See *Advent.*)
Justice of God. (See *God, his perfections.*)
Justification from the free grace of God, 27, 104.

Kingdom of Christ, 2, 56, 66, 68, 89, 106. (See *Christ, Epiphany.*)
Knowledge, spiritual, desired, 97, verse 5, &c.; part v., part xvii., &c.

Law of God, its excellence, consolations, delight in it, &c., 15, 97, part i., part v., part xiii., part xvi.
Lent, psalms proper for. (See *Penitential Psalms.*)
Liberality to the poor, 35, first three verses; 91, verse 3, &c.
Life, its shortness and frailty, 33, 69.
——, uncertainty of, 33.
Longing after God, 36, 37, 49.
Lord's-Day, 49, first three stanzas, 74, 75, 79, 96, verse 12, to the end.
Love to our neighbour, 12.
——, brotherly, 107.

Majesty of God, 53. (See *God.*)
Man, his dominion, 7, verse 5, &c.
——, his mortality, 33, 69, part i.; 80, part i.

Nation's safety is the Church, 42.
National deliverance, 59, 100.
—— desolations, the Church and people of God safe in them, 40.

Obedience, sincere, 27, last two verses; 113, last verse.
Old Age, 69, part i., verse 9, 10.
Omnipresence of God, 113. (See *God.*)
Omnipotence of God, 68, verse 6, and following. (See *God.*)
Omniscience of God, 113. (See *God.*)

Pardon, mercy, and grace prayed for, 6, 20, 27, 44, 64, 104, 107. (See *Penitential Psalms, Repentance.*)
Passion-week, psalms proper for, 17, 45, 54. (See *Christ, his sufferings and death.*)
Patience under afflictions and persecutions, 31, 33, 104.
Peace and holiness, urged, 29, part ii.
——, return of, after war, 77, 96.
Penitential Psalms, 6, 27, 32, 44, 80, part i.; 104, 115.
Perfections of God extolled, 30, 90, 117, 118, 119, 120, 121. (See *God.*)
Persecution, prayer in the time of, 55, 115.
——————, courage in time of, 40, 73, part ii.
——————, deliverance from, 8, 73, part ii.
Pestilence, preservation in it, 70.
Piety, instruction in, 29, part ii.
Poor, charity to. (See *Almsgiving.*)
Portion, God our, 4, last three verses; 57.
Power of Christ, 39.
—— of God, 53, 68. (See *God.*)
Praise, psalms of, 51, 79, 81, 82, 90, 112, 117, 118, 119, 120.
—— for creation and providence, 28, 83.
—— from all creatures, 122.

TABLE OF SUBJECTS.

Praise for temporal blessings, 53, 120.
——— for eminent deliverances, 29, 96.
——— for the victories by which God effected our redemption, 77.
——— for health restored, 25, 94.
——— for hearing prayer, 51, last three verses.
——— to the Messiah, 39.
——— from all nations, 95.
——— for protection, grace, and truth, 47.
——— for rain, 50, part ii.
Prayer, 4, 50.
———, in time of war, 16.
Preservation, daily, 98.
———, in time of public danger and calamity, 40, 70, 91, last verse.
———, from sin and its punishments, 15, part ii., verse 7; 20, 23, 34.
Preserver. (See *God*.)
Priestly office of Christ, 89.
Propagation of the Gospel, 39, 41, 53, 56, 117, 118.
Prophetical psalms, 2, 13, 17, 34, 39, 53, 56, 66, 96.
Prosperous sinners, their fearful end, 31.
Protection of God, extended to the righteous, 29, verse 4, &c.; 31, 70, 101.
Providence, its wisdom and equity, 8, last verse; 75, 76.
——— and grace, 30, 121.
——— in the works of creation, 28, 50, part ii.; 68, 84, 87, 109, 110, 121.
Punishment of sinners. (See *Prosperous sinners, Sinners warned*.)

Qualifications of a Christian, 12, 19.
Quickening grace. (See *Grace*.)

Rain, 50, part ii.; 121, part i., verse 6.
Redemption, the mercies of, celebrated, 81, 82, 87, part i.
Recovery from sickness. (See *Sickness*.)
Relative duties, 12, 107.
Religious education. (See *Education*.)
Renovation, 44, verse 6, &c.; 97, part v. (See *Grace*.)
Repentance, relative to, 6, 27, 32, 44, 80, part i.; 104, 115.
Resignation, 33, 105.
Restoring grace, 18, verse 3. (See *Grace*.)
Resurrection of Christ and of the saints predicted, 13, verse 3, &c.; 25, 96, verse 11, &c. (See *Christ, Easter-Eve, Easter*.)
Reverence in worship. (See *Worship*.)
Righteous, character of, 12. (See *Holiness*.)
———, protected by God, 29, verse 4, &c.; 31, 70.
———, blessings promised to, 1, 27, last verse; 103. (See *Saints*.)
Righteousness of Christ trusted in, 55.
———, from God, 55.

Safety in danger, 70. (See *Preservation*.)
Saints, character of, 12, 19.
———, protection promised to, 29, verse 4, &c.; 31, 70, 101.
———, blessings promised to, 1, 27, 71, verses 8, 9; 103.
Salvation, and eternal joys, 13, 19, 23, 30, 43, part i., third stanza; 48, 63, 64, 66, 76.
Scripture, excellence of, 15, 97.
Seasons of the year, 50, part ii.; 121.
Self-examination, 21, 113, last verse.

TABLE OF SUBJECTS.

Shepherd. (See *God.*)
Sickness, 6, 25, 32, 33, 94.
Sin, confession of, 27, 32, 44, 104, 115. (See *Penitential Psalms, Repentance.*)
Sincerity, 21, 113, last verse.
——— proved and rewarded, 14, part ii.
Sinners warned, 74, last verse.
——— punished, 1, verse 4, &c.; 9, 31.
Slander, deliverance from it, 26.
Sovereignty of God. (See *God.*)
Spirit. (See *Grace, Holy Spirit.*)
Spiritual enemies overcome, 3, 14.
Submission. (See *Resignation.*)
Sufferings of Christ, 17, 35, 45, 54.
Sunday. (See *Lord's-day.*)
Support and counsel from God, 13, verse 1; 45, last verse; 73, part ii.

Temporal business and comforts, blessings on, prayed for, 102.
Temptations overcome, 3, 14.
Thanksgiving. (See *Praise.*)
Thunder and storm, 24, verse 3, &c.
Trinity-Sunday, psalms proper for, 39, 41, 89.
Trust in God, 57. (See *Hope.*)
——— in creatures vain, 120.
Truth of God celebrated, 117, 118, 120.

Unbelief and envy cured, 31.
Unchangeable God. (See *God.*)
Unity, advantages of, celebrated, 107.

Vanity of man, 33, 69, verse 3, &c.

War, psalms in time of, 14, 16, 40.
Watchfulness, 15, part ii., last three verses; 33, 46, 114.
Whit-sunday, 42, 53, 117, 118. (See *Grace, Holy Spirit.*)
Wickedness of man, 11, 44.
Winter and summer, 121.
Works of Creation, Providence, and Grace, 15, 121. (See *Creation, Providence, Grace.*)
Worship and order of the Church, 42.
———, delight in it, 63, 68, 78.
———, public, 49, 63, 74, 79, 99, 106.

Zeal, prayer for, 97, part ii., verse 2, &c.
Zion. (See *Church.*)

HYMNS,

SUITED TO

THE FEASTS AND FASTS

OF

THE CHURCH,

AND

OTHER OCCASIONS OF PUBLIC WORSHIP.

PRINTED BY G. E. EYRE AND W. SPOTTISWOODE.
Warehouses:
NEW YORK, 626, BROADWAY.
LONDON, 43, FLEET STREET, E. C.; EDINBURGH, 16, ELDER STREET.

HYMNS.

I. THE HOLY SCRIPTURES.
HYMN 1. C. M.

GREAT God, with wonder and with praise,
  On all thy works I look;
But still thy wisdom, power, and grace,
  Shine brightest in thy book.

2 The stars that in their courses roll,
  Have much instruction given;
But thy good word informs my soul
  How I may soar to heaven.

3 The fields provide me food, and show
  The goodness of the Lord;
But fruits of life and glory grow
  In thy most holy word.

4 Here are my choicest treasures hid,
  Here my best comfort lies;
Here my desires are satisfied,
  And here my hopes arise.

5 Lord, make me understand thy law,
  Show what my faults have been;
And from thy Gospel let me draw
  Pardon for all my sin.

6 Here would I learn how Christ has died
  To save my soul from hell;
Not all the books on earth beside,
  Such heavenly wonders tell.

7 Then let me love my Bible more,
  And take a fresh delight,
By day to read these wonders o'er,
  And meditate by night.

HYMN 2. C. M.

FATHER of mercies! in thy word
  What endless glory shines!
For ever be thy Name adored
  For these celestial lines.

2 Here may the wretched sons of want
    Exhaustless riches find;
Riches above what earth can grant,
    And lasting as the mind.
3 Here the fair tree of knowledge grows,
    And yields a free repast;
Sublimer sweets than nature knows
    Invite the longing taste.
4 Here the Redeemer's welcome voice
    Spreads heavenly peace around;
And life and everlasting joys
    Attend the blissful sound.
5 O may these heavenly pages be
    My ever dear delight;
And still new beauties may I see,
    And still increasing light.
6 Divine Instructor, gracious Lord,
    Be thou for ever near;
Teach me to love thy sacred word,
    And view my Saviour there.

II. CREATION.
HYMN 3. C. M.

GREAT first of beings! mighty Lord
    Of all this wondrous frame!
Produced by thy creating word,
    The world from nothing came.
2 Thy voice sent forth the high command,
    'Twas instantly obey'd:
And through thy goodness all things stand
    Which by thy power were made.
3 Lord, for thy glory shine the whole;
    They all reflect thy light:
For this, in course the planets roll,
    And day succeeds the night.
4 For this, the sun dispenses heat
    And beams of cheering day;
And distant stars, in order set,
    By night thy power display.

5 For this, the earth its produce yields;
    For this, the waters flow;
And blooming plants adorn the fields,
    And trees aspiring grow.

6 Inspired with praise, our minds pursue
    This wise and noble end;
That all we think, and all we do,
    Shall to thine honour tend.

HYMN 4. C. M.
Genesis i.

LET heaven arise, let earth appear,
    Proclaim th' Eternal Lord:
The heaven arose, the earth appear'd,
    At his creating word.

2 But formless was the earth, and void,
    Dark, sluggish, and confused;
Till o'er the mass the Spirit moved,
    And quickening power diffused.

3 Then spake the Lord Omnipotent
    The mandate, "Be there light:"
Light darted forth in vivid rays,
    And scatter'd ancient night.

4 The glorious firmament he spread,
    To part the earth and sky;
And fix'd the upper elements
    Within their spheres on high.

5 He bade the seas together flow;
    They left the solid land:
And herbs, and plants, and fruitful trees,
    Sprung forth at his command.

6 Above, he form'd the stars; and placed
    Two greater orbs of light;
The radiant sun to rule the day,
    The moon to rule the night.

7 To all the varied living tribes
    He gave their wondrous birth:

Some form'd within the watery deep,
   Some from the teeming earth.
8 Then, chief o'er all his works below,
   Man, honour'd man, was made;
   His soul with God's pure image stamp'd,
   With innocence array'd.
9 Completed now the mighty work,
   God his creation view'd;
   And, pleased with all that he had made,
   Pronounced it " very good."

HYMN 5. II. 1.
Psalm cxlviii.
Praise from Living Creatures.

BEGIN, my soul, th' exalted lay;
   Let each enraptured thought obey,
     And praise th' Almighty's Name:
Let heaven and earth, and seas and skies,
In one melodious concert rise,
   To swell th' inspiring theme.

2 Ye angels, catch the thrilling sound,
   While all the adoring thrones around
     His boundless mercy sing;
   Let every listening saint above
   Wake all the tuneful soul of love,
     And touch the sweetest string.

3 Whate'er this living world contains,
   That wings the air or treads the plains,
     United praise bestow;
   Ye tenants of the ocean wide,
   Proclaim Him through the mighty tide,
     And in the deeps below.

4 Let man, by nobler passions sway'd,
   The feeling heart, the judging head,
     In heavenly praise employ;
   Spread HIS tremendous Name around,
   While heaven's broad arch rings back the
       sound,
     The general burst of joy.

HYMN 6. II. 1.
Psalm cxlviii.
Praise from the Elements and Worlds.

YE fields of light, celestial plains,
　Where pure, serene, effulgence reigns,
　　Ye scenes divinely fair,
Your Maker's wondrous power proclaim,
Tell how he form'd your shining frame,
　　And breathed the fluid air.

2 Join, all ye stars, the vocal choir;
Thou dazzling orb of liquid fire,
　　The mighty chorus aid;
And, soon as evening veils the plain,
Thou moon, prolong the hallow'd strain,
　　And praise Him in the shade.

3 Thou heaven of heavens, his vast abode,
Proclaim the glories of thy God;
　　Ye worlds, declare his might:
He spake the word, and ye were made,
Darkness and dismal chaos fled,
　　And nature sprung to light.

4 Let every element rejoice;
Ye thunders, burst with awful voice
　　To Him who bids you roll;
His praise in softer notes declare,
Each whispering breeze of yielding air,
　　And breathe it to the soul.

HYMN 7. L. M.
Psalm xix.

THE spacious firmament on high,
　With all the blue ethereal sky,
And spangled heavens, a shining frame,
　Their great Original proclaim.

2 Th' unwearied sun, from day to day,
Does his Creator's power display,
And publishes to every land
The work of an Almighty hand.

3 Soon as the evening shades prevail,
The moon takes up the wondrous tale;

     And, nightly, to the listening earth,
     Repeats the story of her birth;
4 Whilst all the stars that round her burn,
     And all the planets in their turn,
     Confirm the tidings as they roll,
     And spread the truth from pole to pole.
5 What though in solemn silence all
     Move round this dark terrestrial ball;
     What though no real voice nor sound
     Amidst their radiant orbs be found;
6 In reason's ear they all rejoice,
     And utter forth a glorious voice;
     For ever singing as they shine,
     "The hand that made us is divine."

III. PROVIDENCE.

HYMN 8. L. M.

ETERNAL Source of every joy!
     Well may thy praise our lips employ
     While in thy temple we appear,
     To hail thee Sovereign of the year.
2 Wide as the wheels of nature roll,
     Thy hand supports and guides the whole:
     The sun is taught by thee to rise,
     And darkness when to veil the skies.
3 The flowery spring at thy command
     Perfumes the air, and paints the land;
     The summer rays with vigour shine,
     To raise the corn, and cheer the vine.
4 Thy hand in autumn richly pours
     Through all our coasts redundant stores;
     And winters, soften'd by thy care,
     No more the face of horror wear.
5 Seasons, and months, and weeks, and days,
     Demand successive songs of praise;
     And be the grateful homage paid,
     With morning light, and evening shade.

6 Here in thy house let incense rise,
And circling sabbaths bless our eyes,
Till to those lofty heights we soar,
Where days and years revolve no more.

HYMN 9. II. 3.
Psalm xxiii.

THE Lord my pasture shall prepare,
And feed me with a shepherd's care;
His presence shall my wants supply,
And guard me with a watchful eye;
My noon-day walks he shall attend,
And all my midnight hours defend.

2 When in the sultry glebe I faint,
Or on the thirsty mountain pant,
To fertile vales and dewy meads
My weary wandering steps he leads,
Where peaceful rivers, soft and slow,
Amid the verdant landscape flow.

3 Though in the paths of death I tread,
With gloomy horrors overspread;
My steadfast heart shall fear no ill,
For thou, O Lord, art with me still:
Thy friendly crook shall give me aid,
And guide me through the dreadful shade.

HYMN 10. C. M.

WHEN all thy mercies, O my God,
My rising soul surveys,
Transported with the view, I'm lost
In wonder, love, and praise.

2 O how shall words with equal warmth
The gratitude declare,
That glows within my ravish'd heart!
But thou canst read it there.

3 Thy providence my life sustain'd,
And all my wants redrest,
When in the silent womb I lay,
And hung upon the breast.

4 To all my weak complaints and cries
Thy mercy lent an ear,

  Ere yet my feeble thoughts had learnt
   To form themselves in prayer.

5 Unnumber'd comforts to my soul
  Thy tender care bestow'd,
Before my infant heart conceived
  From whom those comforts flow'd.

6 When in the slippery paths of youth
  With heedless steps I ran,
Thine arm, unseen, convey'd me safe,
  And led me up to man.

7 Through hidden dangers, toils, and deaths,
  It gently clear'd my way,
And through the pleasing snares of vice,
  More to be fear'd than they.

8 When worn with sickness, oft hast thou
  With health renew'd my face;
And, when in sins and sorrows sunk,
  Revived my soul with grace.

9 Thy bounteous hand with worldly bliss
  Has made my cup run o'er;
And in a kind and faithful friend
  Has doubled all my store.

10 Ten thousand thousand precious gifts
  My daily thanks employ;
Nor is the least a cheerful heart,
  That tastes those gifts with joy.

11 Through every period of my life
  Thy goodness I'll pursue;
And after death, in distant worlds,
  The glorious theme renew.

12 When nature fails, and day and night
  Divide thy works no more,
My ever grateful heart, O Lord,
  Thy mercy shall adore.

13 Through all eternity, to thee
  A joyful song I'll raise;
But O! eternity's too short
  To utter all thy praise.

HYMN 11. III. 1.
Psalm xxxi. 15.
"My times are in thy hand."

SOVEREIGN Ruler of the skies,
Ever gracious, ever wise,
All our times are in thy hand,
All events at thy command.

2 He that form'd us in the womb,
He shall guide us to the tomb;
All our ways shall ever be
Order'd by his wise decree.

3 Times of sickness, times of health,
Blighting want, and cheerful wealth,
All our pleasures, all our pains,
Come, and end, as God ordains.

4 May we always own thy hand,
Still to thee surrender'd stand,
Know that thou art God alone,
We and ours are all thy own!

HYMN 12. C. M.

GOD moves in a mysterious way
His wonders to perform;
He plants his footsteps in the sea,
And rides upon the storm.

2 Deep in unfathomable mines,
With never-failing skill,
He treasures up his bright designs,
And works his gracious will.

3 Ye fearful saints, fresh courage take;
The clouds ye so much dread
Are big with mercy, and shall break
In blessings on your head.

4 Judge not the Lord by feeble sense,
But trust him for his grace:
Behind a frowning providence
He hides a smiling face.

5 His purposes will ripen fast,
Unfolding every hour:

The bud may have a bitter taste,
  But sweet will be the flower.
6 Blind unbelief is sure to err,
  And scan his work in vain:
God is his own interpreter,
  And he will make it plain.

IV. REDEMPTION.

HYMN 13. S. M.
Job ix. 2—6.

AH, how shall fallen man
  Be just before his God!
If he contend in righteousness,
  We sink beneath his rod.

2 If he our ways should mark,
  With strict inquiring eyes,
Could we for one of thousand faults
  A just excuse devise?

3 All-seeing, powerful God!
  Who can with thee contend?
Or who that tries th' unequal strife,
  Shall prosper in the end?

4 The mountains, in thy wrath,
  Their ancient seats forsake:
The trembling earth deserts her place,
  Her rooted pillars shake;

5 Ah, how shall guilty man
  Contend with such a God?
None, none can meet him, and escape,
  But through the Saviour's blood.

HYMN 14. L. M.
Job ix. 30—33.

THOUGH I should seek to wash me clean
  In water of the driven snow,
My soul would yet its spot retain,
  And sink in conscious guilt and woe:

2 The Spirit, in his power divine,
    Would cast my vaunting soul to earth,
Expose the foulness of its sin,
    And show the vileness of its worth.

3 Ah, not like erring man is God,
    That men to answer him should dare;
Condemn'd, and into silence awed,
    They helpless stand before his bar.

4 There, must a Mediator plead,
    Who, God and man, may both embrace;
With God, for man to intercede,
    And offer man the purchased grace.

5 And lo! the Son of God is slain
    To be this Mediator crown'd:
In Him, my soul, be cleansed from stain,
    In Him thy righteousness be found!

HYMN 15. L. M.

ALL glorious God, what hymns of praise
    Shall our transported voices raise:
What ardent love and zeal are due,
While heaven stands open to our view.

2 Once we were fallen, and O how low!
Just on the brink of endless woe:
When Jesus, from the realms above,
Borne on the wings of boundless love,

3 Scatter'd the shades of death and night,
And spread around his heavenly light:
By him what wondrous grace is shown
To souls impoverish'd and undone.

4 He shows, beyond these mortal shores,
A bright inheritance as ours;
Where saints in light our coming wait,
To share their holy, happy state.

HYMN 16. C. M.

SALVATION! O the joyful sound,
    Glad tidings to our ears;
A sovereign balm for every wound,
    A cordial for our fears.

2 Salvation! buried once in sin,
    At hell's dark door we lay;
  But now we rise by grace divine,
    And see a heavenly day.
3 Salvation! let the echo fly
    The spacious earth around;
  While all the armies of the sky
    Conspire to raise the sound.
4 Salvation! O thou bleeding Lamb,
    To thee the praise belongs:
  Our hearts shall kindle at thy Name,
    Thy Name inspire our songs.

Chorus for the end of each verse.
  Glory, honour, praise, and power,
    Be unto the Lamb for ever!
  Jesus Christ is our Redeemer!
    Hallelujah, praise the Lord!

HYMN 17. C. M.

TO our Redeemer's glorious Name
    Awake the sacred song:
  O may his love (immortal flame)
    Tune every heart and tongue.
2 His love, what mortal thought can reach;
    What mortal tongue display!
  Imagination's utmost stretch
    In wonder dies away.
3 He left his radiant throne on high,
    Left the bright realms of bliss,
  And came to earth to bleed and die!
    Was ever love like this?
4 Dear Lord, while we adoring pay
    Our humble thanks to thee,
  May every heart with rapture say,
    "The Saviour died for me."
5 O may the sweet, the blissful theme,
    Fill every heart and tongue;
  Till strangers love thy charming Name,
    And join the sacred song.

HYMN 18. III. 3.

SAVIOUR, source of every blessing,
    Tune my heart to grateful lays;
Streams of mercy, never ceasing,
    Call for ceaseless songs of praise.

2 Teach me some melodious measure,
    Sung by raptured saints above;
Fill my soul with sacred pleasure,
    While I sing redeeming love.

3 Thou didst seek me when a stranger,
    Wandering from the fold of God;
Thou, to save my soul from danger,
    Didst redeem me with thy blood.

4 By thy hand restored, defended,
    Safe through life thus far I've come;
Safe, O Lord, when life is ended,
    Bring me to my heavenly home.

HYMN 19. C. M.
Titus iii. 4—7.

MY grateful soul, for ever praise,
    For ever love his Name,
Who turn'd thee from the fatal paths
    Of folly, sin, and shame.

2 Vain and presumptuous is the trust
    Which in our works we place;
Salvation from a higher source
    Flows to our fallen race.

3 'Tis from the love of God through Christ
    That all our hopes begin;
His mercy saved our souls from death
    And wash'd us from our sin.

4 His Spirit, through the Saviour shed,
    His sacred fire imparts,
Removes our dross, and love divine
    Enkindles in our hearts.

5 Thus rais'd from death, we live anew;
    And, justified by grace,

We hope in glory to appear,
  And see our Father's face.

HYMN 20. C. M.

HOW helpless guilty nature lies,
  Unconscious of its load:
The heart unchanged can never rise
  To happiness and God.

2 The will perverse, the passions blind,
  In paths of ruin stray:
Reason debased can never find
  The safe, the narrow way.

3 Can ought beneath a power divine
  The stubborn will subdue?
'Tis thine, Almighty Saviour, thine
  To form the heart anew.

4 'Tis thine the passions to recall,
  And upwards bid them rise;
And make the scales of error fall
  From reason's darken'd eyes.

5 To chase the shades of death away,
  And bid the sinner live,
A beam of heaven, a vital ray,
  'Tis thine alone to give.

6 O change these wretched hearts of ours,
  And give them life divine:
Then shall our passions and our powers,
  Almighty Lord, be thine.

HYMN 21. C. M.

FATHER, to thee my soul I lift,
  On thee my hope depends,
Convinced that every perfect gift
  From thee alone descends.

2 Mercy and grace are thine alone,
  And power and wisdom too;
Without the Spirit of thy Son
  We nothing good can do.

3 Thou all our works in us hast wrought,
    Our good is all divine;
  The praise of every holy thought
    And righteous word is thine.
4 From thee, through Jesus, we receive
    The power on thee to call,
  In whom we are, and move, and live:
    Our God is all in all.

HYMN 22. III. I.

SING, my soul, His wondrous love,
  Who, from yon bright throne above,
Ever watchful o'er our race,
Still to man extends his grace.

2 Heaven and earth by him were made,
  All is by his sceptre sway'd;
  What are we that he should show
  So much love to us below!

3 God, the merciful and good,
  Bought us with the Saviour's blood;
  And, to make our safety sure,
  Guides us by his Spirit pure.

4 Sing, my soul, adore his Name,
  Let his glory be thy theme:
  Praise him till he calls thee home,
  Trust his love for all to come.

HYMN 23. S. M.

GRACE! 'tis a charming sound,
    Harmonious to the ear;
  Heaven with the echo shall resound,
    And all the earth shall hear.

2 Grace first contriv'd a way
    To save rebellious man,
  And all the means that grace display,
    Which drew the wondrous plan.

3 Grace guides my wandering feet
    To tread the heavenly road;

And new supplies each hour I meet
    While pressing on to God.
4 Grace all the work shall crown
    Through everlasting days;
  It lays in heaven the topmost stone,
    And well deserves the praise.

V. THE CHURCH.
HYMN 24. S. M.

LIKE Noah's weary dove,
    That soar'd the earth around,
But not a resting-place above
    The cheerless waters found;

2 O cease, my wandering soul,
    On restless wing to roam;
  All the wide world, to either pole,
    Has not for thee a home.

3 Behold the ark of God,
    Behold the open door;
  Hasten to gain that dear abode,
    And rove, my soul, no more.

4 There, safe thou shalt abide,
    There, sweet shall be thy rest,
  And every longing satisfied,
    With full salvation blest.

5 And, when the waves of ire
    Again the earth shall fill,
  The Ark shall ride the sea of fire;
    Then rest on Sion's hill.

HYMN 25. S. M.

I LOVE thy kingdom, Lord,
    The house of thine abode,
The Church our blest Redeemer saved,
    With his own precious blood.

2 I love thy Church, O God;
    Her walls before thee stand,
  Dear as the apple of thine eye,
    And graven on thy hand.

3 If e'er to bless thy sons,
  My voice or hands deny,
These hands let useful skill forsake,
  This voice in silence die.

4 If e'er my heart forget
  Her welfare or her woe,
Let every joy this heart forsake,
  And every grief o'erflow.

5 For her my tears shall fall;
  For her my prayers ascend;
To her my cares and toils be given,
  Till toils and cares shall end.

6 Beyond my highest joy
  I prize her heavenly ways,
Her sweet communion, solemn vows,
  Her hymns of love and praise.

7 Jesus, thou Friend divine,
  Our Saviour and our King,
Thy hand from every snare and foe
  Shall great deliverance bring.

8 Sure as thy truth shall last,
  To Sion shall be given
The brightest glories earth can yield,
  And brighter bliss of heaven.

HYMN 26. C. M.
Heb. xii. 18, 22—24.

NOT to the terrors of the Lord,
  The tempest, fire, and smoke:
Not to the thunder of that word
  Which God on Sinai spoke:

2 But we are come to Sion's hill,
  The city of our God;
Where milder words declare his will,
  And spread his love abroad.

3 Behold th' innumerable host
  Of angels clothed in light:
Behold the spirits of the just
  Whose faith is changed to sight.

4 Behold the bless'd assembly there
 Whose names are writ in heaven;
Hear God, the Judge of all, declare
 Their sins, through Christ, forgiven.

5 Angels, and living saints, and dead,
 But one communion make:
All join in Christ, their vital Head,
 And of his love partake.

HYMN 27. S. M.

BLEST is the tie that binds
 Our hearts in Christian love:
The fellowship of kindred minds
 Is like to that above.

2 Before our Father's throne
 We pour united prayers;
Our fears, our hopes, our aims are one;
 Our comforts and our cares.

3 We share our mutual woes,
 Our mutual burdens bear;
And often for each other flows
 The sympathizing tear.

4 When we at death must part,
 How keen, how deep the pain:
But we shall still be join'd in heart,
 And hope to meet again.

5 From sorrow, toil, and pain,
 And sin, we shall be free;
And perfect love and friendship reign
 Throughout eternity.

HYMN 28. H. 1.
Psalm cxxii.
The Church in Glory.

WITH joy shall I behold the day
 That calls my willing soul away,
  To dwell among the blest:
For lo! my great Redeemer's power
Unfolds the everlasting door,
  And points me to his rest.

2 Ev'n now, to my expecting eyes
　The heaven-built towers of Salem rise;
　　Their glory I survey;
　I view her mansions that contain
　The angel host, a beauteous train,
　　And shine with cloudless day.

3 Thither, from earth's remotest end,
　Lo! the redeem'd of God ascend,
　　Borne on immortal wing;
　There, crown'd with everlasting joy,
　In ceaseless hymns their tongues employ,
　　Before th' Almighty King.

4 The King a seat hath there prepared,
　High on eternal base uprear'd,
　　For his eternal Son:
　His palaces with joy abound;
　His saints, by him with glory crown'd,
　　Attend and share his throne.

5 Mother of cities! o'er thy head
　Bright peace, with healing wings outspread
　　For evermore shall dwell:
　Let me, blest seat! my name behold
　Among thy citizens enroll'd,
　　And bid the world farewell.

HYMN 29. L. M.
Isaiah lii. 1, 2.

TRIUMPHANT Sion! lift thy head
From dust, and darkness, and the dead:
Though humbled long, awake at length,
And gird thee with thy Saviour's strength.

2 Put all thy beauteous garments on,
　And let thy excellence be known:
　Deck'd in the robes of righteousness,
　The world thy glories shall confess.

3 No more shall foes unclean invade,
　And fill thy hallow'd walls with dread;
　No more shall hell's insulting host
　Their victory and thy sorrows boast.

4 God from on high has heard thy prayer,
His hand thy ruins shall repair:
Nor will thy watchful Monarch cease
To guard thee in eternal peace.

VI. FESTIVALS AND FASTS.

THE LORD'S DAY.
HYMN 30. II. 4.

AWAKE, ye saints, awake,
   And hail this sacred day;
In loftiest songs of praise
   Your joyful homage pay:
Welcome the day that God hath blest,
The type of heaven's eternal rest.

2 On this auspicious morn
   The Lord of life arose;
He burst the bars of death,
   And vanquish'd all our foes:
And now he pleads our cause above,
And reaps the fruits of all his love.

3 All hail, triumphant Lord!
   Heaven with hosannas rings,
And earth, in humbler strains,
   Thy praise responsive sings:
Worthy the Lamb that once was slain,
Through endless years to live and reign.

4 Great King, gird on thy sword,
   Ascend thy conquering car;
While justice, truth, and love,
   Maintain thy glorious war:
This day let sinners own thy sway,
And rebels cast their arms away.

HYMN 31. C. M.

THIS is the day the Lord hath made,
   Let young and old rejoice:
To him be vows and homage paid,
   Whose service is our choice.

2 This is the temple of the Lord:
    How dreadful is this place!
With meekness let us hear his word,
    With reverence seek his face.

3 This is the homage he requires;
    The voice of praise and prayer,
The soul's affections, hopes, desires,
    Ourselves and all we are.

4 While rich and poor for mercy call,
    Propitious from the skies,
The Lord, the Maker of them all,
    Accepts the sacrifice.

5 Well pleased, through Jesus Christ his Son,
    From sin he grants release;
According to their faith 'tis done,
    He bids them go in peace.

HYMN 32. S. M.

WELCOME, sweet day of rest,
    That saw the Lord arise;
Welcome to this reviving breast,
    And these rejoicing eyes.

2 The King himself comes near,
    To feast his saints to-day;
Here may we sit, and see him here,
    And love, and praise, and pray.

3 One day amidst the place
    Where Jesus is within,
Is better than ten thousand days
    Of pleasure and of sin.

4 My willing soul would stay
    In such a frame as this,
Till it is call'd to soar away
    To everlasting bliss.

HYMN 33. L. M.

ANOTHER six days' work is done,
Another Lord's day has begun;
Return, my soul, enjoy thy rest,
Improve the hours thy God hath blest.

2 This day may our devotion rise,
  As grateful incense to the skies;
  And heaven that sweet repose bestow,
  Which none but they who feel it know.

3 This peaceful calm within the breast
  Is the sure pledge of heavenly rest,
  Which for the Church of God remains,
  The end of cares, the end of pains.

4 In holy duties, let the day,
  In holy pleasures pass away:
  How sweet a sabbath thus to spend,
  In hope of one that ne'er shall end.

HYMN 34. II. 3.

GREAT God, this sacred day of thine
  Demands the soul's collected powers;
Gladly we now to thee resign
  These solemn, consecrated hours:
O may our souls adoring own
The grace that calls us to thy throne.

2 All-seeing God! thy piercing eye
  Can every secret thought explore;
May worldly cares our bosoms fly,
  And, where thou art, intrude no more:
O may thy grace our spirits move,
And fix our minds on things above.

3 Thy Spirit's powerful aid impart,
  And bid thy word, with life divine,
Engage the ear, and warm the heart:
  Then shall the day indeed be thine;
Then shall our souls adoring own
The grace that calls us to thy throne.

HYMN 35. II. 4.

IN loud exalted strains,
  The King of Glory praise;
O'er heaven and earth he reigns,
  Through everlasting days;
But Sion, with his presence blest,
Is his delight, his chosen rest.

2 O King of Glory, come;
    And with thy favour crown
This temple as thy home,
    This people as thy own:
Beneath this roof vouchsafe to show
How God can dwell with men below.

3 Now let thine ear attend
    Our supplicating cries;
Now let our praise ascend,
    Accepted to the skies:
Now let thy Gospel's joyful sound
Spread its celestial influence round.

4 Here may the listening throng
    Imbibe thy truth and love;
Here Christians join the song
    Of seraphim above:
Till all who humbly seek thy face,
Rejoice in thy abounding grace.

HYMN 36. L. M.

FAR from my thoughts, vain world, begone;
    Let my religious hours alone:
From flesh and sense I would be free,
And hold communion, Lord, with thee.

2 My heart grows warm with holy fire,
And kindles with a pure desire
To see thy grace, to taste thy love,
And feel thine influence from above.

3 When I can say that God is mine,
When I can see thy glories shine,
I'll tread the world beneath my feet,
And all that men call rich and great.

4 Send comfort down from thy right hand,
To cheer me in this barren land;
And in thy temple let me know
The joys that from thy presence flow.

HYMN 37. L. M.

MY opening eyes with rapture see
    The dawn of thy returning day;

My thoughts, O God, ascend to thee,
  While thus my early vows I pay.

2 I yield my heart to thee alone,
    Nor would receive another guest;
  Eternal King! erect thy throne,
    And reign sole monarch in my breast.

3 O bid this trifling world retire,
    And drive each carnal thought away;
  Nor let me feel one vain desire,
    One sinful thought, through all the day.

4 Then, to thy courts when I repair,
    My soul shall rise on joyful wing,
  The wonders of thy love declare,
    And join the strains which angels sing.

HYMN 38. III. 1.

TO thy temple I repair;
  Lord, I love to worship there:
While thy glorious praise is sung,
Touch my lips, unloose my tongue.

2 While the prayers of saints ascend,
  God of love, to mine attend;
  Hear me, for thy Spirit pleads;
  Hear, for Jesus intercedes.

3 While I hearken to thy law,
  Fill my soul with humble awe,
  Till thy Gospel bring to me
  Life and immortality.

4 While thy ministers proclaim
  Peace and pardon in thy Name,
  Through their voice, by faith, may I
  Hear thee speaking from on high.

5 From thy house when I return,
  May my heart within me burn;
  And at evening let me say,
  "I have walk'd with God to-day."

HYMN 39. L. M.
After Sermon.

ALMIGHTY Father, bless the word,
Which, through thy grace, we now have heard;
O may the precious seed take root,
Spring up, and bear abundant fruit.

2 We praise thee for the means of grace,
Thus in thy courts to seek thy face:
Grant, Lord, that we who worship here,
May all, at length, in heaven appear.

HYMN 40. III. 5.

LORD, dismiss us with thy blessing,
  Fill our hearts with joy and peace;
Let us each, thy love possessing,
  Triumph in redeeming grace;
    O refresh us,
Travelling through this wilderness.

2 Thanks we give, and adoration,
  For the Gospel's joyful sound;
May the fruits of thy salvation
  In our hearts and lives abound:
    May thy presence
With us evermore be found.

ADVENT.
HYMN 41. C. M.

HARK! the glad sound, the Saviour comes,
  The Saviour promised long:
Let every heart prepare a throne,
  And every voice a song.

2 On him the Spirit, largely pour'd,
  Exerts his sacred fire;
Wisdom and might, and zeal and love,
  His holy breast inspire.

3 He comes, the prisoners to release,
  In Satan's bondage held;
The gates of brass before him burst,
  The iron fetters yield.

4 He comes, from thickest films of vice
    To clear the mental ray;
And on the eyes oppress'd with night,
    To pour celestial day.

5 He comes, the broken heart to bind,
    The bleeding soul to cure,
And with the treasures of his grace,
    T' enrich the humble poor.

6 Our glad hosannas, Prince of Peace,
    Thy welcome shall proclaim;
And heaven's eternal arches ring
    With thy beloved Name.

HYMN 42. III. 3.

HAIL! thou long-expected Jesus,
    Born to set thy people free:
From our sins and fears release us,
    Let us find our rest in thee.

2 Israel's strength and consolation,
    Hope of all the saints, thou art;
Long desired of every nation,
    Joy of every waiting heart.

3 Born thy people to deliver,
    Born a child, yet God our King,
Born to reign in us for ever,
    Now thy gracious kingdom bring.

4 By thine own eternal Spirit,
    Rule in all our hearts alone;
By thine all-sufficient merit,
    Raise us to thy glorious throne.

CHRISTMAS.

HYMN 43. C. M.
Luke ii. 8—15.

WHILE shepherds watch'd their flocks by night,
    All seated on the ground,
The angel of the Lord came down,
    And glory shone around.

2 "Fear not," said he, for mighty dread
    Had seized their troubled mind;
"Glad tidings of great joy I bring
    To you, and all mankind.

3 "To you, in David's town, this day
    Is born, of David's line,
The Saviour, who is Christ the Lord,
    And this shall be the sign:

4 "The heavenly babe you there shall find,
    To human view display'd,
All meanly wrapt in swathing bands,
    And in a manger laid."

5 Thus spake the seraph, and forthwith
    Appear'd a shining throng
Of angels, praising God, who thus
    Address'd their joyful song:

6 "All glory be to God on high,
    And to the earth be peace;
Good-will, henceforth, from heaven to men,
    Begin and never cease."

HYMN 44. C. M.

WHILE angels thus, O Lord, rejoice,
    Shall men no anthem raise?
O may we lose these useless tongues,
    When we forget to praise.

2 Then let us swell responsive notes,
    And join the heavenly throng;
For angels no such love have known,
    As we, to wake their song.

3 Good will to sinful dust is shown,
    And peace on earth is given;
For lo! th' incarnate Saviour comes,
    With news of joy from heaven.

4 Mercy and truth, with sweet accord,
    His rising beams adorn;
Let heaven and earth in concert sing,
    "The promised child is born!"

5 Glory to God, in highest strains,
    By highest worlds is paid;
Be glory, then, by us proclaim'd,
    And by our lives display'd;
6 Till we attain those blissful realms,
    Where now our Saviour reigns;
To rival these celestial choirs
    In their immortal strains.

HYMN 45. III. 1.

HARK! the herald angels sing,
    Glory to the new-born King;
Peace on earth, and mercy mild;
God and sinners reconciled.
2 Joyful all ye nations rise,
    Join the triumph of the skies;
With th' angelic host proclaim,
Christ is born in Bethlehem!
3 Christ, by highest heaven adored,
    Christ, the everlasting Lord,
Late in time behold him come,
Offspring of the Virgin's womb.
4 Veil'd in flesh, the Godhead see:
    Hail th' incarnate Deity,
Pleased, as man, with man to dwell;
Jesus, now Emmanuel.
5 Risen with healing in his wings,
    Light and life to all he brings;
Hail the Sun of righteousness!
Hail the heaven-born Prince of Peace!

HYMN 46.
Chorus.

SHOUT the glad tidings, exultingly sing;
    Jerusalem triumphs, Messiah is King!
1 Sion, the marvellous story be telling,
    The Son of the Highest, how lowly his birth!
The brightest archangel in glory excelling,
    He stoops to redeem thee, he reigns upon earth:

Cho. Shout the glad tidings, exultingly sing;
    Jerusalem triumphs, Messiah is King!

2 Tell how he cometh; from nation to nation,
    The heart-cheering news let the earth echo round;
How free to the faithful he offers salvation,
    How his people with joy everlasting are crown'd:

Cho. Shout the glad tidings, exultingly sing;
    Jerusalem triumphs, Messiah is King!

3 Mortals, your homage be gratefully bringing,
    And sweet let the gladsome hosanna arise;
Ye angels, the full hallelujah be singing;
    One chorus resound thro' the earth and the skies:

Cho. Shout the glad tidings, exultingly sing;
    Jerusalem triumphs, Messiah is King!

HYMN 47. C. M.
Isaiah ix. 2—7.

THE race that long in darkness pined,
    Have seen a glorious light;
The people now behold the dawn,
    Who dwelt in death and night.

2 To hail thy rising, Sun of life,
    The gathering nations come;
Joyous as when the reapers bear
    Their harvest treasures home.

3 For thou our burden hast removed;
    Th' oppressor's reign is broke;
Thy fiery conflict with the foe
    Has burst his cruel yoke.

4 To us the promised Child is born;
    To us the Son is given;
Him shall the tribes of earth obey,
    And all the hosts of heaven.

5 His name shall be the Prince of Peace,
    For evermore adored;
The Wonderful, the Counsellor,
    The mighty God and Lord.

6 His power increasing still shall spread,
   His reign no end shall know;
Justice shall guard his throne above,
   And peace abound below.

END OF THE YEAR.
HYMN 48.   C. M.

TIME hastens on; ye longing saints,
   Now raise your voices high;
And magnify that sovereign love
   Which shows salvation nigh.

2 As time departs salvation comes;
   Each moment brings it near:
Then welcome each declining day,
   Welcome each closing year.

3 Not many years their course shall run,
   Not many mornings rise,
Ere all its glories stand reveal'd
   To our transported eyes.

HYMN 49.   C. M.
St. Luke xiii. 6—9.

SEE, in the vineyard of the Lord,
   A barren fig-tree stands;
No fruit it yields, no blossom bears,
   Though planted by His hands.

2 From year to year the tree He views,
   And still no fruit is found;
Then "Cut it down," the Lord commands,
   "Why cumbers it the ground?"

3 But lo! the gracious Saviour pleads;
   "The barren fig-tree spare,
Another year in mercy wait,
   It yet may bloom and bear:

4 "But if my culture prove in vain,
   And still no fruit be found,
I plead no more; destroy the tree,
   And root it from thy ground."

NEW YEAR.
HYMN 50. L. M.

THE God of life, whose constant care
With blessings crowns each opening year,
My scanty span doth still prolong,
And wakes anew mine annual song.

2 How many precious souls are fled
To the vast regions of the dead,
Since to this day the changing sun
Through his last yearly period run!

3 We yet survive; but who can say,
" Or through this year, or month, or day,
I shall retain this vital breath,
Thus far, at least, in league with death?"

4 That breath is thine, eternal God;
'Tis thine to fix my soul's abode;
It holds its life from thee alone,
On earth, or in the world unknown.

5 To thee our spirits we resign,
Make them and own them still as thine;
So shall they live secure from fear,
Though death should blast the rising year.

6 Thy children, panting to be gone,
May bid the tide of time roll on,
To land them on that happy shore,
Where years and death are known no more.

7 No more fatigue, no more distress,
Nor sin, nor hell, shall reach that place;
No groans, to mingle with the songs
Resounding from immortal tongues:

8 No more alarms from ghostly foes;
No cares to break the long repose;
No midnight shade, no clouded sun,
But sacred, high, eternal noon.

9 O, long-expected year! begin;
Dawn on this world of woe and sin;
Fain would we leave this weary road,
To sleep in death, and rest with God.

HYMN. 51. C. M.

AS o'er the past my memory strays,
  Why heaves the secret sigh?
'Tis that I mourn departed days,
  Still unprepared to die.

2 The world, and worldly things beloved,
  My anxious thoughts employ'd;
And time unhallow'd, unimproved,
  Presents a fearful void.

3 Yet, holy Father, wild despair
  Chase from my labouring breast;
Thy grace it is which prompts the prayer,
  That grace can do the rest.

4 My life's brief remnant all be thine;
  And when thy sure decree
Bids me this fleeting breath resign,
  O speed my soul to thee.

EPIPHANY.
HYMN 52. S. M.
Isaiah lii. 7—10.

HOW beauteous are their feet
  Who stand on Sion's hill;
Who bring salvation on their tongues,
  And words of peace reveal.

2 How charming is their voice:
  How sweet their tidings are:
"Sion, behold thy Saviour-King,
  He reigns and triumphs here."

3 How happy are our ears
  That hear this joyful sound,
Which kings and prophets waited for,
  And sought, but never found.

4 How blessed are our eyes
  That see this heavenly light:
Prophets and kings desired it long,
  But died without the sight.

5 The watchmen join their voice,
  And tuneful notes employ;

Jerusalem breaks forth in songs,
  And deserts learn the joy.
6 The Lord makes bare his arm
  Through all the earth abroad:
Let every nation now behold
  Their Saviour and their God.

HYMN 53. II. 5.
Isaiah lx., &c.

RISE, crown'd with light, imperial Salem, rise;
  Exalt thy towering head and lift thine eyes:
See heaven its sparkling portals wide display,
And break upon thee in a flood of day.

2 See a long race thy spacious courts adorn,
See future sons, and daughters yet unborn,
In crowding ranks on every side arise,
Demanding life, impatient for the skies.

3 See barbarous nations at thy gates attend,
Walk in thy light, and in thy temple bend:
See thy bright altars throng'd with prostrate kings,
While every land its joyous tribute brings.

4 The seas shall waste, the skies to smoke decay,
Rocks fall to dust, and mountains melt away;
But fix'd his word, his saving power remains;
Thy realm shall last, thy own Messiah reigns.

HYMN 54. II. 6.
Psalm lxxii.

HAIL to the Lord's Anointed,
  Great David's greater Son;
Hail, in the time appointed,
  His reign on earth begun!
He comes to break oppression,
  To set the captive free,
To take away transgression,
  And rule in equity.

2 He comes with succour speedy,
  To those who suffer wrong,
To help the poor and needy,
  And bid the weak be strong;

To give them songs for sighing,
     Their darkness turn to light,
   Whose souls, condemn'd and dying,
     Were precious in his sight.
3 He shall descend like showers
     Upon the fruitful earth;
   And love and joy, like flowers,
     Spring in his path to birth:
   Before him, on the mountains,
     Shall peace, the herald, go;
   And righteousness, in fountains,
     From hill to valley flow.
4 To him shall prayer unceasing,
     And daily vows ascend;
   His kingdom still increasing,
     A kingdom without end:
   The tide of time shall never
     His covenant remove;
   His name shall stand for ever:
     That Name to us is love.

HYMN 55. C. M.
Isaiah ii. 2—5.

O'ER mountain-tops the mount of God
   In latter days shall rise,
 Above the summits of the hills,
   And draw the wondering eyes.
2 To this the joyful nations round,
   All tribes and tongues, shall flow;
 Up to the mount of God, they'll say,
   And to his house we'll go.
3 The beams that shine from Sion's hill
   Shall lighten every land;
 The King who reigns in Salem's towers
   Shall all the world command.
4 Among the nations he shall judge;
   His judgments truth shall guide:
 His sceptre shall protect the just,
   And crush the sinner's pride.

5 For peaceful implements shall men
    Exchange their swords and spears;
Nor shall they study war again
    Throughout those happy years.
6 Come, O ye house of Jacob! come
    To worship at his shrine;
And, walking in the light of God,
    With holy graces shine.

LENT.
HYMN 56. III. 1.
Litany.

SAVIOUR, when in dust, to Thee,
Low we bow th' adoring knee;
When, repentant, to the skies
Scarce we lift our streaming eyes;
O, by all thy pains and woe,
Suffer'd once for man below,
Bending from thy throne on high,
Hear our solemn litany.

2 By thy birth and early years,
By thy human griefs and fears,
By thy fasting and distress
In the lonely wilderness,
By thy victory in the hour
Of the subtle tempter's power;
Jesus, look with pitying eye;
Hear our solemn litany.

3 By thine hour of dark despair,
By thine agony of prayer,
By the purple robe of scorn,
By thy wounds, thy crown of thorn,
By thy cross, thy pangs and cries,
By thy perfect sacrifice;
Jesus, look with pitying eye;
Hear our solemn litany.

4 By thy deep expiring groan,
By the seal'd sepulchral stone,
By thy triumph o'er the grave,
By thy power from death to save;

Mighty God, ascended Lord,
To thy throne in heaven restored,
Prince and Saviour, hear our cry,
Hear our solemn litany.

HYMN 57. L. M.

MY God, permit me not to be
A stranger to myself and thee:
Amidst a thousand thoughts I rove,
Forgetful of my highest love.

2 Why should my passions mix with earth,
And thus debase my heavenly birth?
Why should I cleave to things below,
And all my purest joys forego?

3 Call me away from flesh and sense;
Thy grace, O Lord, can draw me thence:
I would obey the voice divine,
And all inferior joys resign.

HYMN 58. C. M.

ALAS, what hourly dangers rise,
  What snares beset my way;
To heaven, O let me lift mine eyes,
  And hourly watch and pray.

2 How oft my mournful thoughts complain,
  And melt in flowing tears:
My weak resistance, ah, how vain,
  How strong my foes and fears.

3 O gracious God, in whom I live,
  My feeble efforts aid;
Help me to watch, and pray, and strive,
  Though trembling and afraid.

4 Increase my faith, increase my hope,
  When foes and fears prevail;
And bear my fainting spirit up,
  Or soon my strength will fail.

5 Whene'er temptations fright my heart,
  Or lure my feet aside,
My God, thy powerful aid impart,
  My guardian and my guide.

6 O keep me in thy heavenly way,
   And bid the tempter flee;
And let me never, never stray
   From happiness and thee.

HYMN 59. C. M.

HOW oft, alas! this wretched heart
   Has wander'd from the Lord:
How oft my roving thoughts depart,
   Forgetful of his word.

2 Yet sovereign mercy calls, "Return;"
   Dear Lord, and may I come?
My vile ingratitude I mourn;
   O, take the wanderer home.

3 And canst thou, wilt thou yet forgive,
   And bid my crimes remove?
And shall a pardon'd rebel live
   To speak thy wondrous love?

4 Almighty grace, thy healing power,
   How glorious, how divine;
That can to life and bliss restore
   So vile a heart as mine.

5 Thy pardoning love, so free, so sweet,
   Dear Saviour, I adore:
O keep me at thy sacred feet,
   And let me rove no more.

HYMN 60. L. M.

O THOU, to whose all-searching sight
   The darkness shineth as the light,
Search, prove my heart; it looks to thee,
O burst its bonds, and set it free.

2 Wash out its stains, remove its dross,
Bind my affections to the cross;
Hallow each thought, let all within
Be clean, as thou, my Lord, art clean.

3 If in this darksome wild I stray,
Be thou my light, be thou my way;
No foes, no violence I fear,
No harm, while thou, my God, art near.

4 When rising floods my soul o'erflow,
　When sinks my heart in waves of woe,
　Jesus, thy timely aid impart,
　And raise my head, and cheer my heart.

5 Saviour, where'er thy steps I see,
　Dauntless, untired, I follow thee:
　O let thy hand support me still,
　And lead me to thy holy hill.

[*See Hymns on Repentance.*]

PASSION WEEK AND GOOD FRIDAY.

HYMN 61. III. 4.

Isaiah lxiii. 1—4.

WHO is this that comes from Edom,
　　All his raiment stain'd with blood,
To the captive speaking freedom,
　　Bringing and bestowing good;
Glorious in the garb he wears,
Glorious in the spoil he bears?

2 'Tis the Saviour, now victorious,
　　Travelling onward in his might;
'Tis the Saviour, O how glorious
　　To his people is the sight!
Satan conquer'd, and the grave,
Jesus now is strong to save.

3 Why that blood his raiment staining?
　　'Tis the blood of many slain;
Of his foes there's none remaining,
　　None, the contest to maintain:
Fall'n they are, no more to rise,
All their glory prostrate lies.

4 Mighty Victor! reign for ever,
　　Wear the crown so dearly won;
Never shall thy people, never,
　　Cease to sing what thou hast done:
Thou hast fought thy people's foes;
Thou hast heal'd thy people's woes.

HYMN 62. L. M.

WHEN I survey the wondrous cross,
    On which the Prince of Glory died,
My richest gain I count but loss,
    And pour contempt on all my pride.

2 Forbid it, Lord, that I should boast,
    Save in the cross of Christ my God:
All the vain things that charm me most,
    I sacrifice them to thy blood.

3 See! from his head, his hands, his feet,
    Sorrow and love flow mingled down:
Did e'er such love and sorrow meet?
    Or thorns compose a Saviour's crown?

4 Were the whole realm of nature mine,
    That were a tribute far too small;
Love so amazing, so divine,
    Demands my life, my soul, my all.

HYMN 63. C. M.

BEHOLD the Saviour of mankind
    Nail'd to the shameful tree;
How vast the love that him inclined
    To bleed and die for me!

2 Hark, how he groans! while nature shakes,
    And earth's strong pillars bend;
The temple's vail in sunder breaks,
    The solid marbles rend.

3 'Tis done! the precious ransom's paid;
    "Receive my soul!" he cries;
See where he bows his sacred head!
    He bows his head and dies.

4 But soon he'll break death's envious chain,
    And in full glory shine;
O Lamb of God, was ever pain,
    Was ever love like thine!

HYMN 64. C. M.

MY Saviour hanging on the tree,
    In agonies and blood,

Methought once turn'd his eyes on me,
    As near his cross I stood.
2 Sure, never till my latest breath
    Can I forget that look;
It seem'd to charge me with his death,
    Though not a word he spoke.
3 My conscience felt and own'd the guilt,
    And plung'd me in despair;
I saw my sins his blood had spilt,
    And help'd to nail him there.
4 Alas! I knew not what I did;
    But now my tears are vain:
Where shall my trembling soul be hid?
    For I the Lord have slain.
5 A second look he gave, which said,
    "I freely all forgive;
This blood is for thy ransom paid,
    I die that thou may'st live."
6 Thus, while his death my sin displays
    In all its blackest hue—
Such is the mystery of grace—
    It seals my pardon too.

HYMN 65. C. M.

FROM whence these direful omens round,
    Which heaven and earth amaze?
Wherefore do earthquakes cleave the ground?
    Why hides the sun his rays?
2 Well may the earth astonish'd shake,
    And nature sympathize;
The sun as darkest night be black:
    Their Maker, Jesus, dies!
3 Behold, fast streaming from the tree,
    His all-atoning blood!
Is this the Infinite? 'tis He,
    My Saviour and my God!
4 For me these pangs his soul assail,
    For me this death is borne;

My sins gave sharpness to the nail,
  And pointed every thorn.
5 Let sin no more my soul enslave,
  Break, Lord, its tyrant chain;
O save me, whom thou cam'st to save,
  Nor bleed, nor die in vain.

HYMN 66. L. M.
St. John xix. 30.

'TIS finish'd; so the Saviour cried,
  And meekly bow'd his head and died:
'Tis finish'd : yes, the work is done,
The battle fought, the victory won.

2 'Tis finish'd : all that heaven decreed,
And all the ancient prophets said,
Is now fulfill'd, as long design'd,
In me, the Saviour of mankind.

3 'Tis finish'd : Aaron now no more
Must stain his robes with purple gore :
The sacred vail is rent in twain,
And Jewish rites no more remain.

4 'Tis finish'd : this, my dying groan,
Shall sins of every kind atone :
Millions shall be redeem'd from death,
By this, my last expiring breath.

5 'Tis finish'd : heaven is reconciled,
And all the powers of darkness spoil'd :
Peace, love, and happiness, again
Return and dwell with sinful men.

6 'Tis finish'd : let the joyful sound
Be heard through all the nations round :
'Tis finish'd : let the echo fly
Through heaven and hell, through earth and sky.

HYMN 67. L. M.
For the Jews.

HIGH on the bending willows hung,
  Israel, still sleeps the tuneful string?
Still mute remains the sullen tongue,
  And Zion's song denies to sing?

2 Awake! thy loudest raptures raise,
 Let harp and voice unite their strains:
Thy promised King his sceptre sways;
 Behold, thy own Messiah reigns.

3 By foreign streams no longer roam,
 And, weeping, think on Jordan's flood;
In every clime behold a home;
 In every temple see thy God.

4 No taunting foes the song require,
 No strangers mock thy captive chain;
Thy friends provoke the silent lyre,
 And brethren ask the holy strain.

5 Then why on bending willows hung,
 Israel, still sleeps the tuneful string?
Why mute remains the sullen tongue,
 And Sion's song delays to sing?

EASTER.

HYMN 68.   C. M.

1 Cor. v. 8.—Rom. vi. 9, 10, 11.

SINCE Christ, our Passover, is slain,
 A sacrifice for all,
Let all, with thankful hearts, agree
 To keep the festival:

2 Not with the leaven, as of old,
 Of sin and malice fed;
But with unfeign'd sincerity,
 And truth's unleaven'd bread.

3 Christ being raised by power divine,
 And rescued from the grave,
Shall die no more; death shall on him
 No more dominion have.

4 For that he died, 'twas for our sins
 He once vouchsafed to die;
But that he lives, he lives to God
 For all eternity.

5 So count yourselves as dead to sin,
 But graciously restored,

And made, henceforth, alive to God,
Through Jesus Christ our Lord.

HYMN 69. III. 1.

CHRIST the Lord is risen to-day,
　Sons of men and angels say :
Raise your joys and triumphs high,
Sing, ye heavens, and earth reply.

2 Love's redeeming work is done,
　Fought the fight, the victory won:
Jesus' agony is o'er,
Darkness veils the earth no more.

3 Vain the stone, the watch, the seal,
Christ has burst the gates of hell;
Death in vain forbids him rise,
Christ hath open'd paradise.

4 Soar we now where Christ hath led,
Following our exalted Head;
Made like him, like him we rise;
Ours the cross, the grave, the skies.

HYMN 70. L. M.
Col. iii. 1, 2.

YE faithful souls who Jesus know,
　If risen indeed with him ye are,
Superior to the joys below,
　His resurrection's power declare :

2 Your faith by holy tempers prove,
　　By actions show your sins forgiven,
And seek the glorious things above,
　　And follow Christ, your Head, to heaven.

3 There your exalted Saviour see,
　　Seated at God's right hand again,
In all his Father's majesty,
　　In everlasting power to reign.

4 To him continually aspire,
　　Contending for your destined place
And emulate the angel choir,
　　And only live to love and praise.

HYMN 71. C. M.
1 Cor. xv. 20, 21, 22—Col. iii. 1.

CHRIST from the dead is raised, and made
  The First-Fruits of the tomb;
For, as by man came death, by man
  Did resurrection come.

2 For, as in Adam all mankind
    Did guilt and death derive;
  So, by the righteousness of Christ,
    Shall all be made alive.

3 If then ye risen are with Christ,
    Seek only how to get
  The things which are above, where Christ
    At God's right hand is set.

ASCENSION.
HYMN 72. L. M.

HE dies, the Friend of sinners dies:
  Lo! Salem's daughters weep around;
A solemn darkness veils the skies;
  A sudden trembling shakes the ground.

2 Ye saints, approach, the anguish view,
    Of him who groans beneath your load;
  He gives his precious life for you,
    For you he sheds his precious blood.

3 Here's love and grief beyond degree,
    The Lord of glory dies for men;
  But lo! what sudden joys we see,
    Jesus, the dead, revives again.

4 The rising God forsakes the tomb;
    Up to his Father's court he flies;
  Cherubic legions guard him home,
    And shout him welcome to the skies.

5 Break off your tears, ye saints, and tell
    How high our great Deliverer reigns;
  Sing how he spoil'd the hosts of hell,
    And led the tyrant, Death, in chains.

6 Say, "Live for ever, glorious King,
    Born to redeem, instruct, and save!"

Then ask—" O death, where is thy sting?
  And where thy victory, O grave?"

HYMN 73. L. M.

OUR Lord is risen from the dead,
  Our Jesus is gone up on high;
The powers of hell are captive led,
  Dragg'd to the portals of the sky.

2 There his triumphal chariot waits,
    And angels chant the solemn lay:
  " Lift up your heads, ye heavenly gates,
    Ye everlasting doors, give way."

3 Loose all your bars of massy light,
    And wide unfold the radiant scene;
  He claims those mansions as his right;
    Receive the King of Glory in.

4 " Who is the King of Glory, who?"
    The Lord that all his foes o'ercame,
  The world, sin, death, and hell o'erthrew;
    And Jesus is the conqueror's name.

5 Lo! his triumphal chariot waits,
    And angels chant the solemn lay,
  " Lift up your heads, ye heavenly gates,
    Ye everlasting doors, give way."

6 "Who is the King of Glory, who?"
    The Lord of boundless power possess'd,
  The King of saints and angels too,
    God over all, for ever bless'd.

WHIT-SUNDAY.

HYMN 74. C. M.

COME, Holy Ghost, Creator, come,
  Inspire these souls of thine;
Till every heart which thou hast made,
  Be fill'd with grace divine.

2 Thou art the Comforter, the gift
    Of God, and fire of love;
  The everlasting spring of joy,
    And unction from above.

3 Thy gifts are manifold, thou writ'st
   God's law in each true heart;
 The promise of the Father, thou
   Dost heavenly speech impart.
4 Enlighten our dark souls, till they
   Thy sacred love embrace;
 Assist our minds, by nature frail,
   With thy celestial grace.
5 Drive far from us the mortal foe,
   And give us peace within;
 That, by thy guidance blest, we may
   Escape the snares of sin.
6 Teach us the Father to confess,
   And Son, from death revived,
 And thee, with both, O Holy Ghost,
   Who art from both derived.

HYMN 75. C. M.

COME, Holy Spirit, Heavenly Dove,
   With all thy quickening powers;
 Kindle a flame of sacred love
   In these cold hearts of ours.
2 See how we grovel here below,
   Fond of these earthly toys:
 Our souls, how heavily they go,
   To reach eternal joys.
3 In vain we tune our lifeless songs,
   In vain we strive to rise:
 Hosannas languish on our tongues,
   And our devotion dies.
4 Come, Holy Spirit, Heavenly Dove,
   With all thy quickening powers;
 Come, shed abroad a Saviour's love,
   And that shall kindle ours.

HYMN 76. C. M.

HE'S come, let every knee be bent,
   All hearts new joy resume;
 Sing, ye redeem'd, with one consent,
   "The Comforter is come."

2 What greater gift, what greater love,
   Could God on man bestow?
Angels for this rejoice above,
   Let man rejoice below.
3 Hail, blessed Spirit! may each soul
   Thy sacred influence feel;
Do thou each sinful thought control,
   And fix our wavering zeal.
4 Thou to the conscience dost convey
   Those checks which we should know;
Thy motions point to us the way;
   Thou giv'st us strength to go.

TRINITY-SUNDAY.
HYMN 77. L. M.

O HOLY, holy, holy Lord,
   Bright in thy deeds and in thy Name;
For ever be thy Name adored,
   Thy glories let the world proclaim.
2 O Jesus, Lamb once crucified
   To take our load of sins away,
Thine be the hymn that rolls its tide
   Along the realms of upper day.
3 O Holy Spirit from above,
   In streams of light and glory given,
Thou source of ecstasy and love,
   Thy praises ring through earth and heaven.
4 O God Triune, to thee we owe
   Our every thought, our every song;
And ever may thy praises flow
   From saint and seraph's burning tongue.

HYMN 78. L. M.

FATHER of all, whose love profound
   A ransom for our souls hath found,
Before thy throne we sinners bend;
   To us thy pardoning love extend.
2 Almighty Son, incarnate Word,
   Our Prophet, Priest, Redeemer, Lord,

Before thy throne we sinners bend;
To us thy saving grace extend.

3 Eternal Spirit, by whose breath
The soul is raised from sin and death,
Before thy throne we sinners bend;
To us thy quickening power extend.

4 Jehovah! Father, Spirit, Son,
Mysterious Godhead, Three in One!
Before thy throne we sinners bend;
Grace, pardon, life, to us extend.

HYMN 79. II. 4.

WE give immortal praise
   To God the Father's love,
For all our comforts here,
   And all our hopes above:
     He sent his own
     Eternal Son
   To die for sins
     That man had done.

2 To God the Son belongs
   Immortal glory too,
Who saved us by his blood
   From everlasting woe:
     And now he lives,
     And now he reigns,
   And sees the fruit
     Of all his pains.

3 To God the Spirit, praise
   And endless worship give,
Whose new-creating power
   Makes the dead sinner live:
     His work completes
     The great design,
   And fills the soul
     With joy divine.

4 Almighty God, to thee
   Be endless honours done;

The sacred Persons Three,
   The Godhead only One;
      Where reason fails
         With all her powers,
      There faith prevails,
         And love adores.

FAST-DAY.
HYMN 80. C. M.

ALMIGHTY Lord, before thy throne
   Thy mourning people bend:
'Tis on thy pardoning grace alone,
   Our prostrate hopes depend.

2 Dark judgments, from thy heavy hand,
   Thy dreadful power display;
Yet mercy spares our guilty land,
   And still we live to pray.

3 How changed, alas! are truths divine,
   For error, guilt, and shame;
What impious numbers, bold in sin,
   Disgrace the Christian name.

4 O turn us, turn us, mighty Lord,
   Convert us by thy grace;
Then shall our hearts obey thy word,
   And see again thy face.

5 Then, should oppressing foes invade,
   We will not sink in fear;
Secure of all-sufficient aid,
   When God, our God, is near.

HYMN 81. III. 3.

DREAD Jehovah, God of nations,
   From thy temple in the skies,
Hear thy people's supplications,
   Now for their deliverance rise:

2 Lo! with deep contrition turning,
   Humbly at thy feet we bend;
Hear us, fasting, praying, mourning,
   Hear us, spare us, and defend.

3 Though our sins, our hearts confounding,
    Long and loud for vengeance call,
Thou hast mercy more abounding,
    Jesus' blood can cleanse them all.

4 Let that love veil our transgression,
    Let that blood our guilt efface:
Save thy people from oppression,
    Save from spoil thy holy place.

HYMN 82. L. M.
Prayer and Hope of Victory.

NOW may the God of grace and power
    Attend his people's humble cry;
Defend them in the needful hour,
    And send deliverance from on high.

2 In his salvation is our hope;
    And in the name of Israel's God,
Our troops shall lift their banners up,
    Our navies spread their flags abroad.

3 Some trust in horses train'd for war,
    And some of chariots make their boasts;
Our surest expectations are
    From Thee, the Lord of heavenly hosts.

4 Then save us, Lord, from slavish fear,
    And let our trust be firm and strong,
Till thy salvation shall appear,
    And hymns of peace conclude our song.

THANKSGIVING-DAY.
HYMN 83.
PART I. III. 2.

PRAISE to God, immortal praise,
    For the love that crowns our days;
Bounteous source of every joy,
    Let thy praise our tongues employ:
All to Thee, our God, we owe,
Source whence all our blessings flow.

2 All the blessings of the fields,
    All the stores the garden yields,

Flocks that whiten all the plain,
Yellow sheaves of ripen'd grain:
Lord, for these our souls shall raise
Grateful vows and solemn praise.

3 Clouds that drop their fattening dews,
Suns that genial warmth diffuse,
All the plenty summer pours,
Autumn's rich o'erflowing stores:
Lord, for these our souls shall raise
Grateful vows and solemn praise.

4 Peace, prosperity, and health,
Private bliss and public wealth,
Knowledge, with its gladdening streams,
Pure religion's holier beams:
Lord, for these our souls shall raise
Grateful vows and solemn praise.

PART II. III 2.

5 YET, should rising whirlwinds tear
From its stem the ripening ear;
Though the sickening flock should fall,
And the herd desert the stall:
Still to thee our souls shall raise
Grateful vows and solemn praise.

6 Should thine alter'd hand restrain
The early and the latter rain,
Blast each opening bud of joy,
And the rising year destroy:
Still to thee our souls shall raise
Grateful vows and solemn praise.

7 Life and grace, whate'er our woe,
Still to thee, our God, we owe;
Though of earthly hopes bereft,
Yet our hope of heaven is left;
And for these our souls shall raise
Grateful vows and solemn praise.

HYMN 84. C. M.

FOUNTAIN of mercy, God of love,
How rich thy bounties are:

The rolling seasons, as they move,
  Proclaim thy constant care.

2 When in the bosom of the earth
    The sower hid the grain,
  Thy goodness mark'd its secret birth,
    And sent the early rain.

3 The spring's sweet influence, Lord, was thine,
    The plants in beauty grew;
  Thou gav'st the summer's suns to shine,
    The mild refreshing dew.

4 These various mercies from above
    Matured the swelling grain;
  A kindly harvest crowns thy love,
    And plenty fills the plain.

5 We own and bless thy gracious sway:
    Thy hand all nature hails;
  Seed-time nor harvest, night nor day,
    Summer nor winter fails.

HYMN 85. L. M.

For Publick Mercies and Deliverances.

SALVATION doth to God belong,
His power and grace shall be our song;
From him alone all mercies flow,
His arm alone subdues the foe.

2 Then praise this God, who bows his ear
  Propitious to his people's prayer;
  And though deliverance he may stay,
  Yet answers still in his own day.

3 O may this goodness lead our land,
  Still saved by thine Almighty hand,
  The tribute of its love to bring
  To thee, our Saviour and our King:

4 Till every publick temple raise
  A song of triumph to thy praise;
  And every peaceful, private home,
  To thee a temple shall become.

5 Still be it our supreme delight
  To walk as in thy glorious sight;
  Still in thy precepts and thy fear,
  Till life's last hour, to persevere.

VII. ORDINANCES AND SPECIAL OCCASIONS.

BAPTISM OF INFANTS.
HYMN 86. III. 3.

SAVIOUR, who thy flock art feeding,
  With the shepherd's kindest care,
All the feeble gently leading,
  While the lambs thy bosom share;
2 Now, *these* little *ones* receiving,
    Fold *them* in thy gracious arm;
  There, we know, thy word believing,
    Only there, secure from harm.
3 Never from thy pasture roving,
    Let *them* be the Lion's prey;
  Let thy tenderness so loving,
    Keep *them* all life's dangerous way:
4 Then, within thy fold eternal,
    Let *them* find a resting-place;
  Feed in pastures ever vernal,
    Drink the rivers of thy grace.

HYMN 87. S. M.

THE gentle Saviour calls
  Our children to his breast;
He folds them in his gracious arms,
  Himself declares them blest.
2 "Let them approach," he cries,
    "Nor scorn their humble claim;
  The heirs of heaven are such as these,
    For such as these I came."
3 Gladly we bring them, Lord,
    Devoting them to thee,
  Imploring that, as we are thine,
    Thine may our offspring be.

BAPTISM OF ADULTS.
HYMN 88. S. M.
Ephesians vi. 10, 13.

SOLDIERS of Christ, arise,
  And put your armour on,
Strong in the strength which God supplies,
  Through his eternal Son.

2 Strong in the Lord of hosts,
  And in his mighty power,
Who in the strength of Jesus trusts,
  Is more than conqueror.

3 Stand then in his great might,
  With all his strength endued;
And take, to arm you for the fight,
  The panoply of God.

4 That having all things done,
  And all your conflicts past,
Ye may behold your victory won,
  And stand complete at last.

CONFIRMATION.
HYMN 89. L. M.

O HAPPY day, that stays my choice
  On thee, my Saviour, and my God:
Well may this glowing heart rejoice,
  And tell thy goodness all abroad.

2 O happy bond, that seals my vows,
  To him who merits all my love;
Let cheerful anthems fill his house,
  While to his sacred throne I move.

3 'Tis done, the great transaction's done;
  Deign, gracious Lord, to make me thine:
Help me, through grace, to follow on,
  Glad to confess thy voice divine.

4 Here rest, my oft-divided heart,
  Fix'd on thy God, thy Saviour, rest;
Who with the world would grieve to part?
  When call'd on angels' food to feast?

5 High heaven, that heard the solemn vow,
　　That vow renew'd shall daily hear,
　Till in life's latest hour I bow,
　　And bless in death a bond so dear.

HYMN 90. C. M.

WITNESS, ye men and angels; now
　　Before the Lord we speak;
To him we make our solemn vow,
　A vow we dare not break:

2 That, long as life itself shall last,
　　Ourselves to Christ we yield;
　Nor from his cause will we depart,
　　Or ever quit the field.

3 We trust not in our native strength,
　　But on his grace rely,
　That, with returning wants, the Lord
　　Will all our need supply.

4 Lord, guide our doubtful feet aright,
　　And keep us in thy ways;
　And, while we turn our vows to prayers,
　　Turn thou our prayers to praise.

HYMN 91. C. M.

YOUTH, when devoted to the Lord,
　　Is pleasing in his eyes;
A flower, though offer'd in the bud,
　Is no vain sacrifice.

2 'Tis easier far if we begin
　　To fear the Lord betimes;
　For sinners who grow old in sin,
　　Are harden'd by their crimes.

3 It saves us from a thousand snares
　　To mind religion young;
　Grace will preserve our following years,
　　And make our virtues strong.

4 To thee, Almighty God, to thee
　　Our hearts we now resign:
　'Twill please us to look back and see
　　That our whole lives were thine.

HYMN 92. C. M.

O, IN the morn of life, when youth
With vital ardour glows,
And shines in all the fairest charms
That beauty can disclose;

2 Deep in thy soul, before its powers
Are yet by vice enslaved,
Be thy Creator's glorious Name
And character engraved:

3 Ere yet the shades of sorrow cloud
The sunshine of thy days;
And cares and toils, in endless round,
Encompass all thy ways;

4 Ere yet thy heart the woes of age,
With vain regret, deplore,
And sadly muse on former joys,
That now return no more.

5 True wisdom, early sought and gain'd
In age will give thee rest:
O then, improve the morn of life,
To make its evening blest.

THE LORD'S SUPPER.

HYMN 93. C. M.

Rev. v. 9, 12, 13.

THOU, God, all glory, honour, power,
Art worthy to receive;
Since all things by thy power were made,
And by thy bounty live.

2 And worthy is the Lamb all power,
Honour, and wealth, to gain,
Glory and strength; who for our sins
A sacrifice was slain.

3 All worthy thou, who hast redeem'd
And ransom'd us to God,
From every nation, every coast,
By thy most precious blood.

4 Blessing and honour, glory, power,
    By all in earth and heaven,
To him that sits upon the throne,
    And to the Lamb be given.

HYMN 94. L. M.

MY God, and is thy table spread,
    And does thy cup with love o'erflow?
Thither be all thy children led,
    And let them thy sweet mercies know.

2 Hail! sacred feast, which Jesus makes,
    Rich banquet of his flesh and blood:
Thrice happy he who here partakes
    That sacred stream, that heavenly food.

3 Why are its bounties all in vain
    Before unwilling hearts display'd?
Was not for you the victim slain?
    Are you forbid the children's bread?

4 O let thy table honour'd be,
    And furnish'd well with joyful guests:
And may each soul salvation see,
    That here its holy pledges tastes.

5 Drawn by thy quickening grace, O Lord,
    In countless numbers let them come;
And gather from their Father's board,
    The bread that lives beyond the tomb.

6 Nor let thy spreading Gospel rest,
    Till through the world thy truth has run;
Till with this bread all men be blest,
    Who see the light or feel the sun.

HYMN 95. C. M.

AND are we now brought near to God,
    Who once at distance stood?
And, to effect this glorious change,
    Did Jesus shed his blood?

2 O for a song of ardent praise,
    To bear our souls above:

What should allay our lively hope,
  Or damp our flaming love?

3 Then let us join the heavenly choirs,
    To praise our heavenly King:
  O may that love which spread this board,
    Inspire us while we sing:

4 " Glory to God in highest strains,
    And to the earth be peace;
  Good-will from heaven to men is come,
    And let it never cease."

HYMN 96.   L. M.

TO Jesus, our exalted Lord,
That Name in heaven and earth adored,
Fain would our hearts and voices raise
A cheerful song of sacred praise.

2 But all the notes which mortals know,
Are weak, and languishing, and low;
Far, far above our humble songs,
The theme demands immortal tongues.

3 Yet whilst around his board we meet,
And worship at his sacred feet,
O let our warm affections move,
In glad returns of grateful love.

4 Yes, Lord, we love, and we adore,
But long to know and love thee more;
And whilst we taste the bread and wine,
Desire to feed on joys divine.

5 Let faith our feeble senses aid,
To see thy wondrous love display'd;
Thy broken flesh, thy bleeding veins,
Thy dreadful agonizing pains.

6 Let humble, penitential woe,
With painful, pleasing anguish flow;
And thy forgiving love impart
Life, hope, and joy to every heart.

ORDINATION, OR INSTITUTION OF MINISTERS.

HYMN 97. L. M.
St. Matt. x.

GO forth, ye heralds, in my Name,
　　Sweetly the Gospel trumpet sound;
The glorious jubilee proclaim,
　　Where'er the human race is found.

2 The joyful news to all impart,
　　And teach them where salvation lies;
With care bind up the broken heart,
　　And wipe the tears from weeping eyes.

3 Be wise as serpents, where you go,
　　But harmless as the peaceful dove;
And let your heaven-taught conduct show
　　That ye're commission'd from above.

4 Freely from me ye have received,
　　Freely, in love, to others give;
Thus shall your doctrines be believed,
　　And, by your labours, sinners live.

HYMN 98. L. M.
St. Mark. xvi. 15, &c., and St. Matt. xxviii. 18, &c.

"GO, preach my gospel," saith the Lord,
　　"Bid the whole earth my grace receive:
Explain to them my sacred word,
　　Bid them believe, obey, and live.

2 "I'll make my great commission known,
　　And ye shall prove my Gospel true,
By all the works that I have done,
　　And all the wonders ye shall do.

3 "Go, heal the sick, go, raise the dead;
　　Go cast out devils in my Name;
Nor let my prophets be afraid,
　　Though Greeks reproach, and Jews blaspheme.

4 "While thus ye follow my commands,
　　I'm with you till the world shall end
All power is trusted in my hands,
　　I can destroy, and can defend."

5 He spake, and light shone round his head;
  On a bright cloud to heaven he rode:
They to the farthest nations spread
  The grace of their ascended God.

HYMN 99. L. M.

THE Saviour, when to heaven he rose,
In splendid triumph o'er his foes,
Scatter'd his gifts on men below,
And wide his royal bounties flow.

2 Hence sprang the Apostle's honour'd name,
Sacred beyond heroic fame;
Hence dictates the Prophetic sage,
And hence the Evangelic page.

3 In lower forms, to bless our eyes,
Pastors from hence and Teachers rise;
Who, though with feebler rays they shine,
Still mark a long-extended line.

4 From Christ their varied gifts derive,
And, fed by him, their graces live:
Whilst, guarded by his potent hand,
Amidst the rage of hell they stand.

5 So shall the bright Succession run,
Through all the courses of the sun;
Whilst unborn churches, by their care,
Shall rise and flourish, large and fair.

6 Jesus, our Lord, their hearts shall know,
The spring whence all these blessings flow;
Pastors and people shout his praise,
Through the long round of endless days.

HYMN 100. L. M.

FATHER of mercies, bow thine ear,
  Attentive to our earnest prayer;
We plead for those who plead for thee,
Successful pleaders may they be.

2 How great their work, how vast their charge;
Do thou their anxious souls enlarge:

Their best acquirements are our gain ;
We share the blessings they obtain.

3 Clothe, then, with energy divine,
Their words, and let those words be thine;
To them thy sacred truth reveal,
Suppress their fear, inflame their zeal.

4 Teach them to sow the precious seed,
Teach them thy chosen flock to feed ;
Teach them immortal souls to gain,
Souls that will well reward their pain.

5 Let thronging multitudes around,
Hear from their lips the joyful sound ;
In humble strains thy grace implore,
And feel thy new-creating power.

6 Let sinners break their massive chains,
Distressed souls forget their pains ;
Let light through distant realms be spread,
And Sion rear her drooping head.

CONSECRATION OF A CHURCH.

HYMN 101. L. M.

AND wilt thou, O Eternal God,
On earth establish thine abode ?
Then look propitious from thy throne,
And take this temple for thine own.

2 These walls we to thine honour raise,
Long may they echo in thy praise;
And thou, descending, fill the place
With the rich tokens of thy grace.

3 Here may the great Redeemer reign,
With all the graces of his train ;
While power divine his word attends,
To conquer foes and cheer his friends.

4 And in the last decisive day,
When God the nations shall survey,
May it before the world appear,
Thousands were born for glory here.

MISSIONS.
HYMN 102. L. M.

JESUS shall reign where'er the sun
  Does his successive journeys run;
His kingdom spread from shore to shore,
Till moons shall wax and wane no more.

2 To him shall endless prayer be made,
  And praises throng to crown his head;
His Name like sweet perfume shall rise
With every morning sacrifice.

3 People and realms, of every tongue,
  Dwell on his love with sweetest song;
And infant voices shall proclaim
Their early blessings on his Name.

4 Blessings abound where'er he reigns;
  The prisoner leaps to burst his chains,
The weary find eternal rest,
And all the sons of want are blest.

5 Where he displays his healing power,
  Death and the curse are known no more:
In him the tribes of Adam boast
More blessings than their father lost.

6 Let every creature rise, and bring
  Peculiar honours to our King:
Angels descend with songs again,
And earth repeat the loud Amen.

HYMN 103. L. M.
Psalm cxvii.

FROM all that dwell below the skies,
  Let the Creator's praise arise;
Jehovah's glorious Name be sung
Through every land, by every tongue.

2 Eternal are thy mercies, Lord,
  And truth eternal is thy Word:
Thy praise shall sound from shore to shore,
Till suns shall rise and set no more.

HYMN 104. L. M.

O SPIRIT of the living God,
  In all thy plenitude of grace,
Where'er the foot of man hath trod,
  Descend on our apostate race.

2 Give tongues of fire and hearts of love,
    To preach the reconciling word;
  Give power and unction from above,
    Where'er the joyful sound is heard.

3 Be darkness, at thy coming, light;
    Confusion, order, in thy path;
  Souls without strength inspire with might;
    Bid mercy triumph over wrath.

4 Convert the nations; far and nigh
    The triumphs of the cross record;
  The name of Jesus glorify,
    Till every people call him Lord.

HYMN 105. H. 1.

For Missions to the New Settlements in the United States.

WHEN, Lord, to this our western land,
  Led by thy providential hand,
    Our wandering fathers came,
  Their ancient homes, their friends in youth,
  Sent forth the heralds of thy truth,
    To keep them in thy Name.

2 Then, through our solitary coast,
  The desert features soon were lost;
    Thy temples there arose;
  Our shores, as culture made them fair,
  Were hallow'd by thy rites, by prayer,
    And blossom'd as the rose.

3 And O, may we repay this debt
  To regions solitary yet,
    Within our spreading land:
  There, brethren, from our common home,
  Still westward, like our fathers, roam;
    Still guided by thy hand.

4 Saviour, we own this debt of love:
  O shed thy Spirit from above,
    To move each Christian breast;
  Till heralds shall thy truth proclaim,
  And temples rise to fix thy Name,
    Through all our desert west.

HYMN 106. C. M.
Isaiah xxxv. 2.

ON Sion, and on Lebanon,
  On Carmel's blooming height,
On Sharon's fertile plains, once shone
  The glory, pure and bright:
2 From thence its mild and cheering ray
    Stream'd forth from land to land;
  And empires now behold its day;
    And still its beams expand.
3 Its brightest splendours, darting west,
    Our happy shores illume;
  Our farther regions, once unblest,
    Now like a garden bloom:
4 But ah, our deserts deep and wild
    See not this heavenly light;
  No sacred beams, no radiance mild,
    Dispel their dreary night.
5 Thou, who didst lighten Sion's hill,
    On Carmel who didst shine,
  Our deserts let thy glory fill,
    Thy excellence divine.
6 Like Lebanon, in towering pride,
    May all our forests smile;
  And may our borders blossom wide
    Like Sharon's fruitful soil.

HYMN 107. II. 6.

FROM Greenland's icy mountains,
  From India's coral strand,
Where Afric's sunny fountains
  Roll down their golden sand;

From many an ancient river,
  From many a palmy plain,
They call us to deliver
  Their land from error's chain.

2 What though the spicy breezes
  Blow soft o'er Ceylon's isle;
Though every prospect pleases,
  And only man is vile:
In vain with lavish kindness
  The gifts of God are strewn;
The heathen in his blindness
  Bows down to wood and stone.

3 Shall we, whose souls are lighted
  With wisdom from on high;
Shall we to men benighted
  The lamp of life deny?
Salvation, oh, Salvation,
  The joyful sound proclaim,
Till each remotest nation
  Has learnt Messiah's Name.

4 Waft, waft, ye winds, his story,
  And you, ye waters, roll,
Till, like a sea of glory,
  It spreads from pole to pole:
Till o'er our ransom'd nature,
  The Lamb for sinners slain,
Redeemer, King, Creator,
  In bliss returns to reign.

HYMN 108. L. M.

For the Jews.

DISOWN'D of heaven, by man oppress'd,
  Outcasts from Sion's hallow'd ground,
Wherefore should Israel's sons, once bless'd,
  Still roam the scorning world around?

2 Lord, visit thy forsaken race,
  Back to thy fold the wanderers bring;
Teach them to seek thy slighted grace,
  And hail in Christ their promis'd King.

3 The veil of darkness rend in twain,
    Which hides their Shiloh's glorious light;
The sever'd olive branch again
    Firm to its parent-stock unite.

4 Hail, glorious day, expected long!
    When Jew and Greek one prayer shall pour;
With eager feet one temple throng,
    With grateful praise one God adore.

HYMN 109. IV. 1.
Rev. xv. 3, 4.

HOW wondrous and great
    Thy works, God of praise;
How just, King of saints,
    And true are thy ways:
O who shall not fear thee,
    And honour thy Name:
Thou only art holy,
    Thou only supreme.

2 To nations long dark
    Thy light shall be shown;
Their worship and vows
    Shall come to thy throne:
Thy truth and thy judgments
    Shall spread all abroad,
Till earth's every people
    Confess thee their God.

FOR SUNDAY AND CHARITY SCHOOLS.

HYMN 110. II. 4.
Children and Congregation.

Children.

COME let our voices join
    In one glad song of praise;
To God, the God of love,
    Our grateful hearts we raise:

Congregation.

To God alone your praise belongs;
His love demands your earliest songs.

Children.
2 Now we are taught to read
    The book of life divine;
  Where our Redeemer's love,
    And brightest glories shine:

Congregation.
  To God alone the praise is due,
  Who sends his word to us and you.

Children.
3 Within these hallow'd walls,
    Our wandering feet are brought;
  Where prayer and praise ascend,
    And heavenly truths are taught:

Congregation.
  To God alone your offerings bring;
  Here in his church his praises sing.

Children.
4 For blessings such as these,
    Our gratitude receive;
  Lord, here accept our hearts,
    'Tis all that we can give:

Congregation.
  Great God, accept their infant songs;
  To thee alone their praise belongs.

Both.
5 Lord, bid this work of love
    Be crown'd with meet success;
  May thousands yet unborn
    This institution bless:
  Thus shall the praise resound to thee,
  Now, and through all eternity.

HYMN 111. III. 1.

GLORY to the Father give,
  God in whom we move and live;
Children's prayers he deigns to hear,
Children's songs delight his ear.

2 Glory to the Son we bring,
   Christ our Prophet, Priest and King;
   Children, raise your sweetest strain
   To the Lamb, for he was slain.
3 Glory to the Holy Ghost,
   He reclaims the sinner lost;
   Children's minds may he inspire,
   Touch their tongues with holy fire.
4 Glory in the highest be
   To the blessed Trinity,
   For the Gospel from above,
   For the word that " God is love."

HYMN 112. C. M.

WHEN Jesus left his heavenly throne,
   He chose an humble birth;
Like us unhonour'd and unknown,
   He came to dwell on earth:
2 Like him, may we be found below,
   In wisdom's paths of peace;
Like him, in grace and knowledge grow,
   As years and strength increase.
3 Sweet were his words and kind his look,
   When mothers round him press'd;
Their infants in his arms he took,
   And on his bosom bless'd:
4 Safe from the world's alluring harms,
   Beneath his watchful eye,
O, thus encircled in his arms,
   May we for ever lie.

HYMN 113. L. M.

LORD, how delightful 'tis to see
   A whole assembly worship thee:
At once they sing, at once they pray;
They hear of heaven, and learn the way.
2 I have been there, and still would go,
   'Tis like a little heaven below;
Not all that earth and sin can say,
Shall tempt me to forget this day.

3 O write upon my memory, Lord,
　The text and doctrine of thy word;
　That I may break thy laws no more,
　But love thee better than before.

4 With thoughts of Christ and things divine,
　Fill up this sinful heart of mine;
　That hoping pardon through his blood,
　I may lie down and wake with God.

HYMN 114. C. M.

MERCY, descending from above,
　　In softest accents pleads;
　O may each tender bosom move,
　　When mercy intercedes.

2 Children our kind protection claim,
　　And God will well approve,
　When infants learn to lisp his Name,
　　And their Creator love.

3 Delightful work, young souls to win,
　　And turn the rising race
　From the deceitful paths of sin,
　　To seek their Saviour's face.

4 Almighty God, thine influence shed
　　To aid this blest design;
　The honour of thy Name be spread,
　　And all the glory thine.

CHARITABLE OCCASIONS.

HYMN 115. C. M.

BLEST is the man whose softening heart
　　Feels all another's pain;
　To whom the supplicating eye
　　Is never raised in vain:

2 Whose breast responds with generous warmth,
　　A stranger's woe to feel;
　Who weeps in pity o'er the wound
　　He wants the power to heal.

3 To gentle offices of love
　　His feet are never slow;

He views, through mercy's melting eye,
  A brother in a foe.

4 To him protection shall be shown;
  And mercy, from above,
Descend on those who thus fulfil
  The Christian law of love.

HYMN 116. C. M.

RICH are the joys which cannot die,
  With God laid up in store;
Treasures beyond the changing sky,
  Brighter than golden ore.

2 The seeds which piety and love
  Have scatter'd here below,
In the fair fertile fields above
  To ample harvests grow.

3 The mite my willing hands can give,
  At Jesus' feet I lay;
Grace shall the humble gift receive,
  Abounding grace repay.

HYMN 117. III. 3.

LORD of life, all praise excelling,
  Thou, in glory unconfined,
Deign'st to make thy humble dwelling
  With the poor of humble mind.

2 As thy love, through all creation,
  Beams like thy diffusive light;
So the high and humble station
  Both are equal in thy sight.

3 Thus thy care, for all providing,
  Warm'd thy faithful prophet's tongue;
Who, the lot of all deciding,
  To thy chosen Israel sung:

4 When thy harvest yields thee pleasure,
  Thou the golden sheaf shalt bind;
To the poor belongs the treasure
  Of the scatter'd ears behind:

Chorus. These thy God ordains to bless,
  The widow and the fatherless.

5 When thine olive-plants increasing
 Pour their plenty o'er thy plain,
Grateful, thou shalt take the blessing,
 But not search the bough again :
   Chorus. These, &c.

6 When thy favour'd vintage flowing,
 Gladdens thine autumnal scene,
Own the bounteous hand bestowing,
 But thy vines the poor shall glean.
   Chorus. These, &c.

7 Still we read thy word declaring
 Mercy, Lord, thine own decree ;
Mercy, every sorrow sharing,
 Warms the heart resembling thee.

8 Still the orphan and the stranger,
 Still the widow owns thy care ;
Screen'd by thee in every danger,
 Heard by thee in every prayer.
   Hallelujah, Amen.

TO BE USED AT SEA.

HYMN 118. L. M.

GOD of the seas, thine awful voice
 Bids all the rolling waves rejoice ;
And one soft word of thy command
Can sink them silent on the sand.

2 The smallest fish that swims the seas,
 Sportful, to thee a tribute pays ;
And largest monsters of the deep,
 At thy command, or rage or sleep.

3 Thus is thy glorious power adored
 Among the watery nations, Lord :
Yet men, who trace the dangerous waves,
 Forget the mighty God who saves.

HYMN 119. IV. 5.
"Save, Lord, or we perish."

St. Matt. viii. 25.

WHEN thro' the torn sail the wild tempest is streaming,
When o'er the dark wave the red lightning is gleaming,
Nor hope lends a ray the poor seaman to cherish,
We fly to our Maker: "Save, Lord, or we perish."

2 O Jesus, once rock'd on the breast of the billow,
Aroused, by the shriek of despair, from thy pillow,
Now seated in glory, the mariner cherish,
Who cries in his anguish, "Save, Lord, or we perish."

3 And O! when the whirlwind of passion is raging,
When sin in our hearts its wild warfare is waging,
Then send down thy Spirit, thy ransom'd to cherish,
Rebuke the destroyer; "Save, Lord, or we perish."

HYMN 120. C. M.
Which may be used at Sea or on Land.

LORD, for the just thou dost provide,
  Thou art their sure defence;
Eternal wisdom is their guide,
  Their help, Omnipotence.

2 Though they thro' foreign lands should roam,
  And breathe the tainted air
In burning climates, far from home,
  Yet Thou, their God, art there.

3 Thy goodness sweetens every soil,
  Makes every country please;
Thou on the snowy hills dost smile,
  And smooth'st the rugged seas.

4 When waves on waves, to heaven uprear'd,
  Defied the pilot's art;
When terror in each face appear'd,
  And sorrow in each heart;

5 To thee I raised my humble prayer,
    To snatch me from the grave:
  I found thine ear not slow to hear,
    Nor short thine arm to save.

6 Thou gav'st the word, the winds did cease,
    The storms obey'd thy will,
  The raging sea was hush'd in peace,
    And every wave was still.

7 For this, my life, in every state,
    A life of praise shall be;
  And death, when death shall be my fate,
    Shall join my soul to Thee.

FOR THE SICK.
HYMN 121. L. M.

WHEN dangers, woes, or death are nigh,
    Past mercies teach me where to fly:
Thine arm, Almighty God, can aid
When sickness grieves, and pains invade.

2 To all the various helps of art
Kindly thy healing power impart;
Bethesda's bath refused to save,
Unless an angel bless'd the wave.

3 All med'cines act by thy decree,
Receive commission all from thee;
And not a plant which spreads the plains,
But teems with health, when heaven ordains.

4 Clay and Siloam's pool, we find,
At heaven's command restored the blind;
And Jordan's waters hence were seen
To wash a Syrian leper clean.

5 But grant me nobler favours still,
Grant me to know and do thy will;
Purge my foul soul from every stain,
And save me from eternal pain.

6 Can such a wretch for pardon sue?
My crimes, my crimes arise in view,
Arrest my trembling tongue in prayer,
And pour the horrors of despair.

7 But thou, regard my contrite sighs,
　My tortured breast, my streaming eyes:
　To me thy boundless love extend,
　My God, my Father, and my Friend.

8 These lovely names I ne'er could plead,
　Had not thy Son vouchsafed to bleed;
　His blood procures our fallen race
　Admittance to the throne of grace.

9 When sin has shot its poison'd dart,
　And conscious guilt corrodes the heart,
　His blood is all-sufficient found
　To draw the shaft and heal the wound.

10 What arrows pierce so deep as sin?
　What venom gives such pain within?
　Thou great Physician of the soul,
　Rebuke my pangs, and make me whole.

11 O, if I trust thy sovereign skill,
　And bow submissive to thy will,
　Sickness and death shall both agree
　To bring me, Lord, at last to thee.

HYMN 122. C. M.

On Recovery from Sickness.

WHEN we are raised from deep distress,
　　Our God deserves our song;
　We take the pattern of our praise
　　From Hezekiah's tongue.

2 The gates of the devouring grave
　　Are open'd wide in vain,
　If he that holds the keys of death,
　　Command them fast again.

3 When he but speaks the healing word,
　　Then no disease withstands;
　Fevers and plagues obey the Lord,
　　And fly, as he commands.

4 If half the strings of life should break,
　　He can our frame restore,

   And cast our sins behind his back,
     And they are found no more.

5 To him I cried, " Thy servant save,
     Thou ever good and just;
   Thy power can rescue from the grave,
     Thy power is all my trust."

6 He heard, and saved my soul from death,
     And dried my falling tears:
   Now to his praise I'll spend my breath,
     Through my remaining years.

HYMN 123. L. M.

On the same.

MY God, since thou hast raised me up,
     Thee I'll extol with thankful voice;
   Restored by thine Almighty power,
     With fear before thee I'll rejoice.

2 With troubles worn, with pain opprest,
     To thee I cried, and thou didst save;
   Thou didst support my sinking hopes,
     My life didst rescue from the grave.

3 Wherefore, ye saints, rejoice with me,
     With me sing praises to the Lord;
   Call all his goodness to your mind,
     And all his faithfulness record.

4 His anger is but short: his love,
     Which is our life, hath certain stay;
   Grief may continue for a night,
     But joy returns with rising day.

5 Then, what I vow'd in my distress,
     In happier hours I now will give,
   And strive that in my grateful verse,
     His praises may for ever live.

6 To Father, Son, and Holy Ghost,
     The blest and undivided Three;
   The One sole giver of all life,
     Glory and praise for ever be.

FUNERALS.
HYMN 124. C. M.

HEAR what the voice from heaven declares
  To those in Christ who die:
Released from all their earthly cares,
  They'll reign with him on high.

2 Then why lament departed friends,
  Or shake at death's alarms?
Death's but the servant Jesus sends
  To call us to his arms.

3 If sin be pardon'd, we're secure,
  Death hath no sting beside;
The law gave sin its strength and power;
  But Christ, our ransom, died.

4 The graves of all his saints he bless'd,
  When in the grave he lay;
And, rising thence, their hopes he raised
  To everlasting day.

5 Then, joyfully, while life we have,
  To Christ, our life, we'll sing,
"Where is thy victory, O grave?
  And where, O death, thy sting?"

HYMN 125. C. M.

WHEN those we love are snatch'd away
  By death's resistless hand,
Our hearts the mournful tribute pay
  That friendship must demand.

2 While pity prompts the rising sigh,
  With awful power imprest;
May this dread truth, "I too must die,"
  Sink deep in every breast.

3 Let this vain world allure no more;
  Behold the opening tomb;
It bids us use the present hour,
  To-morrow death may come.

4 The voice of this instructive scene
  May every heart obey;

Nor be the faithful warning vain
  Which calls to watch and pray.
5 O let us to that Saviour fly,
  Whose arm alone can save:
Then shall our hopes ascend on high,
  And triumph o'er the grave.

HYMN 126. C. M.
Death of a Young Person.

HOW short the race our friend has run,
  Cut down in all *his* bloom:
The course but yesterday begun
  Now finish'd in the tomb.

2 Thou joyous youth, hence learn how soon
  Thy years may end their flight:
Long, long before life's brilliant noon,
  May come death's gloomy night.

3 To serve thy God no longer wait,
  To-day his voice regard;
To-morrow, mercy's open gate
  May be for ever barr'd.

4 And thus the Lord reveals his grace,
  Thy youthful love to gain:
The soul that early seeks my face,
  Shall never seek in vain.

HYMN 127. L. M.
Death of an Infant.

AS the sweet flower that scents the morn,
  But withers in the rising day;
Thus lovely was this infant's dawn,
  Thus swiftly fled its life away.

2 It died ere its expanding soul
  Had ever burnt with wrong desires,
Had ever spurn'd at heaven's control,
  Or ever quench'd its sacred fires.

3 It died to sin, it died to cares,
  But for a moment felt the rod:
O mourner, such, the Lord declares,
  Such are the children of our God.

VIII. INVITATION AND WARNING.

HYMN 128. III. 1.

SINNERS, turn, why will ye die?
  God, your Maker, asks you why:
God, who did your being give,
Made you with himself to live:
He the fatal cause demands,
Asks the works of his own hands:
Why, ye thankless creatures, why
Will ye cross his love, and die?

2 Sinners, turn, why will ye die?
God, your Saviour, asks you why:
He, who did your souls retrieve,
Died himself that ye might live.
Will you let him die in vain?
Crucify your Lord again?
Why, ye ransom'd sinners, why
Will ye slight his grace, and die?

3 Sinners, turn, why will ye die?
God, the Spirit, asks you why:
He who all your lives hath strove,
Woo'd you to embrace his love.
Will ye not his grace receive?
Will ye still refuse to live?
O, ye dying sinners, why,
Why will ye for ever die?

HYMN 129. III. 1.

HASTEN, sinner, to be wise;
  Stay not for the morrow's sun:
Wisdom, if you still despise,
  Harder is it to be won.

2 Hasten, mercy to implore;
   Stay not for the morrow's sun;
Lest thy season should be o'er,
   Ere this evening's stage be run.

3 Hasten, sinner, to return;
   Stay not for the morrow's sun;

    Lest thy lamp should cease to burn,
      Ere salvation's work is done.
4 Hasten, sinner, to be blest;
      Stay not for the morrow's sun;
    Lest perdition thee arrest,
      Ere the morrow is begun.

HYMN 130. II. 3.

PEACE, troubled soul, whose plaintive moan
    Hath taught each scene the note of woe;
Cease thy complaint, suppress thy groan,
    And let thy tears forget to flow:
Behold, the precious balm is found,
To lull thy pain, and heal thy wound.

2 Come, freely come, by sin opprest,
    On Jesus cast thy weighty load;
In him thy refuge find, thy rest,
    Safe in the mercy of thy God:
Thy God's thy Saviour, glorious word;
O hear, believe, and bless the Lord.

HYMN 131. S. M.
Rev. xxii. 17—20.

THE Spirit, in our hearts,
    Is whispering, sinner, Come:
The Bride, the Church of Christ, proclaims
    To all his children, Come.

2 Let him that heareth say
    To all about him, Come:
Let him that thirsts for righteousness
    To Christ, the fountain, come.

3 Yes, whosoever will,
    O let him freely come,
And freely drink the stream of life;
    'Tis Jesus bids him come.

4 Lo, Jesus, who invites,
    Declares, I quickly come.
Lord! even so; I wait thy hour:
    Jesus, my Saviour, come.

HYMN 132. C. M.

YE humble souls, approach your God
   With songs of sacred praise;
For he is good, supremely good,
   And kind are all his ways.

2 All nature owns his guardian care,
   In him we live and move;
But nobler benefits declare
   The wonders of his love.

3 He gave his Son, his only Son,
   To ransom rebel worms;
'Tis here he makes his goodness known
   In its diviner forms.

4 To this dear refuge, Lord, we come,
   'Tis here our hope relies;
A safe defence, a peaceful home,
   When storms of trouble rise.

5 Thine eye beholds, with kind regard,
   The souls who trust in thee;
Their humble hope thou wilt reward
   With bliss divinely free.

6 Great God, to thy almighty love,
   What honours shall we raise!
Not all th' angelic songs above
   Can render equal praise.

IX. CHRISTIAN DUTIES AND AFFECTIONS.

PRAYER.

HYMN 133. C. M.

APPROACH, my soul, the mercy-seat,
   Where Jesus answers prayer;
There humbly fall before his feet,
   For none can perish there.

2 Thy promise is my only plea,
   With this I venture nigh;

Thou callest burden'd souls to thee,
  And such, O Lord, am I.
3 Bow'd down beneath a load of sin,
  By Satan sorely press'd,
By war without, and fear within,
  I come to thee for rest.
4 Be thou my shield and hiding-place;
  That, shelter'd near thy side,
I may my fierce accuser face,
  And tell him, " Thou hast died."
5 O, wondrous love, to bleed and die,
  To bear the cross and shame,
That guilty sinners, such as I,
  Might plead thy gracious Name.

HYMN 134. C. M.

PRAYER is the soul's sincere desire,
  Utter'd or unexpress'd;
The motion of a hidden fire,
  That trembles in the breast.
2 Prayer is the burden of a sigh,
  The falling of a tear;
The upward glancing of an eye,
  When none but God is near.
3 Prayer is the simplest form of speech
  That infant lips can try;
Prayer, the sublimest strains that reach
  The Majesty on high.
4 Prayer is the Christian's vital breath,
  The Christian's native air,
The watch-word at the gates of death;
  He enters heaven with prayer.
5 Prayer is the contrite sinner's voice,
  Returning from his ways;
While angels in their songs rejoice,
  And cry, " Behold, he prays!"
6 In prayer, on earth, the saints are one;
  They're one in word and mind,

When with the Father and the Son
Sweet fellowship they find.

7 O Thou, by whom we come to God,
The Life, the Truth, the Way,
The path of prayer thyself hast trod;
Lord, teach us how to pray.

REPENTANCE.

HYMN 135. L. M.

O THOU that hear'st when sinners cry,
Though all my crimes before thee lie,
Behold them not with angry look,
But blot their memory from thy book.

2 Create my nature pure within,
And form my soul averse to sin:
Let thy good Spirit ne'er depart,
Nor hide thy presence from my heart.

3 I cannot live without thy light,
Cast out and banish'd from thy sight:
Thy holy joys, my God, restore,
And guard me that I fall no more.

4 Though I have grieved thy Spirit, Lord,
Thy help and comfort still afford;
And let a wretch come near thy throne,
To plead the merits of thy Son.

5 A broken heart, my God, my King,
Is all the sacrifice I bring;
The God of grace will ne'er despise
A broken heart for sacrifice.

6 My soul lies humbled in the dust,
And owns thy dreadful sentence just;
Look down, O Lord, with pitying eye,
And save the soul condemn'd to die.

7 Then will I teach the world thy ways;
Sinners shall learn thy sovereign grace:
I'll lead them to my Saviour's blood,
And they shall praise a pardoning God.

8 O may thy love inspire my tongue,
  Salvation shall be all my song:
  And all my powers shall join to bless
  The Lord, my strength and righteousness.

HYMN 136. L. M.

STAY, thou insulted Spirit, stay,
  Though I have done thee such despite;
Nor cast the sinner quite away,
  Nor take thine everlasting flight.

2 Though I have most unfaithful been,
    And long in vain thy grace received;
  Ten thousand times thy goodness seen,
    Ten thousand times thy goodness grieved;

3 Yet, O, the mourning sinner spare,
    In honour of my great High-priest;
  Nor in thy righteous anger swear,
    T' exclude me from thy people's rest.

4 My weary soul, O God, release;
    Uphold me with thy gracious hand;
  Guide me into thy perfect peace,
    And bring me to the promised land.

HYMN 137. L. M.

OH, that my load of sin were gone,
  Oh, that I could at last submit
At Jesus' feet to lay it down,
  To lay my soul at Jesus' feet.

2 Rest for my soul I long to find;
    Saviour of all, if mine thou art,
  Give me thy meek and lowly mind,
    And stamp thine image on my heart.

3 Break off the yoke of inbred sin,
    And fully set my spirit free;
  I cannot rest, till pure within,
    Till I am wholly lost in thee.

4 Fain would I learn of thee, my God;
    Thy light and easy burden prove,
  The cross, all stain'd with hallow'd blood,
    The labour of thy dying love.

5 I would, but thou must give the power,
   My heart from every sin release;
Bring near, bring near the joyful hour,
   And fill me with thy perfect peace.

HYMN 138. C. M.

Penitential Gratitude.

RISE, O my soul, the hours review,
   When, awed by guilt and fear,
To heaven for grace thou durst not sue,
   And found no rescue here.

2 Thy tears are dried, thy griefs are fled,
   Dispell'd each bitter care;
For heaven itself has lent its aid
   To save thee from despair.

3 Here, then, O God, thy work fulfil,
   And, from thy mercy's throne,
Vouchsafe me strength to do thy will,
   And to resist mine own;

4 So shall my soul each power employ
   Thy mercy to adore;
While heaven itself proclaims with joy,
   One pardon'd sinner more.

FAITH.

HYMN 139. III. 2.

ROCK of Ages, cleft for me,
   Let me hide myself in thee;
Let the water and the blood,
From thy side, a healing flood,
Be of sin the double cure,
Save from wrath, and make me pure.

2 Should my tears for ever flow,
Should my zeal no languor know,
This for sin could not atone,
Thou must save, and thou alone;
In my hand no price I bring,
Simply to thy cross I cling.

3 While I draw this fleeting breath,
　When mine eyelids close in death,
　When I rise to worlds unknown,
　And behold thee on thy throne,
　Rock of Ages, cleft for me,
　Let me hide myself in thee.

HYMN 140. L. M.

FAITH is the Christian's evidence
　Of things unseen by mortal eye;
It passes all the bounds of sense,
　And penetrates the inmost sky.

2 Things absent it can set in view,
　　And bring far distant prospects home;
　Events long pass'd it can renew,
　　And long foresee the things to come.

3 With strong persuasion, from afar
　　The heavenly region it surveys,
　Embraces all the blessings there,
　　And here enjoys the promises.

4 By faith a steady course we steer,
　　Through ruffling storms and swelling seas,
　O'ercome the world, keep down our fear,
　　And still possess our souls in peace.

5 By faith we pass the vale of tears
　　Safe and serene, though oft distress'd;
　By faith subdue the king of fears,
　　And go rejoicing to our rest.

HYMN 141. C. M.
Rom. viii. 31—34.

O LET triumphant faith dispel
　The fears of guilt and woe:
If God be for us, God the Lord,
　Who, who shall be our foe?

2 He who his only Son gave up
　To death, that we might live,
Shall he not all things freely grant,
　That boundless love can give?

3 Who now his people shall accuse?
   'Tis God hath justified:
Who now his people shall condemn?
   The Lamb of God hath died.
4 And He who died hath risen again,
   Triumphant from the grave:
At God's right hand for us he pleads,
   Omnipotent to save.

HYMN 142. C. M.
Dead Faith.

DELUDED souls, that dream of heaven,
   And make their empty boast
Of inward joys, and sins forgiven,
   While they are slaves to lust.
2 Vain are our fancies, vain our flights,
   If faith be cold and dead;
None but a living power unites
   To Christ, the living Head.
3 The faith which new-creates the heart,
   And works by active love,
Will bid all sinful joys depart,
   And lift the thoughts above.
4 God from the curse has set us free,
   To make us pure within;
Nor did he send his Son to be
   The minister of sin.

HYMN 143. III. 1.
Christ our Refuge.

JESUS, Saviour of my soul,
   Let me to thy bosom fly,
While the waves of trouble roll,
   While the tempest still is high:
Hide me, O my Saviour, hide,
   Till the storm of life is past;
Safe into the haven guide;
   O receive my soul at last.

2 Other refuge have I none,
   Hangs my helpless soul on thee:
Leave, ah, leave me not alone,
   Still support and comfort me:
All my trust on thee is stay'd,
   All my hope from thee I bring;
Cover my defenceless head
   With the shadow of thy wing.

HYMN 144. IV. 4.

HOW firm a foundation, ye saints of the Lord,
Is laid for your faith in his excellent word;
What more can he say than to you he hath said?
You who unto Jesus for refuge have fled:

2 Fear not, I am with thee, O be not dismay'd,
I, I am thy God, and will still give thee aid;
I'll strengthen thee, help thee, and cause thee to stand,
Upheld by my righteous, omnipotent hand.

3 When through the deep waters I call thee to go,
The rivers of woe shall not thee overflow;
For I will be with thee, thy troubles to bless,
And sanctify to thee thy deepest distress.

4 When through fiery trials thy pathway shall lie,
My grace, all-sufficient, shall be thy supply;
The flame shall not hurt thee, I only design
Thy dross to consume, and thy gold to refine.

5 The soul that to Jesus hath fled for repose,
I will not, I will not desert to his foes; [shake,
That soul, though all hell shall endeavour to
I'll never—no, never—no, never forsake.

HOPE.
HYMN 145.

RISE, my soul, and stretch thy wings,
   Thy better portion trace;
Rise, from transitory things,
   Towards heaven, thy destined place:
Sun, and moon, and stars decay,
   Time shall soon this earth remove;

Rise, my soul, and haste away
  To seats prepared above.
2 Cease, my soul, O cease to mourn,
    Press onward to the prize;
  Soon thy Saviour will return,
    To take thee to the skies:
  There, is everlasting peace,
    Rest, enduring rest in heaven;
  There, will sorrow ever cease,
    And crowns of joy be given.

HYMN 146. III. 1.

CHILDREN of the heavenly King,
  As we journey, let us sing;
Sing the Saviour's worthy praise,
Glorious in his works and ways.

2 We are travelling home to God,
  In the way the fathers trod;
  They are happy now, and we
  Soon their happiness shall see.

3 Banish'd once, by sin betray'd,
  Christ our Advocate was made;
  Pardon'd now, no more we roam,
  Christ conducts us to our home.

4 Lord, obediently we'll go,
  Gladly leaving all below;
  Only thou our leader be,
  And we still will follow thee.

HYMN 147. C. M.

WHEN I can read my title clear
  To mansions in the skies,
I'll bid farewell to every fear,
  And wipe my weeping eyes.

2 Should earth against my soul engage,
    And fiery darts be hurl'd,
  Then I can smile at Satan's rage,
    And face a frowning world.

3 Let cares like a wild deluge come,
    Let storms of sorrow fall;

So I but safely reach my home,
  My God, my heaven, my all:
4 There, anchor'd safe, my weary soul
    Shall find eternal rest;
  Nor storms shall beat, nor billows roll
    Across my peaceful breast.

JOY.
HYMN 148. C. M.

JOY is a fruit that will not grow
  In nature's barren soil;
All we can boast, till Christ we know,
  Is vanity and toil.

2 A bleeding Saviour, seen by faith,
    A sense of pardoning love,
  A hope that triumphs over death,
    Give joys like those above.

3 These are the joys which satisfy
    And purify the mind;
  Which make the spirit mount on high,
    And leave the world behind.

4 No more, believer, mourn thy lot;
    O thou who art the Lord's,
  Resign to those who know him not,
    Such joy as earth affords.

HYMN 149. S. M.

COME, ye that love the Lord,
  And let your joys be known;
Join in a song with sweet accord,
  And thus surround the throne.

2 Let those refuse to sing
    That never knew our God,
  But children of the heavenly King
    May speak their joys abroad.

3 The God of heaven is ours,
    Our Father and our love;
  His care shall guard life's fleeting hours,
    Then waft our souls above.

4 There shall we see his face,
　　And never, never sin;
　There, from the rivers of his grace,
　　Drink endless pleasures in.
5 Yes, and before we rise
　　To that immortal state,
　The thoughts of such amazing bliss
　　Should constant joys create.
6 Children of grace have found
　　Glory begun below;
　Celestial fruits on earthly ground
　　From faith and hope may grow.
7 The hill of Sion yields
　　A thousand sacred sweets,
　Before we reach the heavenly fields,
　　Or walk the golden streets.
8 Then let our songs abound,
　　And every tear be dry;
　We're travelling through Immanuel's ground,
　　To fairer worlds on high.

LOVE.
HYMN 150.　III. 3.

LORD, with glowing heart I'd praise thee
　For the bliss thy love bestows;
For the pardoning grace that saves me,
　And the peace that from it flows:
Help, O God, my weak endeavour;
　This dull soul to rapture raise:
Thou must light the flame, or never
　Can my love be warm'd to praise.

2 Praise, my soul, the God that sought thee,
　　Wretched wanderer, far astray;
　Found thee lost, and kindly brought thee
　　From the paths of death away:
　Praise, with love's devoutest feeling,
　　Him who saw thy guilt-born fear,
　And, the light of hope revealing,
　　Bade the blood-stain'd cross appear.

3 Lord, this bosom's ardent feeling
   Vainly would my lips express:
Low before thy footstool kneeling,
   Deign thy suppliant's prayer to bless:
Let thy grace, my soul's chief treasure,
   Love's pure flame within me raise;
And, since words can never measure,
   Let my life show forth thy praise.

HYMN 151. III. 1.

LORD, my God, I long to know,
   Oft it causes anxious thought;
Do I love thee, Lord, or no?
   Am I thine, or am I not?

2 Could my heart so hard remain,
   Prayer a task and burden prove,
Any duty give me pain,
   If I knew a Saviour's love?

3 When I turn mine eyes within,
   O how dark, and vain, and wild!
Prone to unbelief and sin,
   Can I deem myself thy child?

4 Yet I mourn my stubborn will,
   Find my sin a grief and thrall:
Should I grieve for what I feel,
   If I did not love at all?

5 Could I love thy saints to meet,
   Choose the ways I once abhorr'd,
Find at times the promise sweet,
   If I did not love thee, Lord?

6 Saviour, let me love thee more,
   If I love at all, I pray;
If I have not loved before,
   Help me to begin to-day.

PRAISE.

HYMN 152.

THE God of Abraham praise,
   Who reigns enthroned above;

Ancient of everlasting days,
  And God of love;
Jehovah, Great I AM,
  By earth and heaven confess'd;
I bow and bless the sacred Name,
  For ever blest.

2 The God of Abraham praise,
  At whose supreme command
From earth I rise, and seek the joys
  At his right hand:
I all on earth forsake,
  Its wisdom, fame, and power;
And him my only portion make,
  My shield and tower.

3 He by himself hath sworn,
  I on his oath depend,
I shall, on angel-wings upborne,
  To heaven ascend:
I shall behold his face,
  I shall his power adore,
And sing the wonders of his grace
  For evermore.

4 There dwells the Lord, our King,
  The Lord, our righteousness,
Triumphant o'er the world and sin,
  The Prince of Peace;
On Sion's sacred height
  His kingdom he maintains,
And, glorious, with his saints in light,
  For ever reigns.

5 The God who reigns on high
  The great archangels sing;
And, "Holy, holy, holy," cry,
  "Almighty King,
Who was, and is the same,
  And evermore shall be;
Jehovah, Father, Great I AM,
  We worship thee."

6 The whole triumphant host
    Give thanks to God on high;
"Hail, Father, Son, and Holy Ghost,"
    They ever cry:
Hail, Abraham's God and mine,
    I join the heavenly lays;
All might and majesty are thine,
    And endless praise.

HYMN 153. IV. 3.
Psalm c.

BE joyful in God, all ye lands of the earth,
    O serve him with gladness and fear;
Exult in his presence with music and mirth,
    With love and devotion draw near.

2 For Jehovah is God, and Jehovah alone,
    Creator and ruler o'er all;
And we are his people, his sceptre we own;
    His sheep, and we follow his call.

3 O enter his gates with thanksgiving and song,
    Your vows in his temple proclaim;
His praise with melodious accordance prolong,
    And bless his adorable Name.

4 For good is the Lord, inexpressibly good,
    And we are the work of his hand;
His mercy and truth from eternity stood,
    And shall to eternity stand.

HYMN 154. L. M.
Psalm c.

BEFORE Jehovah's awful throne,
    Ye nations, bow with sacred joy;
Know that the Lord is God alone;
    He can create, and he destroy.

2 His sovereign power, without our aid,
    Made us of clay, and form'd us men;
And when like wandering sheep we stray'd,
    He brought us to his fold again.

3 We are his people, we his care,
    Our souls, and all our mortal frame;
  What lasting honours shall we rear,
    Almighty Maker, to thy Name?

4 We'll crowd thy gates with thankful songs,
    High as the heaven our voices raise;
  And earth, with her ten thousand tongues,
    Shall fill thy courts with sounding praise.

5 Wide as the world is thy command,
    Vast as eternity thy love;
  Firm as a rock thy truth must stand,
    When rolling years shall cease to move.

HYMN 155. III. 1.
Songs of Praise.

SONGS of praise the angels sang;
  Heaven with hallelujahs rang,
When Jehovah's work begun,
When he spake and it was done.

2 Songs of praise awoke the morn,
  When the Prince of Peace was born;
  Songs of praise arose, when he
  Captive led captivity.

3 Heaven and earth must pass away;
  Songs of praise shall crown that day:
  God will make new heavens and earth;
  Songs of praise shall hail their birth.

4 And shall man alone be dumb,
  Till that glorious kingdom come?
  No; the Church delights to raise
  Psalms, and hymns, and songs of praise.

5 Saints below, with heart and voice,
  Still in songs of praise rejoice;
  Learning here, by faith and love,
  Songs of praise to sing above.

6 Borne upon their latest breath,
  Songs of praise shall conquer death;
  Then, amidst eternal joy,
  Songs of praise their powers employ.

CONTENTMENT.
HYMN 156. C. M.

FATHER, whate'er of earthly bliss
  Thy sovereign will denies,
Accepted at thy throne, let this,
  My humble prayer, arise:

2 Give me a calm and thankful heart,
    From every murmur free;
  The blessings of thy grace impart,
    And make me live to thee:

3 Let the sweet hope that thou art mine
    My life and death attend;
  Thy presence through my journey shine,
    And crown my journey's end.

HYMN 157. L. M.

BE still my heart, these anxious cares
  To thee are burdens, thorns, and snares;
They cast dishonour on thy Lord,
And contradict his gracious word.

2 Brought safely by his hand thus far,
  Why wilt thou now give place to fear?
  How canst thou want if he provide,
  Or lose thy way with such a guide?

3 When first before his mercy-seat,
  Thou didst to him thy all commit;
  He gave thee warrant from that hour,
  To trust his wisdom, love, and power.

4 Did ever trouble yet befall,
  And he refuse to hear thy call?
  And has he not his promise past,
  That thou shalt overcome at last?

5 Though rough and thorny be the road,
  It leads thee home, apace, to God;
  Then count thy present trials small,
  For heaven will make amends for all.

IN AFFLICTION.
HYMN 158.   C. M.

HEAR, gracious God, my humble moan,
  To thee I breathe my sighs:
When will the mournful night be gone?
  When shall my joys arise?

2 Yet though my soul in darkness mourns,
  Thy promise is my stay;
Here would I rest till light returns,
  Thy presence makes my day.

3 Come, Lord, and with celestial peace,
  Relieve my aching heart;
O smile, and bid my sorrows cease,
  And all their gloom depart.

4 Then shall my drooping spirit rise,
  And bless thy healing rays,
And change these deep complaining sighs
  For songs of sacred praise.

HYMN 159.   II. 3.
Psalm xlii.

AS, panting in the sultry beam,
  The hart desires the cooling stream,
So to thy presence, Lord, I flee,
So longs my soul, O God, for thee;
Athirst to taste thy living grace,
And see thy glory, face to face.

2 But rising griefs distress my soul,
And tears on tears successive roll;
For many an evil voice is near,
To chide my woe, and mock my fear;
And silent memory weeps alone
O'er hours of peace and gladness flown.

3 For I have walk'd the happy round
That, circles Sion's holy ground,
And gladly swell'd the choral lays,
That hymn'd my great Redeemer's praise,
What time the hallow'd arches rung
Responsive to the solemn song.

4 Ah, why, by passing clouds opprest,
  Should vexing thoughts distract thy breast?
  Turn, turn to Him, in every pain,
  Whom suppliants never sought in vain;
  Thy strength, in joy's ecstatic day,
  Thy hope, when joy has pass'd away.

HYMN 160. II. 3.
A compassionate High-Priest.
Hebrews iv. 15.

WHEN gathering clouds around I view,
  And days are dark, and friends are few,
On Him I lean, who, not in vain,
Experienced every human pain;
He feels my griefs, he sees my fears,
And counts and treasures up my tears.

2 If aught should tempt my soul to stray
  From heavenly wisdom's narrow way,
  To fly the good I would pursue,
  Or do the ill I would not do;
  Still He, who felt temptation's power,
  Shall guard me in that dangerous hour.

3 When vexing thoughts within me rise,
  And, sore dismay'd, my spirit dies;
  Then He, who once vouchsafed to bear
  The sickening anguish of despair,
  Shall sweetly soothe, shall gently dry,
  The throbbing heart, the streaming eye.

4 When sorrowing o'er some stone I bend,
  Which covers all that was a friend,
  And from his voice, his hand, his smile,
  Divides me for a little while;
  Thou, Saviour, seest the tears I shed,
  For thou didst weep o'er Lazarus dead.

5 And, oh, when I have safely past
  Through every conflict but the last,
  Still, still unchanging, watch beside
  My bed of death, for Thou hast died:
  Then point to realms of endless day,
  And wipe the latest tear away.

HYMN 161. L. M.
Sanctified Affliction.

LORD, unafflicted, undismay'd,
In pleasure's path how long I stray'd:
But thou hast made me feel thy rod,
And turn'd my soul to thee, my God.

2 What though it pierced my fainting heart,
I bless thy hand that caused the smart;
It taught my tears awhile to flow,
But saved me from eternal woe.

3 O, hadst thou left me unchastised,
Thy precepts I had still despised,
And still the snare in secret laid,
Had my unwary feet betray'd.

4 I love thy chastenings, O my God,
They fix my hopes on thy abode;
Where, in thy presence fully blest,
Thy stricken saints for ever rest.

DAILY DEVOTION.
HYMN 162. H. 3.
Daily Dependence.

WHEN, streaming from the eastern skies,
The morning light salutes mine eyes,
O Sun of Righteousness divine,
On me with beams of mercy shine;
Chase the dark clouds of sin away,
And turn my darkness into day.

2 When to heaven's great and glorious King
My morning sacrifice I bring;
And, mourning o'er my guilt and shame
Ask mercy, Saviour, in thy Name;
My conscience sprinkle with thy blood,
And be my advocate with God.

3 As every day thy mercy spares
Will bring its trials and its cares,
O Saviour, till my life shall end,
Be thou my counsellor and friend:

  Teach me thy precepts, all divine,
  And be thy pure example mine.

4 When pain transfixes every part,
 Or languor settles at the heart;
 When on my bed, diseased, oppress'd,
 I turn, and sigh, and long for rest;
 O great Physician, see my grief,
 And grant thy servant sweet relief.

5 Should poverty's destructive blow
 Lay all my worldly comforts low;
 And neither help nor hope appear,
 My steps to guide, my heart to cheer;
 Lord, pity and supply my need,
 For thou, on earth, wast poor indeed.

6 Should Providence profusely pour
 Its varied blessings on my store;
 O keep me from the ills that wait
 On such a seeming prosperous state:
 From hurtful passions set me free,
 And humbly may I walk with thee.

7 When each day's scenes and labours close,
 And wearied nature seeks repose,
 With pardoning mercy richly blest,
 Guard me, my Saviour, while I rest:
 And, as each morning sun shall rise,
 O lead me onward to the skies.

8 And, at my life's last setting sun,
 My conflicts o'er, my labours done,
 Jesus, thy heavenly radiance shed,
 To cheer and bless my dying bed;
 And, from death's gloom my spirit raise,
 To see thy face and sing thy praise.

HYMN 163. L. M.
"I have set God always before me." Psalm xvi. 9.

SAVIOUR, when night involves the skies,
 My soul, adoring, turns to thee;
Thee, self-abased in mortal guise,
 And wrapt in shades of death for me.

2 On thee my waking raptures dwell,
    When crimson gleams the east adorn,
Thee, victor of the grave and hell,
    Thee, source of life's eternal morn.

3 When noon her throne in light arrays,
    To thee my soul triumphant springs;
Thee, throned in glory's endless blaze,
    Thee, Lord of lords, and King of kings.

4 O'er earth, when shades of evening steal,
    To death and thee my thoughts I give;
To death, whose power I soon must feel,
    To thee, with whom I trust to live.

HYMN 164. L. M.
Morning Hymn.

AWAKE, my soul, and with the sun
Thy daily course of duty run;
Shake off dull sloth, and early rise
To pay thy morning sacrifice.

2 Redeem thy mis-spent time that's past;
Live this day, as if 'twere thy last;
To improve thy talents take due care;
'Gainst the great day thyself prepare.

3 Let all thy converse be sincere,
Thy conscience as the noon-day clear;
Think how the all-seeing God, thy ways
And all thy secret thoughts surveys.

4 Wake, and lift up thyself, my heart,
And with the angels bear thy part;
Who all night long unwearied sing,
"Glory to thee, eternal King."

5 I wake, I wake, ye heavenly choir;
May your devotion me inspire;
That I like you my age may spend,
Like you may on my God attend.

6 May I like you in God delight,
Have all day long my God in sight;

Perform like you my Maker's will:
  Oh, may I never more do ill.

7 Glory to thee, who safe hast kept,
  And hast refresh'd me while I slept:
  Grant, Lord, when I from death shall wake,
  I may of endless life partake.

8 Lord, I my vows to thee renew;
  Scatter my sins as morning dew;
  Guard my first spring of thought and will,
  And with thyself my spirit fill.

9 Direct, control, suggest this day,
  All I design, or do, or say,
  That all my powers, with all their might,
  In thy sole glory may unite.

10 Praise God, from whom all blessings flow,
   Praise him, all creatures here below;
   Praise him above, angelic host;
   Praise Father, Son, and Holy Ghost.

HYMN 165. L. M.

Morning.

ARISE, my soul, with rapture rise,
  And, fill'd with love and fear, adore
The awful Sovereign of the skies,
  Whose mercy lends me one day more.

2 And may this day, indulgent Power,
    Not idly pass, nor fruitless be;
  But may each swiftly-flying hour
    Still nearer bring my soul to Thee.

3 But can it be? that Power divine
    Is throned in light's unbounded blaze;
  And countless worlds and angels join
    To swell the glorious song of praise—

4 And will He deign to lend an ear,
    When I, poor abject mortal, pray?
  Yes, boundless goodness, He will hear,
    Nor cast the meanest wretch away.

5 Then let me serve Thee all my days,
　　And may my zeal with years increase:
　For pleasant, Lord, are all thy ways,
　　And all thy paths are paths of peace.

HYMN 166.　C. M.
Morning.

TO Thee let my first offerings rise,
　　Whose sun creates the day,
　Swift as his gladdening influence flies,
　　And spotless as his ray.
2 This day thy favouring hand be nigh,
　　So oft vouchsafed before;
　Still may it lead, protect, supply,
　　And I that hand adore.
3 If bliss thy Providence impart,
　　For which, resign'd, I pray,
　Give me to feel a cheerful heart,
　　And grateful homage pay.
4 Affliction should thy love intend,
　　As vice or folly's cure,
　Patient, to gain that gracious end,
　　May I the means endure.
5 Be this and every future day
　　Still wiser than the past;
　And when I all my life survey,
　　May grace sustain at last.

HYMN 167.　III. 1.
Morning.

NOW the shades of night are gone;
　　Now the morning light is come;
　Lord, may we be thine to-day;
　Drive the shades of sin away.
2 Fill our souls with heavenly light,
　Banish doubt and clear our sight;
　In thy service, Lord, to-day,
　May we labour, watch, and pray.

3 Keep our haughty passions bound;
 Save us from our foes around;
 Going out and coming in,
 Keep us safe from every sin.

4 When our work of life is past,
 O receive us then at last;
 Night and sin will be no more,
 When we reach the heavenly shore.

HYMN 168. L. M.
Evening Hymn.

GLORY to thee, my God, this night,
 For all the blessings of the light:
 Keep me, O keep me, King of kings,
 Under thine own Almighty wings.

2 Forgive me, Lord, for thy dear Son,
 The ills that I this day have done;
 That with the world, myself, and Thee,
 I, ere I sleep, at peace may be.

3 Teach me to live, that I may dread
 The grave as little as my bed;
 Teach me to die, that so I may
 Triumphing rise at the last day.

4 O may my soul on thee repose,
 And with sweet sleep mine eyelids close:
 Sleep, that may me more vigorous make
 To serve my God, when I awake.

5 When in the night I sleepless lie,
 My soul with heavenly thoughts supply:
 Let no ill dreams disturb my rest,
 No powers of darkness me molest.

6 O when shall I, in endless day,
 For ever chase dark sleep away,
 And hymns divine with angels sing,
 Glory to thee, eternal King.

7 Praise God, from whom all blessings flow,
 Praise him, all creatures here below;
 Praise him above, angelic host;
 Praise Father, Son, and Holy Ghost.

HYMN 169. L. M.
Evening.

GREAT God, to thee my evening song,
  With humble gratitude I raise:
O let thy mercy tune my tongue,
  And fill my heart with lively praise.

2 My days unclouded as they pass,
  And every onward rolling hour,
Are monuments of wondrous grace,
  And witness to thy love and power.

3 And yet this thoughtless, wretched heart,
  Too oft regardless of thy love,
Ungrateful, can from thee depart,
  And from the path of duty rove.

4 Seal my forgiveness in the blood
  Of Christ, my Lord; his Name alone
I plead for pardon, gracious God,
  And kind acceptance at thy throne.

5 With hope in him mine eyelids close,
  With sleep refresh my feeble frame;
Safe in thy care may I repose,
  And wake with praises to thy Name.

HYMN 170. C. M.
Evening.

NOW from the altar of our hearts,
  Let flames of love arise;
Assist us, Lord, to offer up
  Our evening sacrifice.

2 Minutes and mercies multiplied
  Have made up all this day;
Minutes came quick, but mercies were
  More swift, more free than they.

3 New time, new favours, and new joys,
  Do a new song require;
Till we shall praise Thee as we would,
  Accept our hearts' desire.

HYMN 171. S. M.
Evening.

THE day is past and gone;
  The evening shades appear:
O may we all remember well
  The night of death draws near.

2 We lay our garments by,
  Upon our beds to rest;
So death shall soon disrobe us all
  Of what is here possest.

3 Lord, keep us safe this night,
  Secure from all our fears;
May angels guard us while we sleep,
  Till morning light appears.

HYMN 172. III. 1.
Psalm cxli. 2.

SOFTLY now the light of day
  Fades upon my sight away;
Free from care, from labour free,
Lord, I would commune with thee.

2 Thou, whose all-pervading eye
  Naught escapes, without, within,
Pardon each infirmity,
  Open fault, and secret sin.

3 Soon, for me, the light of day
Shall for ever pass away;
Then, from sin and sorrow free,
Take me, Lord, to dwell with thee.

4 Thou who, sinless, yet hast known
  All of man's infirmity;
Then, from thine eternal throne,
  Jesus, look with pitying eye.

HYMN 173. IV. 2.
Evening.

INSPIRER and hearer of prayer,
  Thou shepherd and guardian of thine,

My all to thy covenant care,
  I, sleeping or waking, resign.
2 If thou art my shield and my sun,
  The night is no darkness to me;
And, fast, as my minutes roll on,
  They bring me but nearer to thee.
3 A sovereign protector I have,
  Unseen, yet for ever at hand;
Unchangeably faithful to save,
  Almighty to rule and command.
4 His smiles and his comforts abound,
  His grace, as the dew, shall descend;
And walls of salvation surround
  The soul he delights to defend.

X. THE CHRISTIAN LIFE.

HYMN 174.   C. M.

Renouncing the World.

LET worldly minds the world pursue,
  It has no charms for me;
Once I admired its follies too,
  But grace has set me free.
2 Those follies now no longer please,
  No more delight afford;
Far from my heart be joys like these,
  Now I have known the Lord.
3 As by the light of opening day
  The stars are all conceal'd,
So earthly pleasures fade away
  When Jesus is reveal'd.
4 Creatures no more divide my choice,
  I bid them all depart;
His Name, and love, and gracious voice
  Shall fix my roving heart.
5 Now, Lord, I would be thine alone,
  And wholly live to thee;

Yet worthless still myself I own,
Thy worth is all my plea.

HYMN 175. L. M.
Not ashamed of Christ.

JESUS, and shall it ever be,
A mortal man ashamed of thee:
Ashamed of thee, whom angels praise,
Whose glories shine through endless days?

2 Ashamed of Jesus! sooner far
Let night disown each radiant star;
'Tis midnight with my soul, till he,
Bright Morning Star, bid darkness flee.

3 Ashamed of Jesus! O, as soon
Let morning blush to own the sun;
He sheds the beams of light divine
O'er this benighted soul of mine.

4 Ashamed of Jesus! that dear Friend
On whom my hopes of heaven depend:
No; when I blush, be this my shame,
That I no more revere his Name.

5 Ashamed of Jesus! empty pride;
I'll boast a Saviour crucified;
And, O, may this my portion be,
My Saviour not ashamed of me.

HYMN 176. S. M.
Prayer for Christian Graces.

JESUS, my strength, my hope,
 On thee I cast my care,
With humble confidence look up,
 And know thou hear'st my prayer:
Give me on thee to wait,
 Till I can all things do;
On thee, Almighty to create,
 Almighty to renew.

2 I want a sober mind,
 A self-renouncing will,

That tramples down and casts behind
　　The baits of pleasing ill;
A soul inured to pain,
　　To hardship, grief, and loss;
Ready to take up and sustain
　　The consecrated cross.

3　I want a godly fear,
　　A quick, discerning eye,
That looks to thee when sin is near,
　　And sees the tempter fly;
A spirit still prepared,
　　And arm'd with jealous care,
For ever standing on its guard,
　　And watching unto prayer.

4　I want a heart to pray,
　　To pray and never cease,
Never to murmur at thy stay,
　　Or wish my sufferings less;
This blessing, above all,
　　Always to pray I want,
Out of the deep on thee to call,
　　And never, never faint.

5　I want a true regard,
　　A single, steady aim,
Unmoved by threatening or reward,
　　To thee and thy great Name;
A jealous, just concern
　　For thine immortal praise;
A pure desire that all may learn
　　And glorify thy grace.

6　I rest upon thy word,
　　The promise is for me;
My succour and salvation, Lord,
　　Shall surely come from thee:
But let me still abide,
　　Nor from my hope remove,
Till thou my patient spirit guide
　　Into thy perfect love.

HYMN 177. III. 3.
Prayer for Guidance.

GUIDE me, O thou great Jehovah,
  Pilgrim through this barren land;
I am weak, but thou art mighty;
  Hold me with thy powerful hand.

2 Open now the crystal fountains
  Whence the living waters flow;
Let the fiery, cloudy pillar,
  Lead me all my journey through.

3 Feed me with the heavenly manna
  In this barren wilderness;
Be my sword, and shield, and banner;
  Be the Lord my righteousness.

4 When I tread the verge of Jordan,
  Bid my anxious fears subside;
Death of death, and hell's destruction,
  Land me safe on Canaan's side.

HYMN 178. L. M.
Following the Example of Christ.

WHENE'ER the angry passions rise,
  And tempt our thoughts or tongues to strife,
To Jesus let us lift our eyes,
  Bright pattern of the Christian life.

2 O how benevolent and kind,
  How mild, how ready to forgive:
Be this the temper of our mind,
  And these the rules by which we live.

3 To do his heavenly Father's will
  Was his employment and delight;
Humility and holy zeal
  Shone through his life divinely bright.

4 Dispensing good where'er he came,
  The labours of his life were love;
Then, if we bear the Saviour's name,
  By his example let us move.

5 But, ah, how blind, how weak we are,
  How frail, how apt to turn aside;

Lord, we depend upon thy care;
 We ask thy Spirit for our guide.
6 Thy fair example may we trace,
 To teach us what we ought to be;
Make us, by thy transforming grace,
 O Saviour, daily more like thee.

HYMN 179. S. M.
Duties.

A CHARGE to keep I have,
 A God to glorify;
A never-dying soul to save,
 And fit it for the sky:
2 From youth to hoary age,
 My calling to fulfil:
O may it all my powers engage
 To do my Master's will.
3 Arm me with jealous care,
 As in thy sight to live,
And, oh! thy servant, Lord, prepare
 A strict account to give.
4 Help me to watch and pray,
 And on thyself rely;
Assured if I my trust betray,
 I shall for ever die.

HYMN 180. C. M.
"Forgetting those things which are behind," &c.—Phil. iii. 13, 14.

AWAKE, my soul, stretch every nerve,
 And press with vigour on;
A heavenly race demands thy zeal,
 And an immortal crown.
2 A cloud of witnesses around
 Hold thee in full survey;
Forget the steps already trod,
 And onward urge thy way.
3 'Tis God's all-animating voice
 That calls thee from on high,
'Tis his own hand presents the prize
 To thine uplifted eye.

4 Then wake, my soul, stretch every nerve,
    And press with vigour on;
  A heavenly race demands thy zeal,
    And an immortal crown.

HYMN 181. C. M.
Doubting.

THE Lord will happiness divine
    On contrite hearts bestow:
  Then tell me, gracious God, is mine
    A contrite heart, or no?

2 I hear, but seem to hear in vain,
    Insensible as steel;
  If aught is felt, 'tis only pain
    To find I cannot feel.

3 My best desires are faint and few,
    I fain would strive for more;
  But when I cry, "My strength renew,"
    Seem weaker than before.

4 I see thy saints with comfort fill'd,
    When in thy house of prayer;
  But still in bondage I am held,
    And find no comfort there.

5 O make this heart rejoice or ache;
    Decide this doubt for me;
  And if it be not broken, break;
    And heal it, if it be.

HYMN 182. C. M.
Desires after renewed Holiness.

OH for a closer walk with God,
    A calm and heavenly frame;
  A light to shine upon the road
    That leads me to the Lamb.

2 Where is the blessedness I knew,
    When first I saw the Lord?
  Where is the soul-refreshing view
    Of Jesus and his word?

3 What peaceful hours I then enjoy'd;
    How sweet their memory still;

But now I feel an aching void
　　　The world can never fill.
4 Return, O holy Dove, return,
　　　Sweet messenger of rest;
　I hate the sins that made thee mourn,
　　　And drove thee from my breast.
5 The dearest idol I have known,
　　　Whate'er that idol be,
　Help me to tear it from thy throne,
　　　And worship only thee.
6 So shall my walk be close with God,
　　　Calm and serene my frame;
　So purer light shall mark the road
　　　That leads me to the Lamb.

HYMN 183. III. 1.
Trials.

'TIS my happiness below
　　Not to live without the cross;
But the Saviour's power to know,
　　Sanctifying every loss.
2 Trials must and will befal;
　　But with humble faith to see
　Love inscribed upon them all—
　　This is happiness to me.
3 Did I meet no trials here,
　　No chastisement by the way,
　Might I not with reason fear
　　I should be a cast-away?
4 Trials make the promise sweet;
　　Trials give new life to prayer;
　Bring me to my Saviour's feet,
　　Lay me low, and keep me there.

HYMN 184. C. M.
Habitual Devotion.

WHILE thee I seek, protecting Power,
　　Be my vain wishes still'd:
And may this consecrated hour
　　With better hopes be fill'd.

2 Thy love the power of thought bestow'd,
    To thee my thoughts would soar:
  Thy mercy o'er my life has flow'd,
    That mercy I adore.
3 In each event of life, how clear
    Thy ruling hand I see:
  Each blessing to my soul more dear,
    Because conferr'd by thee.
4 In every joy that crowns my days,
    In every pain I bear,
  My heart shall find delight in praise,
    Or seek relief in prayer.
5 When gladness wings my favour'd hour,
    Thy love my thoughts shall fill;
  Resign'd, when storms of sorrow lower,
    My soul shall meet thy will.
6 My lifted eye, without a tear,
    The gathering storms shall see;
  My steadfast heart shall know no fear,
    That heart will rest on thee.

HYMN 185.

Walking with God.

SINCE I've known a Saviour's Name,
    And sin's strong fetters broke,
  Careful without care I am,
    Nor feel my easy yoke:
  Joyful now my faith to show,
    I find his service my reward,
  All the work I do below
    Is light, for such a Lord.
2 To the desert or the cell,
    Let others blindly fly,
  In this evil world I dwell,
    Nor fear its enmity;
  Here I find a house of prayer,
    To which I inwardly retire;
  Walking unconcern'd in care,
    And unconsum'd in fire.

3 O that all the world might know
  Of living, Lord, to thee,
 Find their heaven begun below,
  And here thy goodness see;
 Walk in all the works prepared
  By thee to exercise their grace,
 Till they gain their full reward,
  And see thee face to face.

HYMN 186. L. M.
Heaven seen by Faith.

AS, when the weary traveller gains
  The height of some commanding hill,
 His heart revives, if o'er the plains
  He sees his home, though distant still;
2 So, when the Christian pilgrim views
  By faith his mansion in the skies,
 The sight his fainting strength renews,
  And wings his speed to reach the prize.
3 The hope of heaven his spirit cheers;
  No more he grieves for sorrows past;
 Nor any future conflict fears,
  So he may safe arrive at last.
4 O Lord, on thee our hopes we stay,
  To lead us on to thine abode;
 Assured thy love will far o'erpay
  The hardest labours of the road.

HYMN 187. IV. 4.
"I would not live alway." Job vii. 16.

I WOULD not live alway: I ask not to stay
  Where storm after storm rises dark o'er the way;
 The few lurid mornings that dawn on us here,
 Are enough for life's woes, full enough for its cheer.
2 I would not live alway, thus fetter'd by sin,
 Temptation without, and corruption within:
 E'en the rapture of pardon is mingled with fears,
 And the cup of thanksgiving with penitent tears.
3 I would not live away; no, welcome the tomb,
 Since Jesus hath lain there, I dread not its gloom;

There, sweet be my rest, till he bid me arise
To hail him in triumph descending the skies.
4 Who, who would live alway, away from his God;
Away from you heaven, that blissful abode,
Where the rivers of pleasure flow o'er the bright plains,
And the noontide of glory eternally reigns:
5 Where the saints of all ages in harmony meet,
Their Saviour and brethren, transported to greet;
While the anthems of rapture unceasingly roll,
And the smile of the Lord is the feast of the soul.

XI. DEATH.

HYMN 188. C. M.
Job xiv. 1, 2—5, 6.

FEW are thy days, and full of woe,
  O man, of woman born;
Thy doom is written, "Dust thou art,
  To dust thou shalt return."

2 Behold the emblem of thy state
  In flowers that bloom and die;
Or in the shadow's fleeting form
  That mocks the gazer's eye.

3 Determined are the days that fly
  Successive o'er thy head;
The number'd hour is on the wing,
  That lays thee with the dead.

4 Great God, afflict not, in thy wrath,
  The short allotted span,
That bounds the few and weary days
  Of pilgrimage to man.

HYMN 189. C. M.

HARK! from the tombs a mournful sound;
  Mine ears attend the cry;
Ye living men, come view the ground
  Where you must shortly lie.

2 Princes, this clay must be your bed,
  In spite of all your towers;

The tall, the wise, the reverent head
  Must lie as low as ours.
3 Great God, is this our certain doom?
  And are we still secure?
Still walking downward to the tomb,
  And yet prepare no more?
4 Grant us the power of quickening grace
  To raise our souls to thee,
That we may view thy glorious face
  To all eternity.

HYMN 190. S. M.
Job xiv. 11—14.

THE mighty flood that rolls
  Its torrents to the main,
Can ne'er recall its waters lost
  From that abyss again:

2 So days, and years, and time,
  Descending down to night,
Can thenceforth never more return
  Back to the sphere of light:

3 And man, when in the grave,
  Can never quit its gloom,
Until th' eternal morn shall wake
  The slumber of the tomb.

4 O may I find in death
  A hiding-place with God,
Secure from woe and sin; till call'd
  To share his blest abode.

5 Cheer'd by this hope, I wait,
  Through toil, and care, and grief,
Till my appointed course is run,
  And death shall bring relief.

HYMN 191.

VITAL spark of heavenly flame,
  Quit, O quit this mortal frame;
Trembling, hoping, lingering, flying,
  O, the pain, the bliss of dying!

Cease, fond nature, cease thy strife,
And let me languish into life.
2 Hark, they whisper, angels say,
Sister spirit, come away!
What is this absorbs me quite,
Steals my senses, shuts my sight,
Drowns my spirit, draws my breath?
Tell me, my soul, can this be death?
3 The world recedes, it disappears:
Heaven opens on my eyes; my ears
With sounds seraphic ring:
Lend, lend your wings; I mount, I fly:
O grave, where is thy victory,
O death, where is thy sting?

XII. JUDGMENT.

HYMN 192. C. M.

WHEN, rising from the bed of death,
O'erwhelm'd with guilt and fear,
I see my Maker, face to face;
O, how shall I appear!
2 If yet, while pardon may be found,
And mercy may be sought,
My heart with inward horror shrinks,
And trembles at the thought;
3 When thou, O Lord, shalt stand disclosed
In majesty severe,
And sit in judgment on my soul,
O, how shall I appear!
4 But thou hast told the troubled mind,
Who does her sins lament,
That faith in Christ's atoning blood
Shall endless woe prevent.
5 Then never shall my soul despair
Her pardon to procure,
Who knows thine only Son has died
To make that pardon sure.

HYMN 193. S. M.

AND will the Judge descend?
  And must the dead arise?
And not a single soul escape
  His all-discerning eyes?

2 And from his righteous lips
    Shall this dread sentence sound;
  And through the numerous guilty throng
    Spread black despair around?

3 Depart from me, accursed,
    To everlasting flame,
  For rebel angels first prepared,
    Where mercy never came.

4 How will my heart endure
    The terrors of that day,
  When earth and heaven before his face
    Astonish'd shrink away?

5 But, ere the trumpet shakes
    The mansions of the dead,
  Hark! from the Gospel's cheering sound,
    What joyful tidings spread.

6 Ye sinners, seek his grace,
    Whose wrath ye cannot bear;
  Fly to the shelter of his cross,
    And find salvation there.

7 So shall that curse remove,
    By which the Saviour bled;
  And the last awful day shall pour
    His blessings on your head.

HYMN 194. H. 7.

GREAT God, what do I see and hear!
  The end of things created:
The Judge of man I see appear,
  On clouds of glory seated.
The trumpet sounds, the graves restore
The dead which they contain'd before;
  Prepare, my soul, to meet him.

2 The dead in Christ shall first arise
   At the last trumpet's sounding,
Caught up to meet him in the skies,
   With joy their Lord surrounding:
No gloomy fears their souls dismay,
His presence sheds eternal day
   On those prepared to meet him.

3 But sinners, fill'd with guilty fears,
   Behold his wrath prevailing;
For they shall rise, and find their tears
   And sighs are unavailing.
The day of grace is past and gone;
Trembling they stand before the throne,
   All unprepared to meet him.

4 Great God, what do I see and hear!
   The end of things created:
The Judge of man I see appear,
   On clouds of glory seated:
Beneath his cross I view the day
When heaven and earth shall pass away,
   And thus prepare to meet him.

HYMN 195. III. 1.
St Luke xiii. 24—27.

SEEK, my soul, the narrow gate,
   Enter ere it be too late:
Many ask to enter there
When too late to offer prayer.

2 God from mercy's seat shall rise,
   And for ever bar the skies:
Then, though sinners cry without,
He will say, "I know you not."

3 Mournfully will they exclaim;
   "Lord, we have profess'd thy Name;
We have ate with thee, and heard
Heavenly teaching in thy word."

4 Vain, alas, will be their plea,
   Workers of iniquity;
Sad their everlasting lot;
Christ will say, "I know you not."

XIII. ETERNITY.
HYMN 196. S. M.

O, WHERE shall rest be found,
  Rest for the weary soul:
'Twere vain the ocean's depths to sound,
  Or pierce to either pole.

2 The world can never give
  The bliss for which we sigh:
'Tis not the whole of life to live,
  Nor all of death to die.

3 Beyond this vale of tears
  There is a life above,
Unmeasured by the flight of years;
  And all that life is love.

4 There is a death, whose pang
  Outlasts the fleeting breath:
O what eternal horrors hang
  Around the second death.

5 Lord God of truth and grace,
  Teach us that death to shun,
Lest we be driven from thy face,
  For evermore undone.

HYMN 197. C. M.
2 Cor. iv. 18.

HOW long shall earth's alluring toys
  Detain our hearts and eyes,
Regardless of immortal joys,
  And strangers to the skies.

2 These transient scenes will soon decay,
  They fade upon the sight;
And quickly will their brightest day
  Be lost in endless night.

3 Their brightest day, alas, how vain,
  With conscious sighs we own;
While clouds of sorrow, care, and pain,
  O'ershade the smiling noon.

4 O, could our thoughts and wishes fly
  Above these gloomy shades,

To those bright worlds beyond the sky,
　　　　Which sorrow ne'er invades!
5 There, joys unseen by mortal eyes,
　　　Or reason's feeble ray,
　In ever blooming prospects rise,
　　　Unconscious of decay.
6 Lord, send a beam of light divine,
　　　To guide our upward aim:
　With one reviving touch of thine
　　　Our languid hearts inflame.
7 Then shall, on faith's sublimest wing,
　　　Our ardent wishes rise,
　To those bright scenes where pleasures spring
　　　Immortal in the skies.

HYMN 198.　C. M.

COME, Lord, and warm each languid heart,
　　　Inspire each lifeless tongue;
　And let the joys of heaven impart
　　　Their influence to our song.
2 Sorrow, and pain, and every care,
　　　And discord there shall cease;
　And perfect joy, and love sincere,
　　　Adorn the realms of peace.
3 The soul from sin for ever free,
　　　Shall mourn its power no more;
　But, clothed in spotless purity,
　　　Redeeming love adore.
4 There, on a throne (how dazzling bright!)
　　　Th' exalted Saviour shines;
　And beams ineffable delight
　　　On all the heavenly minds.
5 There, shall the followers of the Lamb
　　　Join in immortal songs;
　And endless honours to his Name
　　　Employ their tuneful tongues.
6 Lord, tune our hearts to praise and love,
　　　Our feeble notes inspire;
　Till, in thy blissful courts above,
　　　We join th' angelic choir.

HYMN 199. C. M.

THERE is a land of pure delight,
  Where saints immortal reign;
Eternal day excludes the night,
  And pleasures banish pain.

2 There, everlasting spring abides,
    And never-fading flowers,
  Death, like a narrow sea, divides
    This heavenly land from ours.

3 Bright fields, beyond the swelling flood,
    Stand dress'd in living green;
  So to the Jews fair Canaan stood,
    While Jordan roll'd between.

4 But timorous mortals start, and shrink
    To cross the narrow sea:
  And linger, trembling on the brink,
    And fear to launch away.

5 Oh, could we make our doubts remove,
    Those gloomy doubts that rise,
  And see the Canaan that we love,
    With faith's illumined eyes;

6 Could we but climb where Moses stood,
    And view the landscape o'er,
  Not Jordan's stream nor death's cold flood
    Should fright us from the shore.

HYMN 200. C. M.

SHOULD nature's charms, to please the eye,
  In sweet assemblage join,
All nature's charms would droop and die,
  Jesus, compared with thine.

2 Vain were her fairest beams display'd
    And vain her blooming store;
  Her brightness languishes to shade,
    Her beauty is no more.

3 But, ah, how far from mortal sight
    The Lord of glory dwells:
  A veil of interposing night
    His radiant face conceals.

4 Oh, could my longing spirit rise
    On strong immortal wing,
And reach thy palace in the skies,
    My Saviour and my King!

5 There, thousands worship at thy feet,
    And there, divine employ,
The triumphs of thy love repeat
    In songs of endless joy.

6 Thy presence beams eternal day
    O'er all the blissful place;
Who would not drop this load of clay,
    And die to see thy face?

HYMN 201. III. 1.
Rev. vii. 9, &c.

WHO are these in bright array?
    This innumerable throng
Round the altar, night and day,
    Tuning their triumphant song?
Worthy is the Lamb once slain,
    Blessing, honour, glory, power,
Wisdom, riches, to obtain;
    New dominion every hour.

2 These through fiery trials trod;
    These from great affliction came;
Now before the throne of God,
    Seal'd with his eternal Name:
Clad in raiment pure and white,
    Victor palms in every hand,
Through their great Redeemer's might
    More than conquerors they stand.

3 Hunger, thirst, disease, unknown,
    On immortal fruits they feed;
Them the Lamb amidst the throne
    Shall to living fountains lead:
Joy and gladness banish sighs;
    Perfect love dispels their fears;
And, for ever from their eyes
    God shall wipe away their tears.

XIV. MISCELLANEOUS.

HYMN 202. C. M.
Gen. xxviii. 20, 21.

GOD of our fathers, by whose hand
  Thy people still are blest,
Be with us through our pilgrimage;
  Conduct us to our rest.

2 Through each perplexing path of life
  Our wandering footsteps guide;
Give us each day our daily bread,
  And raiment fit provide.

3 O spread thy sheltering wings around,
  Till all our wanderings cease,
And, at our Father's loved abode,
  Our souls arrive in peace.

4 Such blessings from thy gracious hand
  Our humble prayers implore;
And thou, the Lord, shalt be our God,
  And portion evermore.

HYMN 203. III. 3.
1 Chron. xxix. 10—13.

BLESS'D be thou, the God of Israel,
  Thou, our Father, and our Lord;
Bless'd thy Majesty for ever,
  Ever be thy Name adored.

2 Thine, O Lord, are power and greatness,
  Glory, victory, are thine own;
All is thine in earth and heaven,
  Over all thy boundless throne.

3 Riches come of thee, and honour;
  Power and might to thee belong;
Thine it is to make us prosper,
  Only thine to make us strong.

4 Lord our God, for these, thy bounties,
  Hymns of gratitude we raise;
To thy Name, for ever glorious,
  Ever we address our praise.

HYMN 204. C. M.
Prov. iii. 13—17.

O, HAPPY is the man who hears
    Religion's warning voice,
And who celestial wisdom makes
    His early, only choice.

2 For she has treasures greater far
    Than east or west unfold;
More precious are her bright rewards
    Than gems, or stores of gold.

3 Her right hand offers to the just
    Immortal, happy days;
Her left, imperishable wealth,
    And heavenly crowns displays.

4 And, as her holy labours rise,
    So her rewards increase;
Her ways are ways of pleasantness,
    And all her paths are peace.

HYMN 205. L. M.
Isaiah xl. 6—8.

THE morning flowers display their sweets,
    And gay their silken leaves unfold;
As careless of the noon-day heats,
    And fearless of the evening cold.

2 Nipp'd by the wind's unkindly blast,
    Parch'd by the sun's more fervent ray,
The momentary glories waste,
    The short-lived beauties die away.

3 So blooms the human face divine,
    When youth its pride of beauty shows;
Fairer than spring the colours shine,
    And sweeter than the opening rose.

4 But, worn by slowly-rolling years,
    Or broke by sickness in a day,
The fading glory disappears,
    The short-lived beauties die away.

5 Yet these, new rising from the tomb,
    With lustre brighter far shall shine;

Revive with ever-during bloom,
  Safe from diseases and decline.
6 Let sickness blast, and death devour,
  If heaven shall recompense our pains;
Perish the grass, and fade the flower,
  If firm the Word of God remains.

HYMN 206. C. M.
Isaiah xl. 27—31.

WHY mournest thou, my anxious soul,
  Despairing of relief,
As if the Lord o'erlook'd thy cares,
  Or pitied not thy grief?
2 Hast thou not known, hast thou not heard,
  That firm remains on high,
The everlasting throne of Him
  Who made the earth and sky?
3 Art thou afraid his power will fail
  In sorrow's evil day?
Can the Creator's mighty arm
  Grow weary or decay?
4 Supreme in wisdom as in power
  The Rock of Ages stands;
Thou canst not search his mind, nor trace
  The working of his hands.
5 He gives the conquest to the weak,
  Supports the fainting heart;
And courage in the evil hour
  His heavenly aids impart.
6 Mere human energy shall faint,
  And youthful vigour cease;
But those who wait upon the Lord,
  In strength shall still increase.
7 They, with unwearied step, shall tread
  The path of life divine;
With glowing ardour onward move,
  With growing brightness shine.
8 On eagles' wings they mount, they soar
  On wings of faith and love;

Till, past the sphere of earth and sin,
　　They rise to heaven above.

HYMN 207. C. M.
Isaiah lvii. 15.

THUS speaks the High and Lofty One:
　　My throne is fix'd on high;
There, through eternity, I hear
　　The praises of the sky:

2 Yet, looking down, I visit oft
　　The humble, hallow'd cell;
And, with the penitent who mourn,
　　'Tis my delight to dwell.

3 My presence heals the wounded heart,
　　The sad in spirit cheers;
My presence from the bed of dust,
　　The contrite sinner rears.

4 I dwell with all my humble saints
　　While they on earth remain;
And they, exalted, dwell with me,
　　With me for ever reign.

HYMN 208. II. 1.
Habakkuk iii. 17—19.

ALTHOUGH the vine its fruit deny,
The budding fig-tree droop and die,
　　No oil the olive yield;
Yet will I trust me in my God,
Yea, bend rejoicing to his rod,
　　And by his grace be heal'd.

2 Though fields, in verdure once array'd,
By whirlwinds desolate be laid,
　　Or parch'd by scorching beam;
Still in the Lord shall be my trust,
My joy; for, though his frown is just,
　　His mercy is supreme.

3 Though from the fold the flock decay,
Though herds lie famish'd o'er the lea,
　　And round the empty stall;

My soul above the wreck shall rise,
Its better joys are in the skies;
  There God is all in all.
4 In God my strength, howe'er distrest,
I yet will hope, and calmly rest,
  Nay, triumph in his love:
My lingering soul, my tardy feet,
Free as the hind he makes, and fleet,
  To speed my course above.

HYMN 209. C. M.
St. John xiv. 6.

THOU art the Way, to thee alone
  From sin and death we flee;
And he who would the Father seek,
  Must seek him, Lord, by thee.
2 Thou art the Truth, thy word alone
  True wisdom can impart;
Thou only canst inform the mind
  And purify the heart.
3 Thou art the Life, the rending tomb
  Proclaims thy conquering arm,
And those who put their trust in thee
  Nor death nor hell shall harm.
4 Thou art the Way, the Truth, the Life;
  Grant us that way to know,
That truth to keep, that life to win,
  Whose joys eternal flow.

HYMN 210. S. M.
Philippians ii. 12, 13.

HEIRS of unending life,
  While yet we sojourn here,
O let us our salvation work
  With trembling and with fear.
2 God will support our hearts
  With might before unknown;
The work to be perform'd is ours
  The strength is all his own.
3 'Tis he that works to will,
  'Tis he that works to do;

His is the power by which we act,
 His be the glory too!

HYMN 211.   III. 1.
Ephesians v. 14—17.

SINNER, rouse thee from thy sleep,
 Wake, and o'er thy folly weep;
Raise thy spirit dark and dead,
Jesus waits his light to shed.

2 Wake from sleep, arise from death,
See the bright and living path:
Watchful tread that path ; be wise,
Leave thy folly, seek the skies.

3 Leave thy folly, cease from crime,
From this hour redeem thy time;
Life secure without delay,
Evil is the mortal day.

4 Be not blind and foolish still;
Call'd of Jesus, learn his will:
Jesus calls from death and night,
Jesus waits to shed his light.

HYMN 212.   C. M.
Hebrews xii. 1, 2.

LO ! what a cloud of witnesses
 Encompass us around;
Men once like us with suffering tried,
 But now with glory crown'd.

2 Let us, with zeal like theirs inspired,
 Strive in the Christian race ;
And, freed from every weight of sin,
 Their holy footsteps trace.

3 Behold a witness nobler still,
 Who trod affliction's path,
Jesus, the author, finisher,
 Rewarder of our faith :

4 He, for the joy before him set,
 And moved by pitying love,
Endured the cross, despised the shame,
 And now he reigns above.

5 Thither, forgetting things behind
   Press we, to God's right hand;
  There, with the Saviour and his saints,
   Triumphantly to stand.

GLORIA PATRI.

N. B. The metre marks, affixed to the Psalms and Hymns, refer to a division of the metres, founded on the nature of the verse, into four Classes, marked—I., II., III., IV.

CLASS I. includes Common, Long, and Short metres, marked C. M., L. M., S. M.

CLASS II. includes the other Iambick metres, eight in number, marked II. 1, II. 2, II. 3, II. 4, &c., which may be named *Two, one; Two, two; Two, three*, &c.

CLASS III. includes the Trochaic metres, being five in number, marked III. 1, III. 2, III. 3, &c., which may be named *Three, one; Three, two*, &c.

CLASS IV. includes the metres consisting chiefly of triplets, being five in number, marked IV. 1, IV. 2, IV. 3, &c., and may be named *Four, one; Four, two*, &c.

CLASS I.
C. M.

TO Father, Son, and Holy Ghost,
   The God whom we adore,
  Be glory, as it was, is now,
   And shall be evermore.

L. M.

To Father, Son, and Holy Ghost,
   The God whom earth and heaven adore,
  Be glory, as it was of old,
   Is now, and shall be evermore.

S. M.

To God the Father, Son,
   And Spirit, glory be,

As 'twas, and is, and shall be so
  To all eternity.

CLASS II.

II. 1.

TO Father, Son, and Holy Ghost,
  The God whom heaven's triumphant host
  And saints on earth adore,
Be glory as in ages past,
As now it is, and so shall last
  When time shall be no more.

II. 2.

2 TO Father, Son, and Holy Ghost,
  The God whom heaven's triumphant host,
    And suffering saints on earth adore;
Be glory as in ages past,
As now it is, and so shall last
  When time itself shall be no more.

II. 3.

TO God the Father, God the Son,
And God the Spirit, Three in One,
Be glory in the highest given,
By all in earth, and all in heaven,
As was through ages heretofore,
Is now, and shall be evermore.

II. 4.

TO God the Father, Son,
  And Spirit, ever bless'd,
Eternal Three in One,
  All worship be address'd,
    As heretofore
      It was, is now,
    And shall be so
    For evermore.

II. 5.

TO God the Father, and to God the Son,
To God the Holy Spirit, Three in One,
Be praise from all on earth and all in heaven,
As was, and is, and ever shall be given.

II. 6.

ETERNAL praise be given,
  And songs of highest worth,
By all the hosts of heaven,
  And all the saints on earth,
To God, supreme confess'd,
  To Christ, his only Son,
And to the Spirit bless'd,
  Eternal Three in One.

II. 7.

TO Father, Son, and Spirit bless'd,
  Supreme o'er earth and heaven,
Eternal Three in One confess'd,
  Be highest glory given,
As was through ages heretofore,
  Is now, and shall be evermore,
  By all in earth and heaven.

II. 8.

BY all on earth and all in heaven,
Be everlasting glory given,
  To God the Father, God the Son,
And God the Spirit; equal Three
In undivided Unity,
  Ere time had yet its course begun:
As was, and is, be highest praise,
As still shall be through endless days.

CLASS III.

III. 1.

HOLY Father, holy Son,
  Holy Spirit, Three in One!
Glory, as of old, to thee,
Now, and evermore shall be!

III. 2.

PRAISE the Name of God most high,
Praise him all below the sky,
Praise him all ye heavenly host,
Father, Son, and Holy Ghost;

As through countless ages past,
Evermore his praise shall last.

III. 3.

PRAISE the Father, earth and heaven,
　Praise the Son, the Spirit praise,
As it was, and is, be given
　Glory through eternal days.

III. 4.

TO the Father, throned in heaven,
　To the Saviour, Christ, his Son,
To the Spirit, praise be given,
　Everlasting Three in One:
As of old, the Trinity
Still is worshipp'd, still shall be.

III. 5.

GREAT Jehovah! we adore thee,
　God the Father, God the Son,
God the Spirit, join'd in glory
　On the same eternal throne:
　Endless praises
　　To Jehovah, Three in One.

CLASS IV.

IV. 1.

BY angels in heaven
　Of every degree,
　And saints upon earth,
　　All praise be address'd
To God in Three Persons,
　One God ever bless'd,
　As it has been, now is,
　And ever shall be.

IV. 2.

ALL praise to the Father, the Son,
　And Spirit, thrice holy and bless'd,
Th' eternal, supreme Three in One,
　Was, is, and shall still be address'd.

GLORIA PATRI.

IV. 3.
ALL praise to the Father, all praise to the Son,
    All praise to the Spirit, thrice bless'd,
The holy, eternal, supreme Three in One,
    Was, is, and shall still be address'd.

IV. 4.
O FATHER, Almighty, to thee be address'd,
With Christ and the Spirit, one God ever bless'd,
All glory and worship from earth and from heaven,
As was, and is now, and shall ever be given.

IV. 5.
ALL glory and praise to the Father be given,
The Son, and the Spirit, from earth and from heaven;
As was, and is now, be supreme adoration,
And ever shall be, to the God of salvation.

For Hymns 145 and 185.

TO the Father, to the Son,
    And Spirit, ever bless'd,
Everlasting Three in One,
    All worship be address'd:

Praise from all above, below,
    As throughout the ages past,
Now is given, and shall be so
    While endless ages last.

When used to Hymn 185, in line 6, read
As was throughout the ages past.

COME, let us adore Him; come, bow at his feet;
    O give Him the glory, the praise that is meet;
Let joyful hosannas unceasing arise,
    And join the full chorus that gladdens the skies.

¶ *Whenever the Hymns are used at the celebration of Divine Service, a certain portion or portions of the Psalms of David in metre shall also be sung.*

A

TABLE OF FIRST LINES,

SHOWING WHERE TO FIND EACH HYMN BY THE BEGINNING.

	Page
A CHARGE to keep I have	242
Ah, how shall fallen man	142
Alas, what hourly dangers rise	168
All glorious God, what hymns of praise	143
Almighty Father, bless the word	157
Almighty Lord, before thy throne	181
Although the vine its fruit deny	259
And are we now brought near to God	189
And wilt thou, O Eternal God	193
And will the Judge descend	250
Another six days' work is done	153
Approach, my soul, the mercy-seat	212
Arise, my soul, with rapture rise	233
As, panting in the sultry beam	228
As, when the weary traveller gains	246
As o'er the past my memory strays	164
As the sweet flower that scents the morn	209
Awake, my soul, and with the sun	232
Awake, my soul, stretch every nerve	242
Awake, ye saints, awake	152
Before Jehovah's awful throne	225
Begin, my soul, th' exalted lay	136
Be joyful in God, all ye lands of the earth	225
Be still, my heart; these anxious cares	227
Bless'd be thou, the God of Israel	256
Blest is the man whose softening heart	201
Blest is the tie that binds	150
Behold the Saviour of mankind	171
Children of the heavenly King	220
Christ from the dead is raised, and made	176
Christ the Lord is risen to-day	175
Come, Holy Ghost, Creator, come	177
Come, Holy Spirit, Heavenly Dove	178
Come, let our voices join	198
Come, Lord, and warm each languid heart	253
Come, ye that love the Lord	221
Deluded souls, that dream of heaven	218
Disown'd of heaven, by man oppress'd	197
Doxologies	262
Dread Jehovah, God of nations	181
Eternal Source of every joy	138

TABLE OF FIRST LINES.

	Page
Faith is the Christian's evidence	217
Far from my thoughts, vain world, begone	155
Father of mercies! in thy word	133
Father of all, whose love profound	179
Father of mercies, bow thine ear	192
Father, to thee my soul I lift	146
Father, whate'er of earthly bliss	227
Few are thy days, and full of woe	247
Fountain of mercy, God of love	183
From all that dwell below the skies	194
From Greenland's icy mountains	196
From whence these direful omens round	172
Glory to thee, my God, this night	235
Glory to the Father give	199
God moves in a mysterious way	141
God of the seas, thine awful voice	203
God of our fathers, by whose hand	256
Go forth, ye heralds, in my Name	191
"Go, preach my Gospel," saith the Lord	191
Grace! 'tis a charming sound	147
Great first of beings! mighty Lord	134
Great God, this sacred day of thine	154
Great God, to thee my evening song	236
Great God, what do I see and hear	250
Great God, with wonder and with praise	133
Guide me, O thou great Jehovah	241
Hail! thou long-expected Jesus	158
Hail to the Lord's Anointed	165
Hark! from the tombs a mournful sound	247
Hark! the glad sound, the Saviour comes	157
Hark! the herald angels sing	160
Hasten, sinner, to be wise	210
Hear, gracious God, my humble moan	228
Hear what the voice from heaven declares	208
He dies, the Friend of sinners dies	176
He's come, let every knee be bent	178
Heirs of unending life	260
High on the bending willows hung	173
How beauteous are their feet	164
How firm a foundation, ye saints of the Lord	219
How long shall earth's alluring toys	252
How helpless guilty nature lies	146
How oft, alas! this wretched heart	169
How short the race our friend has run	209
How wondrous and great	198
I love thy kingdom, Lord	148
In loud exalted strains	154
Inspirer and hearer of prayer	237
I would not live alway; I ask not to stay	246
Jesus, and shall it ever be	239
Jesus, my strength, my hope	239
Jesus, Saviour of my soul	218

TABLE OF FIRST LINES.

	Page
Jesus shall reign where'er the sun	194
Joy is a fruit that will not grow	221
Let heaven arise, let earth appear	135
Let wordly minds the world pursue	238
Like Noah's weary dove	148
Lord, dismiss us with thy blessing	157
Lord, for the just thou dost provide	204
Lord, how delightful 'tis to see	200
Lord, my God, I long to know	223
Lord of life, all praise excelling	202
Lord, unafflicted, undismay'd	230
Lord, with glowing heart I'd praise thee	222
Lo! what a cloud of witnesses	261
Mercy, descending from above	201
My God, and is thy table spread	189
My God, permit me not to be	168
My God, since thou hast raised me up	207
My grateful soul, for ever praise	145
My opening eyes with rapture see	155
My Saviour hanging on the tree	171
Not to the terrors of the Lord	149
Now from the altar of our hearts	236
Now may the God of grace and power	182
Now the shades of night are gone	234
O'er mountain-tops the mount of God	166
O happy day, that stays my choice	186
O, happy is the man who hears	257
Oh for a closer walk with God	243
O holy, holy, holy Lord	179
O, in the morn of life, when youth	188
O let triumphant faith dispel	217
On Sion, and on Lebanon	196
O Spirit of the living God	195
Oh, that my load of sin were gone	215
O thou that hear'st when sinners cry	214
O thou, to whose all-searching sight	169
Our Lord is risen from the dead	177
O, where shall rest be found	252
Peace, troubled soul, whose plaintive moan	211
Praise to God, immortal praise	182
Prayer is the soul's sincere desire	213
Rich are the joys which cannot die	202
Rise, crown'd with light, imperial Salem, rise	165
Rise, my soul, and stretch thy wings	219
Rise, O my soul, the hours review	216
Rock of Ages, cleft for me	216
Salvation doth to God belong	184
Salvation! O the joyful sound	143
Saviour, source of every blessing	145

TABLE OF FIRST LINES.

	Page
Saviour, when in dust, to Thee	167
Saviour, when night involves the skies	231
Saviour, who thy flock art feeding	185
See, in the vineyard of the Lord	162
Seek, my soul, the narrow gate	251
Should nature's charms, to please the eye	254
Shout the glad tidings, exultingly sing	160
Since Christ, our Passover, is slain	174
Since I've known a Saviour's Name	245
Sing, my soul, His wondrous love	147
Sinner, rouse thee from thy sleep	261
Sinners, turn, why will ye die	210
Softly now the light of day	237
Soldiers of Christ, arise	186
Songs of praise the angels sang	226
Sov'reign Ruler of the skies	141
Stay, thou insulted Spirit, stay	215
The day is past and gone	237
The gentle Saviour calls	185
The God of Abraham praise	223
The God of life, whose constant care	163
The Lord my pasture shall prepare	139
The Lord will happiness divine	243
The mighty flood that rolls	248
The morning flowers display their sweets	257
The race that long in darkness pined	161
The Saviour, when to heaven he rose	192
There is a land of pure delight	254
The spacious firmament on high	137
The Spirit, in our hearts	211
This is the day the Lord hath made	152
Thou art the Way, to thee alone	260
Though I should seek to wash me clean	142
Thou, God, all glory, honour, power	188
Thus speaks the High and Lofty One	259
Time hastens on; ye longing saints	162
'Tis finish'd; so the Saviour cried	173
'Tis my happiness below	244
To Jesus, our exalted Lord	190
To our Redeemer's glorious Name	144
To Thee let my first offerings rise	234
To thy temple I repair	156
Triumphant Sion! lift thy head	151
Vital spark of heavenly flame	248
We give immortal praise	180
Welcome, sweet day of rest	153
When all thy mercies, O my God	139
When dangers, woes, or death are nigh	205
When gathering clouds around I view	229
Whene'er the angry passions rise	241
When I can read my title clear	220
When I survey the wondrous cross	171
When Jesus left his heavenly throne	200

TABLE OF FIRST LINES.

	Page
When, Lord, to this our western land	195
When, rising from the bed of death	249
When, streaming from the eastern skies	230
When those we love are snatch'd away	208
When through the torn sail the wild tempest is streaming	204
When we are raised from deep distress	206
While angels thus, O Lord, rejoice	159
While shepherds watch'd their flocks by night	158
While thee I seek, protecting Power	244
With joy shall I behold the day	150
Witness, ye men and angels, now	187
Who are these in bright array	255
Who is this that comes from Edom	170
Why mournest thou, my anxious soul	258
Ye faithful souls who Jesus know	175
Ye fields of light, celestial plains	137
Ye humble souls, approach your God	212
Youth, when devoted to the Lord	187

TABLE,

TO FIND HYMNS SUITED TO PARTICULAR SUBJECTS AND OCCASIONS.

	Page
I. THE HOLY SCRIPTURES	133
II. CREATION	134
III. PROVIDENCE	138
IV. REDEMPTION	142
V. THE CHURCH	148
VI. FESTIVALS AND FASTS	152
The Lord's Day	152
Advent	157
Christmas	158
End of the Year	162
New Year	163
Epiphany	164
Lent	167
Passion Week and Good Friday	170
Easter	174
Ascension	176
Whit-Sunday	177
Trinity-Sunday	179
Fast-day	181
Thanksgiving-day	182
VII. ORDINANCES AND SPECIAL OCCASIONS	185
Baptism of Infants	185
Baptism of Adults	186
Confirmation	186
The Lord's Supper	188
Ordination, or Institution of Ministers	191
Consecration of a Church	193
Missions	194
Sunday and Charity Schools	198
Charitable Occasions	201
To be used at Sea	203
For the Sick	205
Funerals	208
VIII. INVITATION AND WARNING	210
IX. CHRISTIAN DUTIES AND AFFECTIONS	212
Prayer	212
Repentance	214
Faith	216
Hope	219
Joy	221
Love	222
Praise	223
Contentment	227
In Affliction	228
Daily Devotion	230
X. THE CHRISTIAN LIFE	238
XI. DEATH	247
XII. JUDGMENT	249
XIII. ETERNITY	252
XIV. MISCELLANEOUS	256
GLORIA PATRI	262

ADDITIONAL HYMNS

SET FORTH BY THE

HOUSE OF BISHOPS,

AT THE REQUEST OF THE

HOUSE OF CLERICAL AND LAY DEPUTIES,

IN

GENERAL CONVENTION, OCTOBER, 1865:

TO BE USED IN THE CONGREGATIONS OF THE
PROTESTANT EPISCOPAL CHURCH IN THE
UNITED STATES OF AMERICA.

PRINTED FOR THE NEW-YORK
BIBLE AND COMMON PRAYER BOOK SOCIETY,
BY MESSRS. EYRE AND SPOTTISWOODE,
LONDON.

ADDITIONAL HYMNS.

REDEMPTION.

HYMN 213. II. 4.

BLOW ye the trumpet, blow;
   The gladly-solemn sound!
Let all the nations know,
   To earth's remotest bound,
The year of jubilee is come;
Return, ye ransomed sinners, home.

2 Jesus, our great High Priest,
   Hath full atonement made:
Ye weary spirits, rest;
   Ye mournful souls, be glad;
The year of jubilee is come;
Return, ye ransomed sinners, home.

3 Extol the Lamb of God,
   The sin-atoning Lamb;
Redemption by his blood
   Throughout the world proclaim:
The year of jubilee is come;
Return, ye ransomed sinners, home.

4 Ye slaves of sin and hell,
   Your liberty receive,
And safe in Jesus dwell,
   And blest in Jesus live:
The year of jubilee is come;
Return, ye ransomed sinners, home.

5 Ye who have sold for naught
   Your heritage above,
Receive it back unbought,
   The gift of Jesus' love:
The year of jubilee is come;
Return, ye ransomed sinners, home.

6 The gospel trumpet hear,
　　The news of heavenly grace;
　And, saved from earth, appear
　　Before your Saviour's face:
　The year of jubilee is come;
　Return, ye ransomed sinners, home.

HYMN 214.　C. M.

THERE is a fountain filled with blood
　　Drawn from Emmanuel's veins;
　And sinners plunged beneath that flood
　　Lose all their guilty stains.

2 The dying thief rejoiced to see
　　That fountain in his day;
　And there may I, as vile as he,
　　Wash all my sins away.

3 Dear, dying Lamb, Thy precious blood
　　Shall never lose its power,
　Till all the ransomed church of God
　　Be saved, to sin no more.

4 E'er since, by faith, I saw the stream
　　Thy flowing wounds supply,
　Redeeming love has been my theme,
　　And shall be till I die.

5 Then in a nobler, sweeter song,
　　I'll sing Thy power to save;
　When this poor lisping, stammering tongue
　　Lies silent in the grave.

THE CHURCH.

HYMN 215.　III. 3.

GLORIOUS things of thee are spoken,
　　Zion, city of our God:
　He, whose word cannot be broken,
　　Formed thee for his own abode;
　On the rock of ages founded,
　　What can shake thy sure repose?

THE CHURCH.

With salvation's walls surrounded,
  Thou may'st smile at all thy foes.

2 See, the streams of living waters,
  Springing from eternal love,
Well supply,thy sons and daughters,
  And all fear of want remove ;
Who can faint while such a river
  Ever flows their thirst t' assuage ?
Grace, which like the Lord, the Giver,
  Never fails from age to age.

3 Round each habitation hovering,
  See the cloud and fire appear,
For a glory and a covering,
  Showing that the Lord is near.
Blest inhabitants of Zion,
  Washed in the Redeemer's blood !
Jesus, whom their souls rely on,
  Makes them kings and priests to God.

4 Saviour, if of Zion's city
  I through grace a member am,
Let the world deride or pity,
  I will glory in Thy name :
Fading is the worldling's pleasure,
  All his boasted pomp and show ;
Solid joys and lasting treasure,
  None but Zion's children know.

HYMN 216. C. M.

COME, let us join our friends above,
  That have obtained the prize,
And on the eagle wings of love,
  To joys celestial rise :

2 Let all the saints terrestrial sing,
  With those to glory gone :
For all the servants of our King,
  In earth and heaven, are one.

3 One family, we dwell in Him ;
  One church above, beneath ;

Though now divided by the stream,—
The narrow stream of death.

4 One army of the living God,
To His command we bow;
Part of His host have crossed the flood,
And part are crossing now.

5 Ten thousand to their endless home,
This solemn moment fly;
And we are to the margin come,
And we expect to die.

6 Then, Lord of Hosts, be Thou our Guide,
And we, at Thy command,
Through waves that part on either side,
Shall reach Thy blessed land.

HYMN 217. C. M.

THE Son of God goes forth to war,
A kingly crown to gain;
His blood-red banner streams afar:
Who follows in His train?

2 Who best can drink His cup of woe,
And triumph over pain,
Who patient bear His cross below,
He follows in His train.

3 The martyr first, whose eagle eye
Could pierce beyond the grave,
Who saw his Master in the sky,
And called on Him to save.

4 Like Him, with pardon on his tongue,
In midst of mortal pain,
He prayed for them that did the wrong;
Who follows in His train?

5 A glorious band, the chosen few,
On whom the Spirit came:
Twelve valiant saints, their hope they knew,
And mocked the cross and flame.

ADVENT.

6 They met the tyrant's brandished steel,
  The lion's gory mane ;
They bowed their necks the death to feel ;
  Who follows in their train ?

7 A noble army, men and boys,
  The matron and the maid,
Around the Saviour's throne rejoice,
  In robes of light arrayed.

8 They climbed the dizzy steep of heaven,
  Through peril, toil, and pain ;
Oh God ! to us may grace be given
  To follow in their train !

ADVENT.

HYMN 218. III. 3.

HARK ! a thrilling voice is sounding ;
  " Christ is nigh ! " it seems to say,
" Cast away the works of darkness,
  O ye children of the day ! "

2 Wakened by the solemn warning,
  Let the earth-bound soul arise ;
Christ, our Sun, all sloth dispelling,
  Rises in the morning skies.

3 Lo ! the Lamb, so long expected,
  Comes with pardon down from heaven :
Let us haste, in godly sorrow,
  Through His blood to be forgiven.

4 So when next He comes with glory,
  Wrapping all the earth in fear,
May we by His love be shielded !
  May He to forgive draw near !

HYMN 219. III. 3.

SEE, He comes ! whom every nation,
  Taught of God, desired to see,
Filled with hope and expectation
  That He would their Saviour be.

Sing! oh sing, with exultation!
  Haste we to our Father's home!
Peace, redemption, joy, salvation,
  Now from heaven to earth are come!

2 See, He comes! whom kings and sages,
  Prophets, patriarchs of old,
Distant climes, and countless ages,
  Waited eager to behold.
Sing! oh sing with exultation!
  Haste we to our Father's home!
Peace, redemption, joy, salvation,
  Now from heaven to earth are come!

3 See! the Lamb of God appearing!
  God of God, from heaven above!
See the heavenly Bridegroom cheering
  His own Bride with words of love!
Glory to the Eternal Father,
  Glory to the Incarnate Son,
Glory to the Holy Spirit,
  Glory to the Three in One!

HYMN 220. C. M.

NOW gird your patient loins again,
  Your wasting torches trim!
The chief of all the sons of men,
  Who will not welcome Him?

2 Rejoice, the hour is near! At length
  The Journeyer, on His way,
Comes in the greatness of His strength,
  To keep His festal day.

3 Oh let the streams of solemn thought
  Which in His temples rise,
From deeper sources spring, than aught
  Born of the changing skies.

4 Then, though the summer's pride departs,
  And winter's withering chill
Rests on the cheerless woods, our hearts
  Shall be unchanging still.

HYMN 221. C. M.

ONCE more, O Lord, Thy sign shall be
   Upon the heavens displayed,
And earth and its inhabitants
   Be terribly afraid:
For, not in weakness clad, Thou com'st,
   Our woes, our sins to bear,
But girt with all Thy Father's might,
   His judgment to declare.

2 The terrors of that awful day,
   Oh! who can understand?
Or who abide, when Thou in wrath
   Shalt lift Thy holy hand?
The earth shall quake, the sea shall roar,
   The sun in heaven grow pale;
But Thou hast sworn, and wilt not change,
   Thy faithful shall not fail.

3 Then grant us, Saviour, so to pass
   Our time in trembling here,
That when upon the clouds of heaven
   Thy glory shall appear,
Uplifting high our joyful heads,
   In triumph we may rise,
And enter, with Thine angel train,
   Thy palace in the skies.

HYMN 222. L. M.

HOSANNA to the living Lord!
Hosanna to th' incarnate Word!
To Christ, Creator, Saviour, King,
Let earth, let heaven, hosanna sing.

2 Hosanna, Lord! Thine angels cry;
Hosanna, Lord! Thy saints reply:
Above, beneath us, and around,
The dead and living swell the sound.

3 O Saviour! with protecting care,
   Return to this, Thy house of prayer:

Assembled in Thy sacred name,
Here we Thy parting promise claim.

4 But chiefest in our cleansed breast,
Eternal! bid Thy Spirit rest;
And make our secret soul to be
A temple pure, and worthy Thee.

5 So, in the last and dreadful day,
When earth and heaven shall melt away,
Thy flock, redeemed from sinful stain,
Shall swell the sound of praise again.

CHRISTMAS.
HYMN 223.   III. 3.

HARK! what mean those holy voices,
  Sweetly sounding through the skies?
Lo! th' angelic host rejoices;
  Heavenly hallelujahs rise.

2 Cherubs tell the wondrous story,
    Joyous seraphim reply,
  "Glory in the highest, glory!
    Glory be to God most high!

3 Peace on earth, good-will from Heaven,
    Reaching far as man is found;
  Souls redeemed, and sins forgiven!
    Loud our grateful harps shall sound.

4 Christ is born, the great Anointed;
    Heaven and earth His praises sing!
  Oh receive whom God appointed,
    For your Prophet, Priest, and King!

5 Hasten, mortals, to adore Him;
    Learn His name to magnify,
  Till in heaven ye sing before Him,
    Glory be to God most high!"

NEW YEAR.
HYMN 224.   III. 1.

WHILE with ceaseless course the sun
  Hasted through the former year,

EPIPHANY.

Many souls their race have run,
    Never more to meet us here :
Fixed in an eternal state,
    They have done with all below :
We a little longer wait,
    But how little, none can know.

2 As the winged arrow flies
    Speedily the mark to find ;
As the lightning from the skies
    Darts, and leaves no trace behind,
Swiftly thus our fleeting days
    Bear us down life's rapid stream ;
Upward, Lord, our spirits raise ;
    All below is but a dream.

3 Thanks for mercies past receive;
    Pardon of our sins renew ;
Teach us henceforth how to live
    With eternity in view :
Bless Thy word to young and old ;
    Fill us with a Saviour's love ;
And when life's short tale is told,
    May we dwell with Thee above.

EPIPHANY.

HYMN 225. P. M.

BRIGHTEST and best of the sons of the morning!
    Dawn on our darkness, and lend us Thine aid!
Star of the East, the horizon adorning,
    Guide where our infant Redeemer is laid.

2 Cold on His cradle the dew-drops are shining ;
    Low lies His head with the beasts of the stall :
Angels adore Him in slumber reclining,
    Maker, and Monarch, and Saviour of all.

3 Say, shall we yield Him, in costly devotion,
    Odors of Edom, and offerings divine,
Gems of the mountain, and pearls of the ocean,
    Myrrh from the forest, and gold from the mine?

4 Vainly we offer each ample oblation,
    Vainly with gifts would His favor secure ;
Richer, by far, is the heart's adoration,
    Dearer to God are the prayers of the poor.

5 Brightest and best of the sons of the morning !
    Dawn on our darkness, and lend us Thine aid !
Star of the East, the horizon adorning,
    Guide where our infant Redeemer is laid.

LENT.

HYMN 226. P. M.

JESUS, let Thy pitying eye
    Call back a wandering sheep :
Prone, like Peter, to deny,
    Like Peter, I would weep.
Let me be by grace restored ;
    On me be all long-suffering shown ;
Turn, and look upon me, Lord,
    And break my heart of stone.

2 Saviour, Prince, enthroned above,
    Repentance to impart,
Give me, through Thy dying love,
    The humble, contrite heart ;
Give what I have long implored,
    A portion of Thy grief unknown ;
Turn, and look upon me, Lord,
    And break my heart of stone.

3 For Thine own compassion's sake
    The gracious wonder show ;
Cast my sins behind Thy back,
    And wash me white as snow :
Let Thy pity help afford,
    And while I do myself bemoan,
Turn, and look upon me, Lord,
    And break my heart of stone.

PASSION WEEK.

HYMN 227. L. M.

MY dear Redeemer and my Lord,
I read my duty in Thy word;
But in Thy life the law appears,
Drawn out in living characters.

2 Such was Thy truth and such Thy zeal,
Such deference to Thy Father's will,
Such love, and meekness so divine,
I would transcribe and make them mine.

3 Cold mountains and the midnight air
Witnessed the fervor of Thy prayer;
The desert Thy temptations knew,
Thy conflict, and Thy victory too.

4 Be Thou my pattern, make me bear
More of Thy gracious image here;
Then God the Judge shall own my name
Among the followers of the Lamb.

PASSION WEEK.

HYMN 228. C. M.

ALAS! and did my Saviour bleed?
And did my Sovereign die?
Would He devote that sacred head
For such a worm as I?

2 Was it for crimes that I have done
He groaned upon the tree?
Amazing pity! grace unknown!
And love beyond degree!

3 Well might the sun in darkness hide,
And shut his glories in,
When God, the mighty Maker, died,
For man, the creature's sin.

4 Thus might I hide my blushing face,
While His dear cross appears,
Dissolve my heart in thankfulness,
And melt mine eyes in tears.

5 But drops of grief can ne'er repay
   The debt of love I owe:
Here, Lord, I give myself away,
   'Tis all that I can do.

HYMN 229. III. 3.

Hail, Thou once despised Jesus,
   Hail, Thou Galilean King;
Thou didst suffer to release us;
   Thou didst free salvation bring!
Hail, Thou agonizing Saviour,
   Bearer of our sin and shame;
By Thy merit find we favor;
   Life is given through Thy name.

2 Paschal Lamb, by God appointed,
   All our sins on Thee were laid;
By almighty love anointed,
   Thou hast full atonement made.
All Thy people are forgiven,
   Through the virtue of Thy blood,
Opened is the gate of heaven,
   Man is reconciled to God.

3 Jesus, low we bow before Thee,
   Mediator glorified!
All the heavenly hosts adore Thee,
   Seated at Thy Father's side;
There for sinners Thou art pleading,
   There Thou dost our place prepare;
Ever for us interceding,
   Till in glory we appear.

4 Worship, honor, power, and blessing
   Thou art worthy to receive;
Loudest praises, never ceasing,
   Meet it is for us to give.
Help, ye bright angelic spirits,
   Bring your sweetest, noblest lays;
Help to sing our Saviour's merits,
   Help to chant Emmanuel's praise.

GOOD FRIDAY.
HYMN 230. III. 2.

GO to dark Gethsemane,
  Ye that feel the tempter's power,
Your Redeemer's conflict see,
  Watch with Him one bitter hour;
Turn not from His griefs away,
Learn of Jesus Christ to pray.

2 Follow to the judgment hall;
    View the Lord of life arraigned;
  Oh, the wormwood and the gall;
    Oh, the pangs His soul sustained!
  Shun not suffering, shame, or loss;
  Learn of Him to bear the cross.

3 Calvary's mournful mountain climb;
    There, adoring at His feet,
  Mark the miracle of time,
    God's own sacrifice complete;
  "It is finished!"—hear Him cry;
  Learn of Jesus Christ to die.

HYMN 231. II. 6.

OH, sacred head, now wounded!
  With grief and shame weighed down!
Oh, sacred brow, surrounded
  With thorns, Thy only crown!
Oh, sacred head, what glory,
  What bliss, till now was Thine!
Yet though despised and gory,
  I joy to call Thee mine.

2 On me, as Thou art dying,
    Oh turn Thy pitying eye!
  To Thee for mercy crying,
    Before Thy cross I lie.
  Thy grief and Thy compassion
    Were all for sinners' gain;
  Mine, mine was the transgression,
    But Thine the deadly pain.

3 What language shall I borrow
  To praise Thee, dearest Friend,
For this, Thy dying sorrow,
  Thy pity without end!
Oh, make me Thine for ever,
  And should I fainting be,
Lord, let me never, never,
  Outlive my love to Thee.

4 Be near when I am dying;
  Oh, show Thy cross to me!
And to my succor flying,
  Come, Lord, and set me free.
These eyes new faith receiving,
  From Thine eyes shall not move;
For he who dies believing
  Dies safely through Thy love.

HYMN 232. II. 4.

THE atoning work is done,
  The Victim's blood is shed,
And Jesus now is gone
  His people's cause to plead;
He stands in heaven their great High Priest,
And bears their names upon His breast.

2 He sprinkles with His blood
    The mercy-seat above;
  For justice had withstood
    The purposes of love;
  But justice now withstands no more,
  And mercy yields her boundless store.

3 No temple made with hands,
    His place of service is;
  In heaven itself He stands;
    A Heavenly Priesthood His.
  In Him the shadows of the law
  Are all fulfilled, and now withdraw.

4 And though awhile He be
    Hid from the eyes of men,

His people look to see
　Their great High Priest again ;
In brightest glory He will come,
And take His waiting people home.

EASTER.
HYMN 233. III. 1.

JESUS Christ is risen to-day,
　Our triumphant holiday ;
Who did once upon the cross
Suffer to redeem our loss.
　　　　　　Hallelujah !

2 Hymns of praise then let us sing
Unto Christ, our heavenly King :
Who endured the cross and grave,
Sinners to redeem and save.
　　　　　　Hallelujah !

3 But the pains which He endured
Our salvation have procured ;
Now above the sky He's King,
Where the angels ever sing,
　　　　　　Hallelujah !

ASCENSION.
HYMN 234. III. 1.

HAIL the day that sees Him rise,
　Glorious, to His native skies !
Christ, awhile to mortals given,
Enters now the highest heaven.

2 There for Him high triumph waits ;
Lift your heads, eternal gates !
Conqueror over death and sin,
Take the King of glory in.

3 Lo, the heaven its Lord receives !
Yet He loves the earth He leaves :

Though returning to His throne,
Still He calls mankind His own.

4 Still for us He intercedes,
His prevailing death He pleads;
Near Himself prepares our place,
Great Forerunner of our race.

5 Lord, though parted from our sight,
Far above yon azure height,
Grant our hearts may thither rise
Following Thee beyond the skies.

6 Master (will we ever say,)
Taken from our head to-day,
See Thy faithful servants, see,
Ever gazing up to Thee.

HYMN 235. L. M.

WHERE high the heavenly temple stands,
The house of God not made with hands,
A great High-Priest our nature wears,
The guardian of mankind appears.

2 Though now ascended up on high,
He bends to earth a brother's eye;
Partaker of the human name,
He knows the frailty of our frame.

3 Our fellow-sufferer yet retains,
A fellow-feeling for our pains;
And still remembers, in the skies,
His tears, His agonies, and cries.

4 In every pang that rends the heart,
The Man of sorrows had a part;
He sympathizes in our grief,
And to the sufferer sends relief.

5 With boldness, therefore, at the throne,
Let us make all our sorrows known,
And ask the aids of heavenly power,
To help us in the evil hour.

WHITSUNDAY.
HYMN 236. L. M.

CREATOR Spirit! by whose aid
The world's foundations first were laid,
Come, visit every waiting mind;
Come, pour Thy joys on human kind.

2 Thrice Holy Fount, thrice Holy Fire,
Our hearts with heavenly love inspire;
Come, and Thy sacred unction bring
To sanctify us while we sing.

3 O source of uncreated light,
The Father's promised Paraclete!
From sin and sorrow set us free,
And make us temples worthy Thee!

4 Our frailties help, our vice control,
Subdue the senses to the soul;
And when rebellious they are grown,
Then lay Thy hand and hold them down.

5 Chase from our minds th' infernal foe,
And peace, the fruit of love, bestow;
And lest our feet should step astray,
Protect and guide us in the way.

6 Make us eternal truths receive,
And practice all that we believe;
Give us Thyself, that we may see
The Father and the Son, by Thee.

HYMN 237. S. M.

LORD God, the Holy Ghost,
  In this accepted hour,
As on the day of Pentecost,
  Descend in all Thy power;
We meet with one accord
  In our appointed place,
And wait the promise of our Lord,
  The Spirit of all grace.

2 Like mighty, rushing wind
  Upon the waves beneath,

Move with one impulse every mind,
  One soul, one feeling breathe:
The young, the old inspire
  With wisdom from above;
And give us hearts and tongues of fire
  To pray, and praise, and love.

3 Spirit of Light, explore,
    And chase our gloom away,
  With lustre shining more and more
    Unto the perfect day:
  Spirit of Truth be Thou
    In life and death our guide;
  O Spirit of Adoption, now
    May we be sanctified.

HYMN 238. C. M.

SPIRIT of Truth! on this Thy day
  To Thee for help we cry,
To guide us through the dreary way
  Of dark mortality.

2 We ask not, Lord, the cloven flame
    Or tongues of various tone;
  But long Thy praises to proclaim,
    With fervor in our own.

3 We mourn not that prophetic skill
    Is found on earth no more;
  Enough for us to trace Thy will
    In Scripture's sacred lore.

4 Though tongues shall cease and power decay,
    And knowledge empty prove,
  Do Thou Thy trembling servants stay
    With faith, with hope, with love.

TRINITY SUNDAY.
HYMN 239. III. 5.

HOLY Father, great Creator,
  Source of mercy, love, and peace,

TRINITY SUNDAY.

Look upon the Mediator,
   Clothe us with His righteousness ;
     Heavenly Father,
  Through the Saviour, hear and bless.

2 Holy Jesus, Lord of Glory,
   Whom angelic hosts proclaim,
While we hear Thy wondrous story,
   Meet and worship in Thy name,
     Dear Redeemer,
  In our hearts Thy peace proclaim.

3 Holy Spirit, Sanctifier,
   Come with unction from above,
Raise our hearts to raptures higher,
   Fill them with the Saviour's love !
     Source of comfort,
  Cheer us with the Saviour's love !

4 God the Lord, through every nation
   Let Thy wondrous mercies shine !
In the song of Thy salvation
   Every tongue and race combine !
     Great Jehovah,
  Form our hearts and make them Thine.

HYMN 240. P. M.

THOU, whose Almighty word
  Chaos and darkness heard,
   And took their flight !
Hear us, we humbly pray.
And where the gospel day
Sheds not its glorious ray,
  Let there be light !

2 Thou who didst come to bring
  On Thy redeeming wing
   Healing and sight,
Health to the sick in mind,
Light to the spirit-blind,
Oh, now to all mankind
  Let there be light !

3 Spirit of Truth and Love,
  Life-giving, holy Dove,
    Speed forth Thy flight!
  Move on the water's face,
  Spreading the beams of grace,
  And in earth's darkest place
    Let there be light!

4 Blessed and Holy Three,
  Glorious Trinity,
    Grace, Love, and Light!
  Through the world, far and wide,
  Boundless as ocean's tide
  Rolling in fullest pride,
    Let there be light!

THANKSGIVING DAY.
HYMN 241. L. M.

GREAT God, as seasons disappear,
And changes mark the rolling year;
As time with rapid pinions flies,
May every season make us wise.

2 Long has Thy favor crowned our days,
  And summer shed again its rays;
  No deadly cloud our sky has veiled;
  No blasting winds our path assailed.

3 Our harvest months have o'er us rolled,
  And filled our fields with waving gold;
  Our tables spread, our garners stored!
  Where are our hearts to praise the Lord?

4 The solemn harvest comes apace,
  The closing day of life and grace;
  Time of decision, awful hour!
  Around it let no tempests lower!

5 Prepare us, Lord, by grace divine,
  Like stars in heaven to rise and shine;
  Then shall our happy souls above
  Reap the full harvest of Thy love!

THANKSGIVING DAY.

HYMN 242. II. 4.

BEFORE the Lord we bow,
    The God who reigns above,
And rules the world below,
    Boundless in power and love.
        Our thanks we bring
            In joy and praise,
            Our hearts we raise
        To heaven's high King.

2 The nation Thou hast blest
    May well Thy love declare,
From foes and fears at rest,
    Protected by Thy care.
        For this fair land,
            For this bright day,
            Our thanks we pay—
        Gifts of Thy hand.

3 May every mountain height,
    Each vale and forest green,
Shine in Thy word's pure light,
    And its rich fruits be seen!
        May every tongue
            Be tuned to praise,
            And joined to raise
        A grateful song.

4 Earth! hear thy Maker's voice,
    The great Redeemer own,
Believe, obey, rejoice,
    And worship Him alone;
        Cast down thy pride,
            Thy sin deplore,
            And bow before
        The Crucified.

5 And when in power He comes,
    Oh, may our native land,
From all its rending tombs,
    Send forth a glorious band;

A countless throng
Ever to sing
To heaven's high King
Salvation's song.

CONFIRMATION.
HYMN 243.

MY faith looks up to Thee,
Thou Lamb of Calvary,
Saviour divine!
Now hear me while I pray:
Take all my guilt away;
Oh, let me from this day
Be wholly Thine.

2 May Thy rich grace impart
Strength to my fainting heart;
My zeal inspire;
As Thou hast died for me,
Oh, may my love to Thee
Pure, warm, and changeless be,
A living fire.

3 While life's dark maze I tread,
And griefs around me spread,
Be Thou my guide;
Bid darkness turn to day;
Wipe sorrow's tears away,
Nor let me ever stray
From Thee aside.

HYMN 244. C. M.

MY God, accept my heart this day,
And make it always Thine,
That I from Thee no more may stray,
No more from Thee decline.

2 Before the cross of Him who died,
Behold, I prostrate fall;

  Let every sin be crucified,
   Let Christ be all in all.

3 Anoint me with Thy heavenly grace,
 Adopt me for Thine own ;
That I may see Thy glorious face,
 And worship at Thy throne.

4 May the dear blood once shed for me
 My blest atonement prove ;
That I from first to last may be
 The purchase of Thy love !

5 Let every thought, and work, and word,
 To Thee be ever given ;
Then life shall be Thy service, Lord,
 And death the gate of heaven !

THE LORD'S SUPPER.
HYMN 245. P. M.

BREAD of the world, in mercy broken,
 Wine of the soul, in mercy shed,
By whom the words of life were spoken,
 And in whose death our sins are dead:

2 Look on the heart by sorrow broken,
 Look on the tears by sinners shed,
And be Thy feast to us the token
 That by Thy grace our souls are fed.

SUNDAY SCHOOLS.
HYMN 246. C. M.

BY cool Siloam's shady rill
 How fair the lily grows !
How sweet the breath, beneath the hill,
 Of Sharon's dewy rose !

2 Lo, such the child, whose early feet
 The path of peace have trod,
Whose secret heart, with influence sweet,
 Is upward drawn to God.

3 By cool Siloam's shady rill
   The lily must decay;
The rose, that blooms beneath the hill,
   Must shortly fade away.

4 And soon, too soon, the wintry hour
   Of man's maturer age
Will shake the soul with sorrow's power,
   And stormy passion's rage.

5 O Thou, who givest life and breath,
   We seek Thy grace alone,
In childhood, manhood, age, and death,
   To keep us still Thine own.

FUNERALS.
HYMN 247. P. M.

THOU art gone to the grave! but we will not deplore thee,
   Though sorrow and darkness encompass the tomb;
Thy Saviour hath passed through its portals before thee,
   And the lamp of His love was thy guide through the gloom.

2 Thou art gone to the grave! we no longer behold thee,
   Nor tread the rough paths of the world by thy side;
But the wide arms of mercy were spread to enfold thee,
   And sinners may die, for the Sinless hath died.

3 Thou art gone to the grave! and, its mansion forsaking,
   Perhaps thy weak spirit in fear lingered long;
But the mild rays of Paradise dawned on thy waking,
   And the sound which thou heard'st was the seraphim's song.

4 Thou art gone to the grave! but we will not deplore thee,
　Whose God was thy Ransom, thy Guardian and Guide:
He gave thee, He took thee, and He will restore thee;
　And death hath no sting, for the Saviour hath died.

PRAYER.

HYMN 248.　III. 1.

COME, my soul, thy suit prepare,
　Jesus loves to answer prayer;
He Himself has bid thee pray,
Therefore will not say thee nay.

2 Thou art coming to a King,
　Large petitions with thee bring;
For His grace and power are such,
None can ever ask too much.

3 With my burden I begin;
　Lord, remove this load of sin;
Let Thy blood, for sinners spilt.
Set my conscience free from guilt.

4 Lord, I come to Thee for rest,
　Take possession of my breast;
There Thy blood-bought right maintain,
And without a rival reign.

5 While I am a pilgrim here,
　Let Thy love my spirit cheer;
As my Guide, my Guard, my Friend,
Lead me to my journey's end.

6 Show me what I have to do,
　Every hour my strength renew;
Let me live a life of faith,
Let me die Thy people's death.

REPENTANCE.
HYMN 249. III. 1.

DEPTH of mercy! can there be
Mercy still reserved for me?
Can my God His wrath forbear?
Me, the chief of sinners, spare?

2 I have long withstood His grace;
Long provoked Him to His face;
Would not hearken to His calls;
Grieved Him by a thousand falls.

3 Kindled His relentings are;
Me He now delights to spare;
Now my Father's mercies move,
Justice lingers into love.

4 Lo! for me the Saviour stands;
Shows His wounds, and spreads His hands:
God is Love! I know, I feel;
Jesus weeps, and loves me still.

FAITH.
HYMN 250. P. M.

JUST as I am, without one plea,
But that Thy blood was shed for me,
And that Thou bidd'st me come to Thee,
O Lamb of God, I come.

2 Just as I am, and waiting not
To rid my soul of one dark blot;
To Thee, whose blood can cleanse each spot,
O Lamb of God, I come.

3 Just as I am, though tossed about
With many a conflict, many a doubt,
With fears within, and foes without,
O Lamb of God, I come.

4 Just as I am—poor, wretched, blind—
Sight, riches, healing of the mind,
Yea, all I need, in Thee to find,
O Lamb of God, I come.

5 Just as I am, Thou wilt receive,
　Wilt welcome, pardon, cleanse, relieve;
　Because Thy promise I believe,
　　　O Lamb of God, I come.

6 Just as I am, Thy love unknown
　Has broken every barrier down;
　Now to be Thine, yea, Thine alone,
　　　O Lamb of God, I come.

HYMN 251.　C. M.

FOREVER here my rest shall be,
　Close to Thy bleeding side;
This all my hope, and all my plea,
　"For me the Saviour died."

2 My dying Saviour and my God,
　　Fountain for guilt and sin!
　Sprinkle me ever with Thy blood,
　　And cleanse and keep me clean.

3 Wash me, and make me thus Thine own;
　　Wash me, and mine Thou art;
　Wash me, but not my feet alone,
　　My hands, my head, my heart.

4 Th' atonement of Thy blood apply,
　　Till faith to sight improve;
　Till hope in full fruition die,
　　And all my soul be love.

HYMN 252.　L. M.

JESUS, Thy blood and righteousness
　My beauty are, my glorious dress;
Midst flaming worlds in these arrayed,
With joy shall I lift up my head.

2 When from the dust of death I rise
　To take my mansion in the skies,
　E'en then shall this be all my plea,
　"Jesus hath lived and died for me."

3 This spotless robe the same appears
　When ruined nature sinks in years;
　No age can change its glorious hue;
　The robe of Christ is ever new.

4 Oh! let the dead now hear Thy voice;
    Bid, Lord, Thy banished ones rejoice;
    Our beauty this, our glorious dress,
    Jesus, the Lord, our Righteousness.

LOVE.
HYMN 253. C. M.

JESUS! the very thought of Thee
  With sweetness fills my breast;
But sweeter far Thy face to see,
  And in Thy presence rest.

2 No voice can sing, no heart can frame,
    Nor can the memory find,
  A sweeter sound than Jesus' name,
    The Saviour of mankind.

3 Oh, hope of every contrite heart,
    Oh, joy of all the meek,
  To those who fall, how kind Thou art!
    How good to those who seek!

4 But what to those who find? Ah! this
    Nor tongue nor pen can show;
  The love of Jesus, what it is
    None but His loved ones know.

5 Jesus! our only joy be Thou,
    As Thou our prize wilt be;
  Jesus! be Thou our glory now,
    And through eternity.

HYMN 254. C. M.

MY God, I love Thee, not because
  I hope for heaven thereby;
Nor yet because, if I love not,
  I must forever die.

2 But, O my Jesus, Thou didst me
    Upon the cross embrace;
  For me didst bear the nails and spear,
    And manifold disgrace,

3 And griefs and torments numberless,
    And sweat of agony,

E'en death itself; and all for one
      Who was Thine enemy.
4 Then why, O blessed Jesus Christ!
      Should I not love Thee well;
   Not for the sake of winning heaven,
      Or of escaping hell;
5 Not with the hope of gaining aught;
      Not seeking a reward;
   But, as Thyself hast loved me,
      O ever loving Lord!
6 E'en so I love Thee, and will love,
      And in Thy praise will sing;
   Solely because Thou art my God,
      And my eternal King.

HYMN 255.   C. M.

HOW sweet the name of Jesus sounds
      In a believer's ear!
   It soothes his sorrows, heals his wounds,
      And drives away his fear.
2 It makes the wounded spirit whole,
      And calms the troubled breast;
   'Tis manna to the hungry soul,
      And for the weary, rest.
3 Dear name! the rock on which I build,
      My shield and hiding place;
   My never-failing treasury filled
      With boundless stores of grace.
4 By Thee my prayers acceptance gain,
      Although with sin defiled;
   Satan accuses me in vain,
      And I am owned a child.
5 Jesus! my Shepherd, Guardian, Friend,
      My Prophet, Priest, and King,
   My Lord, my Life, my Way, my End,
      Accept the praise I bring.
6 Weak is the effort of my heart,
      And cold my warmest thought;

But when I see Thee as Thou art,
  I'll praise Thee as I ought.

7 Till then, I would Thy love proclaim
  With every fleeting breath;
And may the music of Thy name
  Refresh my soul in death.

PRAISE.

HYMN 256. III. 3.

LORD, Thy glory fills the heaven;
  Earth is with its fulness stored;
Unto Thee be glory given,
  Holy, holy, holy Lord!
Heaven is still with anthems ringing;
  Earth takes up the angels' cry,
"Holy, holy, holy," singing,
  "Lord of hosts, the Lord most High!"

2 Ever thus in God's high praises,
  Brethren, let our tongues unite,
While our thoughts His greatness raises,
  And our love His gifts excite.
With his seraph train before Him,
  With His holy church below,
Thus unite we to adore Him,
  Bid we thus our anthems flow.

3 Lord, Thy glory fills the heaven;
  Earth is with its fulness stored;
Unto Thee be glory given,
  Holy, holy, holy Lord!
Thus Thy glorious name confessing,
  We adopt the angels' cry,
"Holy, holy, holy"—blessing
  Thee, the Lord our God most High!

HYMN 257. L. M.

AWAKE, my soul, to joyful lays,
  And sing Thy great Redeemer's praise,

He justly claims a song from thee ;
His loving-kindness, oh, how free !

2 He saw me ruined in the fall,
Yet loved me notwithstanding all ;
He saved me from my lost estate ;
His loving-kindness, oh, how great !

3 Though numerous hosts of mighty foes,
Though earth and hell my way oppose,
He safely leads my soul along ;
His loving-kindness, oh, how strong !

4 When trouble, like a gloomy cloud,
Has gathered thick, and thundered loud,
He near my soul has always stood ;
His loving-kindness, oh, how good !

5 Often I feel my sinful heart
Prone from my Saviour to depart,
But though I oft have Him forgot,
His loving-kindness changes not.

6 Soon shall I pass the gloomy vale,
Soon all my mortal powers must fail ;
Oh, may my last expiring breath
His loving-kindness sing in death !

7 Then let me mount and soar away
To the bright world of endless day ;
And sing, with rapture and surprise,
His loving-kindness in the skies.

HYMN 258. C. M.

ALL hail the power of Jesus' name !
Let angels prostrate fall,
Bring forth the royal diadem,
And crown Him—Lord of all.

2 Crown Him, ye martyrs of our God,
Who from the Altar call ;
Extol the stem of Jesse's rod,
And crown Him—Lord of all.

3 Hail Him, the Heir of David's line,
Whom David, Lord did call ;

The God incarnate! Man divine!
  And crown Him—Lord of all.

4 Ye chosen seed of Israel's race,
    Ye ransomed from the fall,
  Hail Him who saves you by His grace,
    And crown Him—Lord of all.

5 Sinners, whose love can ne'er forget
    The wormwood and the gall,
  Go, spread your trophies at His feet,
    And crown Him—Lord of all.

6 Let every kindred, every tribe
    On this terrestrial ball,
  To Him all majesty ascribe,
    And crown Him—Lord of all.

HYMN 259.

THE strain upraise of joy and praise:
                                Alleluia.
For the glory of their King,
Shall the ransomed people sing;
                                Alleluia.
And the choirs that dwell on high
Shall re-echo through the sky   Alleluia.
They in the rest of Paradise who dwell,
The blessed ones, with joy the chorus swell.
                                Alleluia.

2 The planets beaming on their heavenly way,
  The shining constellations, join and say.
                                Alleluia.
  Ye clouds that onward sweep,
  Ye thunders echoing loud and deep,
  Ye winds on pinions light,
  Ye lightnings wildly bright,
  In sweet consent unite
                            Your Alleluia.

3 Ye floods and ocean billows,
    Ye storms and winter snow,
  Ye days of cloudless beauty,
    Hoar frost and summer glow,

Ye groves that wave in spring,
And glorious forests, sing
        Alleluia.
First let the birds, with painted plumage gay,
Exalt their great Creator's praise, and say
        Alleluia.
4 Then let the beasts of earth, with varying strain,
Join in creation's hymn and cry again,
        Alleluia.
Here let the mountains thunder forth sonorous
        Alleluia.
Here let the valleys sing in gentler chorus
        Alleluia.
Thou jubilant abyss of ocean cry,
        Alleluia.
Ye tracts of earth and continents reply,
        Alleluia.
5 To God who all creation made,
The frequent hymn be duly paid,
        Alleluia.
This is the strain, the eternal strain, the Lord
  Almighty loves,   Alleluia.
This is the song, the heavenly song, that Christ
  the King approves.   Alleluia.
Therefore we sing, both heart and voice awaking,
        Alleluia.
And children's voices echo, answer making,
        Alleluia.

Now from all men be outpoured
Alleluia to the Lord :
With Alleluia evermore
The Son and Spirit we adore :
Praise be done to the Three in One !
   Alleluia ! Alleluia ! Alleluia ! Amen.

PEACE.
HYMN 260. C. M.
OH for a heart to praise my God,
 A heart from sin set free !

A heart that always feels Thy blood,
  So freely spilt for me;

2 A heart resigned, submissive, meek,
    My great Redeemer's throne;
  Where only Christ is heard to speak,
    Where Jesus reigns alone;

3 An humble, lowly, contrite heart,
    Believing, true and clean;
  Which neither life nor death can part
    From Him that dwells within;

4 A heart in every thought renewed,
    And full of love divine,
  Perfect, and right, and pure, and good,
    A copy, Lord, of Thine!

5 Thy nature, gracious Lord, impart;
    Come quickly from above;
  Write Thy new name upon my heart,
    Thy new, best name of Love.

HYMN 261. C. M.

THERE is a fold whence none can stray,
    And pastures ever green,
  Where sultry sun, or stormy day,
    Or night is never seen.

2 Far up the everlasting hills,
    In God's own light it lies;
  His smile its vast dimension fills
    With joy that never dies.

3 One narrow vale, one darksome wave,
    Divides that land from this;
  I have a Shepherd pledged to save,
    And bear me home to bliss.

4 Soon at His feet my soul will lie,
    In life's last struggling breath;
  But I shall only seem to die,
    I shall not taste of death.

5 Far from this guilty world, to be
    Exempt from toil and strife;
  To spend eternity with Thee,
    My Saviour, this is life!

HYMN 262. C. M.

O LORD, my best desire fulfil,
    And help me to resign
  Life, health, and comfort to Thy will,
    And make Thy pleasure mine.

2 Why should I shrink at Thy command,
    Whose love forbids my fears?
  Or tremble at the gracious hand
    That wipes away my tears?

3 No, rather let me freely yield
    What most I prize to Thee,
  Who never hast a good withheld,
    Or wilt withhold, from me.

4 Thy favour, all my journey through,
    Thou art engaged to grant;
  What else I want, or think I do,
    'Tis better still to want.

5 Wisdom and mercy guide my way,
    Shall I resist them both?
  The poor, blind creature of a day,
    And crushed before the moth!

6 But oh! my inward spirit cries,
    Still bind me to Thy sway!
  Else the next cloud that veils the skies,
    Drives all these thoughts away.

HYMN 263. P. M.

MY Saviour, as Thou wilt!
    Oh, may Thy will be mine!
  Into Thy hand of love
    I would my all resign.
  Through sorrow or through joy,
    Conduct me as Thine own,

And help me still to say,
  My Lord, Thy will be done.

2 My Saviour, as Thou wilt!
   If needy here and poor,
 Give me Thy people's bread,
   Their portion rich and sure.
 The manna of Thy word
   Let my soul feed upon;
 And if all else should fail,
   My Lord, Thy will be done!

3 My Saviour, as Thou wilt!
   Though seen through many a tear,
 Let not my star of hope
   Grow dim or disappear.
 Since Thou on earth hast wept
   And sorrowed oft alone,
 If I must weep with Thee,
   My Lord, Thy will be done.

4 My Saviour, as Thou wilt!
   All shall be well for me:
 Each changing future scene,
   I gladly trust with Thee.
 Straight to my home above,
   I travel calmly on,
 And sing in life or death,
   My Lord, Thy will be done!

DAILY DEVOTION.
HYMN 264. II. 5.

ABIDE with me! fast falls the eventide,
  The darkness deepens; Lord, with me abide;
When other helpers fail, and comforts flee,
Help of the helpless, oh abide with me.

2 Swift to its close ebbs out life's little day;
  Earth's joys grow dim, its glories pass away;
  Change and decay on all around I see;
  O Thou who changest not, abide with me.

3 I need Thy presence every passing hour;
  What but Thy grace can foil the tempter's power?
  Who like Thyself, my guide and stay can be?
  Through cloud and sunshine, Lord, abide with me.

4 I fear no foe, with Thee at hand to bless;
  Ills have no weight, and tears no bitterness.
  Where is death's sting? where, grave, thy victory?
  I triumph still, if Thou abide with me.

5 Hold Thou Thy cross before my closing eyes;
  Shine through the gloom, and point me to the skies;
  Heaven's morning breaks, and earth's vain shadows flee;
  In life, in death, O Lord, abide with me.

HYMN 265. L. M.

FORTH in Thy name, O Lord, I go,
  My daily labor to pursue;
Thee, only Thee, resolved to know,
  In all I think, or speak, or do.

2 Give me to bear Thy easy yoke,
   And every moment watch and pray;
  And still to things eternal look,
   And hasten to that glorious day.

3 Fain would I still for Thee employ
   Whate'er Thy bounteous grace hath given;
  Would run my course with even joy,
   And closely walk with Thee to heaven.

HYMN 266. C. M.

FAR from the world, O Lord, I flee,
  From strife and tumult far;
From scenes where Satan wages still
  His most successful war.

2 The calm retreat, the silent shade,
   With prayer and praise agree;

And seem by Thy sweet bounty made
  For those that follow Thee.

3 There, if Thy Spirit touch the soul,
  And grace her mean abode,
Oh with what peace, and joy, and love,
  She communes with her God!

4 There, like the nightingale, she pours
  Her solitary lays,
Nor asks a witness of her song,
  Nor thirsts for human praise.

5 Author and Guardian of my life!
  Sweet source of life divine,
And—all harmonious names in one—
  My Saviour! Thou art mine.

6 What thanks I owe Thee, and what love,
  A boundless, endless store,
Shall echo through the realms above,
  When time shall be no more.

HYMN 267. P. M.

NEARER, my God, to Thee!
  Nearer to Thee!
E'en though it be a cross
  That raiseth me;
Still all my song shall be,
Nearer, my God, to Thee,
  Nearer to Thee!

2 Though like a wanderer,
  Weary and lone,
Darkness comes over me,
  My rest a stone,
Yet in my dreams I'd be
Nearer, my God, to Thee,
  Nearer to Thee!

3 There let my way appear
  Steps unto heaven;

All that Thou sendest me
　　In mercy given ;
Angels to beckon me,
Nearer, my God, to Thee,
　　Nearer to Thee !

4 Then, with my waking thoughts
　　Bright with Thy praise,
Out of my stony griefs
　　Altars I'll raise ;
So by my woes to be,
Nearer, my God, to Thee,
　　Nearer to Thee !

5 Or, if on joyful wing,
　　Cleaving the sky,
Sun, moon, and stars forgot,
　　Upward I fly ;
Still all my song shall be
Nearer, my God, to Thee,
　　Nearer to Thee !

HYMN 268.　L. M.

SUN of my soul, Thou Saviour dear,
It is not night if Thou be near ;
Oh, may no earth-born cloud arise
To hide Thee from Thy servant's eyes.

2 When the soft dews of kindly sleep
My wearied eye-lids gently steep,
Be my last thought how sweet to rest
For ever on my Saviour's breast.

3 Abide with me from morn till eve,
For without Thee I cannot live ;
Abide with me when night is nigh,
For without Thee I dare not die.

4 If some poor wandering child of Thine
Have spurned to-day the voice divine,
Now, Lord, the gracious work begin ;
Let him no more lie down in sin.

5 Watch by the sick ; enrich the poor
With blessings from Thy boundless store ;
Be every mourner's sleep to-night,
Like infant slumbers, pure and light.

6 Come near and bless us when we wake,
Ere through the world our way we take,
Till in the ocean of Thy love
We lose ourselves in heaven above.

DEATH.

HYMN 269. L. M.

ASLEEP in Jesus ! blessed sleep !
From which none ever wakes to weep ;
A calm and undisturbed repose,
Unbroken by the last of foes.

2 Asleep in Jesus ! oh, how sweet,
To be for such a slumber meet ;
With holy confidence to sing
That death has lost its painful sting.

3 Asleep in Jesus ! peaceful rest !
Whose waking is supremely blest ;
No fear, no woe shall dim that hour
That manifests the Saviour's power.

4 Asleep in Jesus ! oh, for me
May such a blissful refuge be ;
Securely shall my ashes lie,
Waiting the summons from on high.

5 Asleep in Jesus ! far from thee
Thy kindred and their graves may be ;
But there is still a blessed sleep,
From which none ever wakes to weep.

HYMN 270. S. M.

FOR ever with the Lord !
Amen, so let it be :
Life from the dead is in that word,
'Tis immortality.

2 Here in the body pent,
    Absent from Him I roam,
Yet nightly pitch my moving tent
    A day's march nearer home.

3 My Father's house on high,
    Home of my soul, how near
At times to faith's illumined eye
    The golden gates appear!

4 Ah, then my spirit faints
    To reach the land I love,
The bright inheritance of saints,
    Jerusalem above.

5 Yet clouds will intervene,
    And all my prospect flies;
Like Noah's dove, I flit between
    Rough seas and stormy skies.

6 Lord, bid the clouds depart,
    The winds and waters cease,
And sweetly o'er my gladdened heart
    Expand Thy bow of peace.

HYMN 271. C. M.

JERUSALEM, my happy home!
    Name ever dear to me!
When shall my labors have an end,
    In joy, and peace, and Thee!

2 Thy walls are made of precious stones,
    Thy bulwarks diamond-square,
Thy gates are all of orient pearl:
    O God! if I were there!

3 O my sweet home, Jerusalem!
    Thy joys when shall I see?
The King that sitteth on Thy throne
    In His felicity!

4 Thy gardens, and Thy goodly walks
    Continually are green,
Where grow such sweet and pleasant flowers
    As nowhere else are seen.

5 Right through Thy streets, with pleasing sound,
    The living waters flow,
And on the banks on either side,
    The trees of life do grow.

6 Those trees each month yield ripened fruit;
    For evermore they spring,
And all the nations of the earth
    To Thee their honours bring.

7 Oh, mother dear; Jerusalem,
    When shall I come to Thee?
When shall my sorrows have an end?
    Thy joys when shall I see?

HYMN 272. C. M.

ON Jordan's stormy banks I stand,
    And cast a wishful eye
To Canaan's fair and happy land,
    Where my possessions lie.

2 Oh, the transporting, rapturous scene,
    That rises to my sight!
Sweet fields arrayed in living green,
    And rivers of delight!

3 O'er all those wide, extended plains
    Shines one eternal day;
There God the Son forever reigns,
    And scatters night away.

4 No chilling winds, nor poisonous breath,
    Can reach that healthful shore;
Sickness and sorrow, pain and death,
    Are felt and feared no more.

5 When shall I reach that happy place,
    And be forever blest?
When shall I see my Father's face,
    And in His bosom rest?

6 Filled with delight, my raptured soul
    Can here no longer stay;
Though Jordan's waves around me roll,
    Fearless I'd launch away.

JUDGMENT.

HYMN 273. P. M.

DAY of wrath! that day of mourning!
See fulfilled the prophet's warning,
Heaven and earth in ashes burning!

2 Oh, what fear man's bosom rendeth,
When from heaven the Judge descendeth,
On whose sentence all dependeth!

3 Lo! the trumpet's wondrous swelling
Peals through each sepulchral dwelling,
All before the Throne compelling.

4 Death is struck, and nature quaking,
All creation is awaking,
To its Judge an answer making.

5 Lo, the book, exactly worded,
Wherein all hath been recorded;
Thence shall justice be awarded.

6 When the Judge His seat attaineth,
And each hidden deed arraigneth,
Nothing unavenged remaineth.

7 What shall I, frail man, be pleading?
Who for me be interceding,
When the just are mercy needing?

8 King of Majesty tremendous,
Who dost free salvation send us,
Fount of pity! then befriend us!

9 Think, kind Jesus, my salvation
Cost thy wondrous Incarnation;
Leave me not to reprobation!

10 Faint and weary Thou hast sought me,
On the cross of suffering bought me;
Shall such grace in vain be brought me?

11 Righteous Judge! for sin's pollution
Grant Thy gift of absolution,
Ere that day of retribution.

12 Guilty, now I pour my moaning,
   All my shame with anguish owning;
   Spare, O God, Thy suppliant groaning!

13 Thou the harlot gav'st remission,
   Heard'st the dying thief's petition;
   Hopeless else were my condition.

14 Worthless are my prayers and sighing,
   Yet, good Lord, in grace complying,
   Rescue me from fires undying!

15 With Thy favored sheep, oh, place me!
   Nor among the goats abase me;
   But to Thy right hand upraise me.

16 While the wicked are confounded,
   Doomed to flames of woe unbounded,
   Call me, with Thy saints surrounded.

17 Bow my heart in meek submission,
   Strewn with ashes of contrition;
   Help me in my last condition.

18 Day of sorrows, day of weeping,
   When in dust no longer sleeping,
   Man awakes in Thy dread keeping!

19 To the rest Thou didst prepare him
   By Thy Cross, O Christ, upbear him;
   Spare, O God, in mercy spare him.

ETERNITY.

HYMN 274.

LET me not, Thou King Eternal,
   Enter hell's domain infernal!
Where is grieving, where is sadness,
Where is sorrow, where is madness,
Where despair is ever sighing,
Where the worm is never dying,
Where the shameless are astounded,
Where the guilty are confounded.

ETERNITY.   47

2 Me, may Zion welcome, saved ;
   Tranquil city, seat of David ;
   God its builder, light immortal ;
   Orient pearl each blazing portal ;
   Crystal gold its streets ; the nation
   Of the blest its population ;
   Living rock the walls that bound it,
   Christ the guard that dwells around it.

3 With what joyous gratulations
   Throng Thy gates the festive nations !
   What the warmth of their embracing !
   What the gems Thy walls enchasing !
   Through that city's streets are wending,
   Holy throngs, their anthems blending ;
   There may I, with myriads glorious,
   Chant Thy praise in psalms victorious !

HYMN 275.

BRIEF life is here our portion,
   Brief sorrow, short-lived care ;
The life that knows no ending,
   The tearless life is there.
Oh, happy retribution !
   Short toil, eternal rest ;
For mortals and for sinners,
   A mansion with the blest.

2 And now we fight the battle,
     But then shall wear the crown
   Of full and everlasting
     And passionless renown.
   The morning shall awaken,
     The shadows pass away,
   And each true-hearted servant
     Shall shine as doth the day.

3 Oh, sweet and blessed country !
     The home of God's elect !
   Oh, sweet and blessed country,
     That eager hearts expect !

Jesus, in mercy bring us
  To that dear land of rest ;
Who art with God the Father,
  And Spirit, ever blest.

HYMN 276.

JERUSALEM, the golden !
  With milk and honey blest ;
Beneath thy contemplation
  Sink heart and voice opprest.
I know not, oh ! I know not
  What joys await me there ;
What radiancy of glory,
  What bliss beyond compare.

2 They stand, those halls of Zion,
    All jubilant with song,
  And bright with many an angel,
    And all the martyr throng.
  There is the throne of David,
    And there, from toil released,
  The shout of them that triumph,
    The song of them that feast.

3 And they, who with their Leader,
    Have conquered in the fight ;
  Forever, and forever,
    Are clad in robes of white.
  Oh, land that seest no sorrow !
    Oh, state that fear'st no strife !
  Oh, royal land of flowers !
    Oh, realm and home of life !

4 Oh, sweet and blessed country !
    The home of God's elect !
  Oh, sweet and blessed country,
    That eager hearts expect !
  Jesus, in mercy bring us
    To that dear land of rest ;
  Who art, with God the Father,
    And Spirit, ever blest.

HYMN 277.

For thee, oh dear, dear country,
    Mine eyes their vigils keep;
For very love, beholding
    Thy happy name, they weep.
The mention of thy glory
    Is unction to the breast,
And medicine in sickness,
    And love, and life, and rest.

2 Oh one, oh only mansion!
    Oh Paradise of joy!
Where tears are ever banished,
    And smiles have no alloy;
Thou hast no shores, fair ocean!
    Thou hast no time, bright day!
Dear fountain of refreshment
    To pilgrims far away.

3 Oh, sweet and blessed country,
    The home of God's elect!
Oh, sweet and blessed country,
    That eager hearts expect!
Jesus, in mercy bring us
    To that dear land of rest;
Who art, with God the Father,
    And Spirit, ever blest.

INDEX.

		HYMN.
Abide with me! fast falls the eventide	Lyte.	264
Alas! and did my Saviour bleed	Watts.	228
All hail the power of Jesus' name	Duncan.	258
Asleep in Jesus! blessed sleep	Mackay.	269
Awake, my soul, to joyful lays	Medley.	257
Before the Lord we bow	Key.	242
Blow ye the trumpet, blow	Wesley.	213
Bread of the world, in mercy broken	Keble.	245
Brief life is here our portion		275
Brightest and best of the sons of the morning	Heber.	225
By cool Siloam's shady rill	Heber.	246
Come, let us join our friends above	Wesley.	216
Come, my soul, thy suit prepare	Newton.	248
Creator Spirit! by whose aid	Dryden.	236
Day of wrath! that day of mourning	Ancient.	273
Depth of mercy! can there be	Wesley.	249
Far from the world, O Lord, I flee	Cowper.	266
For ever here my rest shall be	Wesley.	251
For ever with the Lord	Montgomery.	270
For thee, oh dear, dear country	Ancient.	277
Forth in Thy name, O Lord, I go	Wesley.	265
Glorious things of thee are spoken	Newton.	215
Go to dark Gethsemane.	Montgomery.	230
Great God, as seasons disappear	Unknown.	241
Hail the day that sees Him rise	Madan.	234
Hail, Thou once despised Jesus	Bakewell.	229
Hark! a thrilling voice is sounding		218
Hark! what mean those holy voices	Cawood.	223
Holy Father, great Creator	Bp. Griswold.	239
Hosanna to the living Lord	Heber.	222
How sweet the name of Jesus sounds	Newton.	255
Jerusalem, my happy home	Unknown.	271
Jerusalem, the golden		276
Jesus Christ is risen to-day	Old English.	233
Jesus, let Thy pitying eye	Wesley.	226
Jesus, the very thought of Thee	St. Bernard.	253
Jesus, Thy blood and righteousness	Zinzendorf.	252
Just as I am, without one plea	Elliott.	250

INDEX.

	HYMN.
Let me not, Thou King Eternal . . . . *Ancient.*	274
Lord God, the Holy Ghost . . . . *Montgomery.*	237
Lord, Thy glory fills the heaven . . . . *Ancient.*	256
My dear Redeemer and my Lord	227
My faith looks up to Thee	243
My God, accept my heart this day . . . *Unknown.*	244
My God, I love Thee, not because . . . *Xavier.*	254
My Saviour, as Thou wilt . . . . *Schmolck.*	263
Nearer, my God, to Thee . . . . *Adams.*	267
Now gird your patient loins again. . . . *Croswell.*	220
Oh! for a heart to praise my God . . . *Wesley.*	260
Oh, sacred head, now wounded . . . *Gerhardt.*	231
O Lord, my best desire fulfil . . . . *Cowper.*	262
Once more, O Lord, Thy sign shall be . . . *Bp. Doane.*	221
On Jordan's stormy banks I stand . . . *Stennet.*	272
See, He comes! whom every nation	219
Spirit of Truth! on this Thy day . . . . *Heber.*	238
Sun of my Soul! Thou Saviour dear . . . *Keble.*	268
The atoning work is done . . . . *Unknown.*	232
The Son of God goes forth to war . . . *Heber.*	217
The strain upraise of joy and praise	259
There is a fold whence none can stray . . . *East.*	261
There is a fountain filled with blood . . . *Cowper.*	214
Thou art gone to the grave! but we will not deplore thee . . . . *Heber.*	247
Thou, whose Almighty word . . . . *Marriott.*	240
Where high the heavenly temple stands . . *Logan.*	235
While with ceaseless course the sun . . . *Newton.*	224

www.ingramcontent.com/pod-product-compliance
Lightning Source LLC
Chambersburg PA
CBHW030742230426
43667CB00007B/807